# BEHAVIORAL FINANCE

## The Second Generation

Meir Statman

CFA Institute
Research
Foundation

## Statement of Purpose

The CFA Institute Research Foundation is a not-for-profit organization established to promote the development and dissemination of relevant research for investment practitioners worldwide.

CFA®, Chartered Financial Analyst®, and GIPS® are just a few of the trademarks owned by CFA Institute. To view a list of CFA Institute trademarks and the Guide for the Use of CFA Institute Marks, please visit our website at www.cfainstitute.org.

Cover photo credit: DigiPub / Moment / Getty Images

ISBN 978-1-944960-85-8

# Biography

**Meir Statman** is the Glenn Klimek Professor of Finance at Santa Clara University. His research focuses on behavioral finance. He attempts to understand how investors and managers make financial decisions and how these decisions are reflected in financial markets. His most recent book is *Finance for Normal People: How Investors and Markets Behave*, which was published by Oxford University Press and rated as an Outstanding Business Reference Source by the American Library Association.

The questions he addresses in his research include the following: What are investors' wants, and how can we help investors balance them? What are investors' cognitive and emotional shortcuts and how can we help them overcome cognitive and emotional errors? How are wants, shortcuts, and errors reflected in choices of saving, spending, and portfolio construction? How are they reflected in asset pricing and market efficiency?

Professor Statman's research has been published in the *Journal of Finance*, the *Journal of Financial Economics*, the *Review of Financial Studies*, the *Journal of Financial and Quantitative Analysis*, the *Financial Analysts Journal*, and the *Journal of Portfolio Management*, among many other journals. The research has been supported by the National Science Foundation, CFA Institute Research Foundation, and the Investment Management Consultants Association.

Professor Statman is a member of the advisory board of the *Journal of Portfolio Management*, the *Journal of Wealth Management*, the *Journal of Retirement*, the *Journal of Investment Consulting*, and the *Journal of Behavioral and Experimental Finance*; an associate editor for the *Journal of Behavioral Finance* and the *Journal of Investment Management*; and a recipient of a Batterymarch Fellowship, a William F. Sharpe Best Paper Award, two Bernstein Fabozzi/Jacobs Levy Awards, a Davis Ethics Award, a Moskowitz Prize for best paper on socially responsible investing, a Matthew R. McArthur Industry Pioneer Award, three Baker IMCA Journal Awards, and three Graham and Dodd Awards. Professor Statman was named one of the 25 most influential people by *Investment Advisor*. He consults with many investment companies and presents his work to academics and professionals in many forums in the United States and abroad.

Professor Statman received his PhD from Columbia University and his BA and MBA from the Hebrew University of Jerusalem.

# Contents

CE Qualified Activity **CFA Institute** This publication qualifies for 5 CE credits under the guidelines of the CFA Institute Continuing Education Program.

# Foreword: Managers, Examine Thyselves

Too frequently, investors—amateurs and professionals alike—unknowingly fall prey to their best investing intentions. Most often, their disappointment stems from a wide array of well-documented behavioral influences. We know that they are harmful to our financial health, yet we persist in them. Why are behavioral dilemmas so sticky to overcome?

Read on:

In my mind, Meir Statman, the distinguished author of the CFA Institute Research Foundation monograph we present here, is an academic detective. He has been fascinated by behavioral finance for many, many years. I met him as young, wide-eyed academic, full of vigor. He has not changed: He is as feisty as ever. I am allured by his academic insights, especially because they are implementable. This book is pure Meir—energetic, practical, understandable, and implementable.

Meir's research books and papers all provide invaluable insights on investment decision making for amateurs and professionals alike. As such, I have been hooked on his insights for many years. Other academics may be equally brilliant, but frankly, I have trouble understanding all those complicated descriptions and formulas. Meir, however, has not lost his touch for making complicated material understandable. He writes books with titles like Finance for Normal People and What Investors Really Want. My long fascination for the knowledge and insights that behavioral finance offers to money managers has been highly influenced by his research.

Behavioral finance has blossomed—and justly so. It is a key to the justification for active portfolio management. If investors were perfectly rational and always acted in their enlightened self-interest, active management would still have a role because different investors have different goals and preferences and may require different portfolios. Roger Ibbotson, with three colleagues, demonstrated in Popularity: A Bridge between Classical and Behavioral Finance that an investment may be popular (and thus offer inferior prospective returns) for perfectly rational reasons—for example, because it offers liquidity or tax savings. And it may be unpopular (and thus offer superior prospective returns) for precisely opposite reasons.

But active management based on investor irrationality—that is, on behavioral finance—is much more interesting and likely to be much more rewarding. It turns us into detectives like Meir, hunting down parts of the market where euphoria, despair, ignorance, greed, fear, and a litany of other behavioral faults reign and prices depart from their fair value. It is in these situations where active managers can add the most value.

I believe that, while some managers have gotten pretty good at combing the market for these opportunities, they have been less skillful at examining themselves for potential cognitive flaws. Meir Statman's book shines a bright light not only on the imperfections of markets but also on the areas where self-evaluation by managers will provide ideas for improvement. For these and many other reasons, the CFA Institute Research Foundation is exceptionally pleased to present Meir Statman's latest work, Behavioral Finance: The Second Generation.

Arnold S. Wood
*Founder and Retired CIO, Martingale Asset Management*
*Former Chair, CFA Institute Research Foundation Board of Trustees*
October 2019

# Introduction

A driver told me his story recently, on our way to the Santiago, Chile, airport. He was a representative of a Swiss pharmaceutical company in California in 2006, on a contract set to expire in 2008. His friends were buying houses with no questions asked and no money down, with subprime mortgage payments no higher than the rents they had been paying. He and his wife bought one as well.

The man's contract was not renewed in 2008, and he failed to find another job. His mortgage banker showed him a tall stack of documents, all describing people in his situation. "Live in your house," said the banker, "until your eviction notice comes."

The man and his wife decided to relocate to Santiago, close to the wife's family. Their teenage son and daughter objected vociferously but had no choice.

A relative offered help in establishing a car service. By the time the man told me his story, he owned five cars and was doing well. His children found it hard to adjust at first, but they are fine now.

We often hear that behavioral finance is nothing more than a collection of stories about people like that man—irrational people lured by cognitive and emotional errors into foolish behavior, buying fancier houses than they can afford, with larger mortgages than they can bear. We often hear that behavioral finance lacks the unified structure of standard finance. We are asked, What is your theory of portfolio construction? Where is your asset pricing theory? Yet today's standard finance is no longer unified because wide cracks have opened between the theory that it embraces and the evidence.

As I described recently, the first generation of behavioral finance, starting in the early 1980s, largely accepted standard finance's notion of investors' wants as "rational" wants—mainly high wealth. That first generation commonly described people as "irrational"—misled by cognitive and emotional errors on their way to their rational wants.[1]

The second generation of behavioral finance describes investors, and people more generally, as "normal"—neither "rational" nor "irrational." We, like the man in the story, are normal. Like him, we want freedom from poverty through steady income, prospects for riches in houses of our own, nurturing

---

[1]Meir Statman, "Financial Advertising in the Second Generation of Behavioral Finance," *Journal of Behavioral Finance* 18, no. 4 (August 2017): 470–77.

our children, helping family and friends, and being helped by them. We, like him, use shortcuts and sometimes commit errors on our way to satisfying our wants. And we, like him, are usually normal-knowledgeable and normal-smart but sometimes normal-ignorant or normal-foolish.

Second-generation behavioral finance, as I related in my 2017 book *Finance for Normal People: How Investors and Markets Behave*, offers behavioral finance as a unified structure that incorporates parts of standard finance, replaces others, and includes bridges between theory, evidence, and practice. It distinguishes normal wants from cognitive and emotional errors and offers guidance on using shortcuts and avoiding errors on the way to satisfying wants.[2]

This book is about the second generation of behavioral finance. It offers knowledge about the behavior of investors, both professionals and amateurs, including wants, shortcuts, and errors, and it offers knowledge about the behavior of markets. Investment professionals can serve investment amateurs by sharing that knowledge with them, transforming them from normal-ignorant to normal-knowledgeable and from normal-foolish to normal-smart.

Standard finance dates back to the late 1950s and early 1960s, celebrated in many Nobel Prizes. In 1952, Harry Markowitz introduced mean–variance portfolio theory.[3] In 1954, Franco Modigliani and Richard Brumberg presented life-cycle theory,[4] and in 1957, Milton Friedman offered a similar "permanent income hypothesis."[5] In 1961, Merton Miller and Franco Modigliani defined rational investors.[6] In 1964, William Sharpe introduced the capital asset pricing model (CAPM).[7] And in 1965, Eugene Fama described efficient markets.[8] All these men except Brumberg won Nobel Prizes.

---

[2]Meir Statman, *Finance for Normal People: How Investors and Markets Behave* (New York: Oxford University Press, 2017).

[3]Harry Markowitz, "Portfolio Selection," *Journal of Finance* 7, no. 1 (March 1952): 77–91.

[4]Franco Modigliani and Richard Brumberg, "Utility Analysis and the Consumption Function: An Interpretation of Cross-Section Data," in *Post Keynesian Economics*, edited by Kenneth Kurihara, 388–436 (New Brunswick, NJ: Rutgers University Press, 1954).

[5]Milton Friedman, *A Theory of the Consumption Function* (Princeton, NJ: Princeton University Press, 1957).

[6]Merton Miller and Franco Modigliani, "Dividend Policy, Growth, and the Valuation of Shares," *Journal of Business* 34, no. 4 (October 1961): 411–33.

[7]William Sharpe, "Capital Asset Prices: A Theory of Market Equilibrium Under Conditions of Risk," *Journal of Finance* 19, no. 3 (September 1964): 425–42.

[8]Eugene F. Fama, "The Behavior of Stock-Market Prices," *Journal of Business* 38, no. 1 (January 1965): 34–105.

As detailed in *Finance for Normal People*, standard finance is built on five foundation blocks:

1. People are rational.

2. People construct portfolios as described by mean–variance portfolio theory, where people's portfolio wants include only high expected returns and low risk.

3. People save and spend as described by standard life-cycle theory, where people find it easy to identify and implement the right way to save and spend.

4. Expected returns of investments are accounted for by standard asset pricing theory, where differences in expected returns are determined only by differences in risk.

5. Markets are efficient, in the sense that price equals value for all securities and in the sense that markets are hard to beat.

Second-generation behavioral finance offers an alternative foundation block for each of the five foundation blocks of standard finance, incorporating knowledge about people's wants and their cognitive and emotional shortcuts and errors. According to second-generation behavioral finance,

1. People are normal.

2. People construct portfolios as described by behavioral portfolio theory, where people's portfolio wants extend beyond high expected returns and low risk, such as wants for social responsibility and social status.

3. People save and spend as described by behavioral life-cycle theory, where impediments, such as weak self-control, make it difficult to save and spend in the right way.

4. Expected returns of investments are accounted for by behavioral asset pricing theory, where differences in expected returns are determined by more than just differences in risk—for example, by levels of social responsibility and social status.

5. Markets are not efficient in the sense that price always equals value in them, but they are efficient in the sense that they are hard to beat.

## The Second Generation of Behavioral Finance

People want three types of benefits—utilitarian, expressive, and emotional—from every activity, product, and service, including financial ones. Utilitarian benefits answer the question, What does something do for me and my wallet? Expressive benefits answer the question, What does something say about me to others and to myself? Emotional benefits answer the question, How does something make me feel?[9]

Consider lottery tickets. Standard finance says that rational people do not buy lottery tickets because they reduce expected wealth by imposing negative expected returns and increase risk, measured as the variance of returns. First-generation behavioral finance says that irrational people buy lottery tickets because they are misled by cognitive errors, exaggerating the odds of winning.

Second-generation behavioral finance says that normal people buy lottery tickets for the expressive benefits of being "players" with a chance of winning, the emotional benefits of the hope of winning, and the utilitarian benefits of the minuscule chance of winning. Lottery ticket buyers are not likely to be dissuaded from buying when told that they are committing a cognitive error in estimating their odds of winning as one in 100 million when their true odds are only one in 200 million.

We see the transition from standard finance to the first and second generations of behavioral finance in the study of advertisements, including financial advertisements. Economists writing within the framework of standard economics and finance presume that consumers reading ads seek information only about utilitarian costs and benefits.[10] Writing within that framework, Nobel Prize–winning economist George Stigler defined advertising as "the provision of information about the availability and quality of a commodity" (p. 243).[11]

Economists writing within the framework of first-generation behavioral economics and finance accept the premise that consumers reading ads seek information only about utilitarian costs and benefits but claim that consumers are misled by cognitive and emotional errors.

Sendhil Mullainathan, Joshua Schwartzstein, and Andrei Shleifer's discussion of advertising is typical of the first generation of behavioral

---

[9]Meir Statman, "Behavioral Finance: Past Battles and Future Engagements," *Financial Analysts Journal* 55, no. 6 (November 1999): 18–27; Meir Statman, "What Do Investors Want?" *Journal of Portfolio Management* 30, no. 5 (September 2004): 153–61; Meir Statman, *What Investors Really Want: Discover What Drives Investor Behavior and Make Smarter Financial Decisions* (New York: McGraw-Hill, 2011); Statman, *Finance for Normal People.*

[10]Statman, "Financial Advertising."

[11]George Stigler, *The Theory of Price*, Fourth Edition (New York: Macmillan Publishing, 1987).

economics and finance.[12] They illustrated their discussion with the Alberto-Culver Natural Silk Shampoo advertising slogan "We put silk in a bottle." The shampoo actually contained some silk threads, but a company spokesman conceded that silk does not really do anything for hair.

Mullainathan et al. argued that Alberto-Culver's ads mislead consumers into the cognitive and emotional errors of attributing the positive quality of silk to its shampoo. They wrote that "the audience might already have some analogy for the product in mind; it already thinks of the product in terms of something else. In this case, one way to persuade is to advertise attributes of the product that are positively related to quality in the analogous situation." (p. 578).[13]

Writing within the framework of second-generation behavioral finance, I argued recently that although it is possible that such ads as Alberto-Culver's mislead consumers into cognitive and emotional errors, it is more likely that consumers are not misled at all. Instead, ads make products and services more valuable to consumers by adding expressive and emotional benefits to their utilitarian benefits.[14]

All shampoos deliver the utilitarian benefits of clean hair, but those who use Alberto-Culver's shampoos also reap the emotional benefits of believing their hair is silky, despite the possibility that Alberto-Culver's products make their hair no silkier than that of people who use generic shampoo.[15]

L'Oréal's slogan, "Because I'm worth it," instead of masking its beauty products' prices, celebrates their prices, highlighting the expressive and emotional benefits of expensive products as symbols of high self-worth. Regarding the slogan, L'Oréal's global brand president was quoted in an article as saying, "This is a celebration of self-esteem and confidence and what we think beauty is."[16]

In an advertisement for Patek Philippe watches, a handsome man stands next to his similarly handsome son in a luxurious setting, with the following caption: "You never actually own a Patek Philippe, you merely look after it for the next generation." The expressive benefits Patek Philippe watch ownership include an expression of refined taste and high social status. The emotional

---

[12]Sendhil Mullainathan, Joshua Schwartzstein, and Andrei Shleifer, "Coarse Thinking and Persuasion," *Quarterly Journal of Economics* 123, no. 2 (May 2008): 577–619.

[13]Mullainathan et al., "Coarse Thinking."

[14]Statman, "Financial Advertising."

[15]Statman, "Financial Advertising."

[16]Statman, "Financial Advertising." The original article about the slogan is Amy Verner, "L'Oréal's 'Because I'm worth it' slogan marks a milestone," *The Globe and Mail* (2 December 2011), www.theglobeandmail.com/life/fashion-and-beauty/beauty/loreals-because-im-worth-it-slogan-marks-a-milestone/article554604/.

benefits include fulfillment and pride. Patek Philippe watches cost between a few thousand dollars and hundreds of thousands of dollars.[17]

Many ads for financial products and services bear great resemblance to ads for cosmetics and watches, addressing wants for utilitarian, expressive, and emotional benefits. One shows a smiling grandfather standing next to his grandson, and the caption says, "I want my grandson to spend my money." Another says, "Feel valued, no matter how much you're worth."

Behavioral finance, like all fields of science, is a work in progress, and there are no sharp timelines separating the second generation of behavioral finance from the first. Indeed, many wants were identified early in behavioral finance. For example, wants for the emotional benefits of pride and avoidance of the emotional costs of regret are central in Hersh Shefrin's and my analysis of the "disposition effect," the disposition to realize gains quickly and procrastinate in the realization of losses.[18]

The nature of behavioral finance as a work in progress is also evident in the changing behavioral finance roles of emotions, mood, and affect. By now, they have assumed roles that are as important as the role of cognition, yet wide acceptance of these roles in behavioral finance is relatively recent. Early work in behavioral finance centered on cognition, particularly cognitive errors. The reluctance to incorporate emotions into behavioral finance earlier reflected the view that emotions are convoluted whereas cognition is straightforward. And it reflected the view that the involvement of emotions necessarily implies emotional errors, rather than possibly emotional benefits. This view is evident in the still common advice to set emotions aside when making financial choices.

Behavioral finance, and finance more generally, is a mosaic. Each tile matters, but a unified image emerges only when the mosaic tiles complement one another.

First-generation behavioral finance centers on shaping and polishing individual tiles. Neurofinance is one tile, using functional magnetic resonance imaging (fMRI) to reflect investor behavior.[19] That tile is especially bright, attracting much attention for its technological wizardry, yet it is only one among many tiles reflecting investor behavior. Other equally illuminating tiles reflect investor behavior by direct observation, questionnaires, and experiments.

---

[17]Statman, "Financial Advertising."

[18]Hersh Shefrin and Meir Statman, "The Disposition to Sell Winners Too Early and Ride Losers Too Long: Theory and Evidence," *Journal of Finance* 40, no. 3 (July 1985): 777–90.

[19]See Jason Zweig, *Your Money and Your Brain: How the New Science of Neuroeconomics Can Help Make You Rich* (New York: Simon & Schuster, 2007).

A jumble of tiles reflects investors' cognitive errors, yet these tiles tend to clash or overlap, obscuring the mosaic's image rather than clarifying it. One list of cognitive errors extends to 175 tiles, including a bizarreness effect, humor effect, Von Restorff effect, picture superiority effect, self-relevance effect, and negativity bias.[20] Other tiles are shaped to reflect more than they can, such as asset pricing models that account for risk but nothing else. Such tiles might be attractive on their own but do not complement adjacent tiles and do not help reveal the mosaic's image.

Tiles that reflect normal wants, such as nurturing children and families, being true to values, and gaining high social status, are commonly missing. Yet these tiles belong at the center of the mosaic and at the center of second-generation behavioral finance, because they complete the image with other tiles, including not only those of cognitive and emotional shortcuts and errors but also those of behavioral portfolios, behavioral life cycle of saving and spending, behavioral asset pricing, and behavioral efficient markets.

---

[20]"List of Cognitive Biases," Wikipedia, accessed 5 September 2019 https://en.wikipedia.org/wiki/List_of_cognitive_biases.

# 1. Normal Investors

People commonly use the term "rational" as a synonym for "normal-smart." They might say, "It is not rational to buy a Patek Philippe watch for $50,000 when you can buy for $50 a Timex watch showing the same time." Some might even describe those who buy Patek Philippe watches as "irrational," using the term as a synonym for "normal-foolish." Financial economists, however, use the term "rational" more narrowly.

Merton Miller and Franco Modigliani described rational investors in their 1961 article about dividends. Rational investors, they wrote, "always prefer more wealth to less and are indifferent as to whether a given increment to their wealth takes the form of cash payments or an increase in the market value of their holdings of shares" (p. 412).[21] This is a starting point for a description of the rational investors of standard finance.

The rational investors of standard finance can be described more completely as immune to all cognitive and emotional errors. Moreover, rational investors distinguish their roles as investors from their roles as consumers. As investors, rational people care only about the utilitarian benefits of wealth. As consumers, they also care about the expressive and emotional benefits of keeping that wealth or spending it.

As I described in *Finance for Normal People*, quoting Miller and Modigliani, rational investors "always prefer more wealth to less." They are never willing to exchange the utilitarian benefits of wealth for a combination of less wealth and expressive and emotional benefits. These include the expressive benefits of social status demonstrated by wearing a Patek Philippe watch rather than a Timex one and the emotional benefits of the pride from being able to afford a Patek Philippe watch. And quoting Miller and Modigliani, rational investors "are indifferent as to whether a given increment to their wealth takes the form of cash payments or an increase in the market value of their holdings of shares." They never commit "framing" errors that mislead many normal investors into perceiving a $1,000 cash dividend as superior to a $1,000 increase in capital (the market value of their shares).

Rational people are also immune to cognitive and emotional errors beyond framing errors. Rational people never commit "availability" cognitive errors that mislead many normal investors into concluding that many or most mutual funds are five-star funds because mutual fund companies advertise mostly

---

[21]Merton Miller and Franco Modigliani, "Dividend Policy, Growth, and the Valuation of Shares," *Journal of Business* 34, no. 4 (October 1961): 411–33.

five-star funds, making them more available to mind than the more numerous two-star funds. Rational investors never commit "representativeness" cognitive errors, which mislead many normal investors into forecasting either continuations of recent stock market trends or reversals of current trends, even though they have no ability to forecast at all. And rational investors never commit emotional errors, such as unwarranted pride or unjustified regret.

As Hersh Shefrin and I detailed in 1984, normal investors do not always perceive a $1,000 cash dividend as equivalent to a $1,000 increase in capital, and they are not always indifferent between the two. Normal investors with weak self-control withstand spending temptations by framing wealth into distinct mental account "buckets"—for example, capital buckets and income (in this case, dividend) buckets. They construct their system of self-control by the rule of "spend dividends but don't dip into capital." Rational investors have no use for such a rule, because they are immune to framing errors, knowing that an increment to their wealth in the form of a cash dividend is no different from an increment to their wealth in the form of a capital gain, and because their perfect self-control is a perfect barrier to spending temptations.[22]

## Cognitive and Emotional Shortcuts and Errors

Which contractor shall we choose to remodel our kitchen? We care about a range of benefits and costs when choosing a contractor, including price, quality, reliability, and distance. Rational homeowners are able to rank all contractors by the full set of benefits and costs quickly and accurately and then to choose the best. But normal homeowners find ranking all contractors by the full set of benefits and costs too complicated. Instead, normal homeowners begin with a cognitive shortcut that simplifies the problem, such as by excluding contractors from outside their city, limiting to three the number of contractors they interview, and setting a maximum price they are willing to pay. They might add an emotional shortcut, accounting for their feelings of ease in interactions with the contractor. Normal homeowners usually choose good contractors, even if not the best, such as medium-cost contractors working in their city, ones who seem easy to interact with.

Investors often use shortcuts by a similar method, whether excluding from consideration mutual funds with fewer than four stars or choosing mutual funds from a "top 10" list in a newspaper or magazine. Investment consultants advising institutional investors use shortcuts by excluding funds that fall short of thresholds, such as $500 million in assets under management and

---

[22]Hersh Shefrin and Meir Statman, "Explaining Investor Preference for Cash Dividends," *Journal of Financial Economics* 13, no. 2 (June 1984): 253–82.

first-quartile rank by recent past returns. A study of shortcuts by investment consultants found that funds just short of the $500 million in assets under management threshold get 20% fewer page views and 5%–9% less in investment flows during the following year than similar funds positioned just above the threshold.[23]

Good shortcuts enable normal homeowners and investors to get close to the best choices, solutions, and answers. A contractor from a neighboring city might have been the best choice if homeowners did not limit their search to contractors from their city, and a fund just short of $500 million in assets under management might have been the best choice if investment consultants did not limit their search to funds with assets under management exceeding $500 million. But the choice of contractors from their own city or funds with assets under management above $500 million might come close enough to their best choice, solution, and answer.

Cognitive and emotional shortcuts turn into cognitive and emotional errors when they take normal people far from their best choices, solutions, and answers. Cognitive shortcuts that simplify choices turn into cognitive errors when they induce homeowners to save time and effort by failing to visit houses remodeled by the contractor. And cognitive shortcuts that simplify choices turn into cognitive errors when they induce investors to save time by failing to examine whether a fund's good recent performance indicates anything more than good luck.

Emotional shortcuts stirred by feelings of affinity turn into emotional errors when they induce normal homeowners to hire a contractor who is an expert at affinity fraud. And emotional shortcuts stirred by feelings of affinity turn into emotional errors when they induce institutional investors to choose a poorly managed fund whose manager graduated from the same school as they did.

## System 1 and System 2

Cognitive and emotional shortcuts are part of the intuitive "blink" system in our minds—System 1. Psychologists Keith Stanovich, Richard West, and Nobel Laureate Daniel Kahneman described System 1 and System 2.[24]

---

[23]Sudheer Chava, Soohun Kim, and Daniel Weagley, "Revealed Heuristics: Evidence from Investment Consultants' Search Behavior," Georgia Tech Scheller College of Business Research Paper No. 18-44; 14th Annual Mid-Atlantic Research Conference in Finance (2 November 2018). Available at SSRN: https://ssrn.com/abstract=3277424 or http://dx.doi.org/10.2139/ssrn.3277424.

[24]Keith E. Stanovich and Richard F. West, "Individual Differences in Reasoning: Implications for the Rationality Debate?" *Behavioral and Brain Sciences* 23, no. 5 (November 2000): 645–65; Daniel Kahneman, *Thinking, Fast and Slow* (New York: Farrar, Straus and Giroux, 2011).

System 1 is fast, automatic, and effortless, whereas System 2 is slow, controlled, and effortful. We know cognitive and emotional shortcuts also as cognitive and emotional *rules of thumb* and as cognitive and emotional *heuristics*.

The intuition of System 1 and its cognitive and emotional shortcuts takes us to good choices, solutions, and answers in most of life. But the reflection of System 2 takes us to better choices, solutions, and answers when the intuition of System 1 misleads us into cognitive and emotional errors. People with knowledge of human behavior and financial facts use cognitive and emotional shortcuts correctly, whereas people lacking such knowledge commit cognitive and emotional errors as they use them incorrectly.

We default to the shortcuts of System 1 because we are "cognitive misers." Using less brain capacity for one task leaves more brain capacity for other tasks that must be completed simultaneously. Yet modern life often requires better choices than those provided by the shortcuts of System 1.

System 2 is easier to use when we are not burdened by heavy cognitive and emotional loads of tasks that must be completed simultaneously, and it is most beneficial when the consequences of poor choices by System 1 are severe. It is a reasonable shortcut to choose fish as your main course by System 1 when a waiter hovers over you and your fellow diners are impatient. But choosing a set of mutual funds for a retirement savings account without System 2 thinking is an error.

Cognitive and emotional loads imposed by many simultaneous tasks impinge on the attention one can give to some of those tasks because we ration our brain capacity. Rationing increases the likelihood of cognitive and emotional errors in tasks allocated insufficient brain capacity.

Personal real estate transactions impose cognitive and emotional loads on asset managers, reducing brain capacity the managers allocate to asset management tasks. Consequences are evident in reduced trading and worse investment performance.[25] High volumes of simultaneous corporate news impose cognitive and emotional loads on investors, especially amateur investors, causing them to overlook possibly relevant news.[26]

We might begin with a System 1 intuitive claim or hypothesis, such as the claim that mutual funds with five-star ratings are best for our retirement

---

[25]David C. Ling, Yan Lu, and Sugata Ray, "How Do Personal Real Estate Transactions Affect Productivity and Risk Taking? Evidence from Professional Asset Managers" (January 2018). Available at SSRN: https://ssrn.com/abstract=3143081 or http://dx.doi.org/10.2139/ssrn.3143081.

[26]Doron Israeli, Ron Kasznik, and Suhas A. Sridharan, "Unexpected Distractions and Investor Attention to Corporate Announcements" (13 May 2019). Available at SSRN: https://ssrn.com/abstract=3057278 or http://dx.doi.org/10.2139/ssrn.3057278.

savings plan. But we subject that claim to the reflective System 2, examining the claim by the tools of science—logic and empirical evidence—in a slow, controlled, and effortful process.

Reflect on the following question: "If John can drink one barrel of water in 6 days, and Mary can drink one barrel of water in 12 days, how long would it take them to drink one barrel of water together?" (p. 151).[27]

The incorrect System 1 intuitive answer is 9 days, the average of 6 and 12, but the correct System 2 reflection answer is 4 days. John drinks 1/6 of a barrel each day, and Mary drinks 1/12, so together they drink 1/4 of a barrel each day, taking 4 days to drink the barrel.

Or reflect on the following question: "Simon decided to invest $8,000 in the stock market one day early in 2008. Six months after he invested, on July 17, the stocks he had purchased were down 50%. Fortunately for Simon, from July 17 to October 17, the stocks he had purchased went up 75%. At this point, Simon has:

a.  broken even in the stock market,

b.  is ahead of where he began,

c.  has lost money" (p. 151).[28]

The incorrect System 1 intuitive answer is b, because 75% is greater than 50%, but by using System 2 reflection, we find that the initial $8,000 declined by 50%, to $4,000, before increasing by 75%, to $7,000, still short of $8,000.

We are fortunate to have brains that use System 1 shortcuts and jump to conclusions. Indeed, jumping to the right conclusions constitutes much of what we call "intelligence." This is what we do when we swerve our cars quickly to avoid a sofa that just fell off the truck in front of us. There are no computers today that can rival our driving ability. But sometimes we crash when we jump to conclusions. A lightning-quick combination of the cognition and emotions prompts a System 1 slam on the brakes when the car ahead of us stops suddenly, but we are unable to coordinate our cognition, emotions, and foot movements fast enough to, instead, pump the brakes, as the older among us remember from driving school. Computers are better at the braking task. The antilock braking systems onboard today's cars function as a System 2, letting us jump to our System 1 conclusions and slam the brakes while they pump the brakes fast enough to avoid a crash. Indeed, computers

---

[27]Maggie E. Toplak, Richard F. West, and Keith E. Stanovich, "Assessing Miserly Information Processing: An Expansion of the Cognitive Reflection Test," *Thinking & Reasoning* 20, no. 2 (October 2014): 147–68.

[28]Toplak et al., "Assessing Miserly Information Processing."

onboard today's cars do not wait for us to slam the brakes; they slow our cars when we approach cars in front of us at unsafe speeds.

Instruments, including computers, antilock brakes, and GPS (Global Positioning System), perform System 2 functions, but instruments are not always effective or sufficient. People perform System 2 functions beyond the ability of instruments. Committees are almost universally dreaded, but people in effective committees perform System 2 functions in controlled, slow, and effortful processes as they probe, challenge, and offer better alternatives than derived by one member's System 1. Similarly, investment professionals perform System 2 functions in controlled, slow, and effortful processes as they probe, challenge, and offer better alternatives than those derived by an investment amateur's System 1.

## Two Kinds of Knowledge

We can divide knowledge in the context of finance into two kinds: financial-facts knowledge and human-behavior knowledge. Financial-facts knowledge includes facts about financial products and services and about financial markets. It includes facts about differences between taxable and tax-deferred accounts, facts about compounding interest rates, and facts about mutual fund fees.

Human-behavior knowledge is about normal people, their wants, cognitive and emotional shortcuts, and cognitive and emotional errors. Human-behavior knowledge includes knowledge of wants for financial security and nurturing children and families. It also includes knowledge of cognitive shortcuts and errors, such as in framing, availability, and representativeness, and emotional shortcuts and errors, such as in pride, regret, sadness, and disgust.

## From Ignorant to Knowledgeable

Ignorant people lack financial-facts knowledge, human-behavior knowledge, or both. They have not learned to proceed from the intuitive System 1 to the reflective System 2, even when errors induced by System 1 impose substantial costs. For example, people lacking financial-facts knowledge fail to understand differences between types of mortgages and thus cannot identify the ones that are best for them. The portfolios of some of them include a small number of stocks because they believe that portfolios composed of stocks of the few companies they know are less volatile or more likely to rise in value than portfolios of mutual funds that hold thousands of stocks of companies they do not know. And they fail to understand that they should assess their investment success by the difference between their returns and market returns, rather than by their returns alone.

People lacking human-behavior knowledge are unaware of their susceptibility to availability cognitive errors and can be easily misled into funds advertised as five-star funds. They are not on guard against representativeness cognitive errors that mislead them into forecasting either continuations or reversals of recent stock market trends. And they are blind to emotional errors, such as unwarranted pride or unjustified regret.

Investment professionals who possess financial-facts and human-behavior knowledge can educate investment amateurs—for example, wealth managers educating their clients or pension fund staff members educating the lay members of their boards.

## Conclusion

The brains of rational people are never full. They can process any amount of information rapidly and accurately, free from cognitive and emotional errors. The brains of normal people, however, are often full, like that of the student in *The Far Side* cartoon who raises his hand and asks, "Mr. Osborne, may I be excused? My brain is full."

Rational people use the reflective System 2 whenever the intuitive System 1 misleads, whereas normal people regularly forgo reflection once they have found an answer using System 1. Yet normal people vary, ranging from ignorant to knowledgeable. Knowledgeable people have learned, imperfectly and with much effort, to pause, reflect, and use System 2 when System 1 misleads.

Knowledge of financial facts and human behavior makes investment professionals effective in performing System 2 functions for investment amateurs. Investment professionals acquire their knowledge by education and experience, such as is acquired on the way to an MBA in finance or a CFA® charter. Education and experience are part of a continuous process, as new knowledge is developed, often overturning old knowledge. Investment professionals must continue to acquire the best available knowledge and share it with investment amateurs.

Education is hard, especially when financial-facts and human-behavior knowledge conflict with System 1 intuition. And too many investment amateurs resist education. But education is possible, and its benefits are great.

# 2. What Investors Really Want

Ask investors what they want from their investments and they are likely to say that all they want is to make money. But what do investors really want? What do investments provide beyond the utilitarian benefits of money? Standard finance does not answer this question, considering it beyond its domain. But this question and its answer are central in the second generation of behavioral finance, which describes investors, and people more generally, as "normal" and encompasses the full range of benefits and costs of investing and investments—utilitarian, expressive, and emotional.

Ask investment professionals, especially asset managers, what they do for their investors and they are likely to say, in the language of investment performance, that they make money for their investors. Yet the work of investment professionals centers on identifying investors' wants and helping satisfy them.

Our wants include the utilitarian, expressive, and emotional benefits of protection from poverty, prospects for riches, nurturing our children and families, staying true to our values, gaining high social status, inclusion, respect, fairness, and more.

Investments are like jobs. The benefits of jobs extend beyond the utilitarian benefits of money, to include expressive and emotional benefits. We express our identities in our jobs, whether a professor, policeman, technician, or physician. We take pride in accomplishments, find satisfaction in contributions to society, and enjoy memberships in communities of colleagues and friends. We lose more than money when we lose our jobs. We lose parts of our identities, pride in our accomplishments, and membership in our communities.

The benefits of investments, like those of jobs, extend beyond the utilitarian benefits of money to include expressive and emotional benefits. We express parts of our identities in our investments, whether those of a retirement saver, a day trader, a socially responsible investor, or an art collector. And we derive emotional benefits and suffer emotional costs from our investments, whether pride or regret, hope or fear.

Marketing efforts devoted to identifying investors' wants and helping to satisfy them are crucial in directing investors to investment professionals. Yet studies of investment professionals rarely explore marketing efforts, such as those of mutual fund companies. Instead, they explore investment performance. In truth, marketing efforts contribute to mutual funds' asset growth more than investment performance. Marketing and sales employees constitute significant shares of all mutual fund employees, and mutual fund companies with higher ratios of marketing employees enjoy higher asset growth, which is not principally driven by better investment performance.[29]

Investment professionals do well to consider their work within the second generation of behavioral finance. Such investment professionals understand the importance of marketing in identifying investors' wants, educating them about financial facts and human behavior, and helping them avoid errors on the way to satisfying wants. Indeed, marketing efforts in the form of advertising offer windows into investor wants.

## We Want Financial Security

Financial security is listed first by investors as the answer to the survey question, "Why is wealth important to you?"[30] As I related recently in "Financial Advertising in the Second Generation of Behavioral Finance," to some, wants for financial security mean wants for retirement with solid investment income and growth.[31] A firm's ad promised to satisfy these wants with growth and income funds, transferring the image of safety provided by a lighthouse to safety by investing in its funds. "Consistency. Experience. Dependability. They drew me to the lighthouse. Like a sailor searching for a safe haven. Or a baby boomer looking for solid growth and income funds."[32]

To others, financial security means freedom from poverty, especially when stock markets crash. An ad at the height of the 2008–09 crisis and the bottom of the stock market shows a silhouette of woman who says, "I'm anxious about retiring in a market like this." The ad reassures her: "Times like these require innovative solutions."[33]

Financial security matters so much because its absence is so painful. The economist Sendhil Mullainathan and the psychologist Eldar Shafir told the story of Sandra Harris, who was always a month ahead on her rent and bills until her husband lost his job. Their car insurance was due, and Sandra's only solution was a payday loan, which started a chain of such loans. Money was tighter the following month, and loan fees added to the amount owed. Sandra bounced checks, her car was repossessed, and she broke down crying. "It takes a lot for me to cry," she said. Sandra's story is typical, wrote Mullainathan and

---

[29]Wenxi Jiang and Mindy Z. Xiaolan, "Growing Beyond Performance" (15 July 2017). Available at SSRN: https://ssrn.com/abstract=3002922 or http://dx.doi.org/10.2139/ssrn.3002922.

[30]SEI Private Wealth Management, "The Generation Gap" (August 2011): 1–4.

[31]Meir Statman, "Financial Advertising in the Second Generation of Behavioral Finance," *Journal of Behavioral Finance* 18, no. 4 (August 2017): 470–77.

[32]Advertisement for Van Kampen, *Money* (December 2006).

[33]Advertisement for Prudential, *Money* (March 2009).

Shafir, illustrating the effects of scarcity: "When faced with scarcity, we borrow when it makes sense in the long run and when it does not" (p. 111).[34]

Another ad from the 2008–09 crisis says, "These days, a little peace of mind is invaluable. Get peace of mind knowing the income from your deferred variable annuity won't go down if the market does."[35] Indeed, "Living stress-free/Peace-of-mind" is at the top of a "What is wealth to you?" list in another survey.[36] People in that survey said they need $1.4 million on average to be "financially comfortable." The amounts grow by age. Millennials said on average that they need $1.3 million, but baby boomers said on average that they need $1.6 million.

Possession of wealth that makes us financially comfortable or even wealthy does not always bestow peace of mind and a sense of financial security. A financial adviser told me about a female client who saved ample money to retire at age 60. Her saving and spending ethos derived from a poor childhood. She was always afraid that she would end up living in a box eating cat food. Her personal statement was "By nature, I'm risk averse." That woman speaks in the language of risk, but she thinks in the language of financial security.

Another adviser told me about a 93-year-old female client living in a comfortable assisted living setting. She was strict about spending only dividend and interest income from a $2.5 million portfolio and income from rental property. Recently, the adviser learned that the woman was refraining from visiting friends because of concern over taxi fares, neglecting her love of the fine arts because of concern over the museum entrance fees, and shunning the idea of a new winter coat.

The adviser finally persuaded the woman to dip into capital at a $500 monthly rate. The woman said that she might just get herself a manicure—something she had not done since she was in her 30s.

## We Want to Nurture Our Children and Families

"Help children become successful" is listed second to "financial security" by investors as the answer to the survey question, "Why is wealth important to you?" "Educate children" is listed third.[37] We want to nurture our families, especially our children.

---

[34]Sendhil Mullainathan and Eldar Shafir, *Scarcity: Why Having Too Little Means So Much* (New York: Times Books, 2013).
[35]Advertisement for Fidelity, *Money* (March 2009).
[36]Suzanne Woolley, "How Much Money Do You Need to Be Wealthy in America?" Bloomberg (15 May 2018). www.bloomberg.com/news/articles/2018-05-15/how-much-money-do-you-need-to-be-wealthy-in-america.
[37]SEI Private Wealth Management, "The Generation Gap."

A commercial shows a young woman taking a cello out of a car, as the camera zooms to the sign on a building that reads "The Juilliard School." "It was not my dream to realize this day," says the financial adviser, "the day a father watched his daughter start at Juilliard. But I embraced that dream with unwavering attention, and made it my own, because that was the dream of my client." We see the proud father listening attentively as his daughter plays.[38]

Parents offer financial support to children long into adulthood. A survey found that 72% of parents said they have put their adult children's interests ahead of their own need to save for retirement. Parents pay for food and groceries, student loans, mobile phones, weddings, medical care, and down payments on homes.[39]

Children negotiate their transition from childhood to adulthood with their parents and themselves. Certain birthdays mark important occasions in the journey to adulthood, such as getting behind the wheel as a licensed driver without mom in the passenger seat, but these birthdays do not always mark transitions to full adulthood.[40] A British survey found that more than 1 in 10 adults did not think of themselves as adults until they reached the age of 27. One said, "Even after a career, two children and being together with my partner for 10 years, it still took being married to make me feel grown up."[41]

Some parents use financial support to control their children long into adulthood. An adviser told me about members of a wealthy family fighting for control. The children love their mother but want financial freedom. The mother has the best interests of her children at heart, but the intense control she attempts to exert over them through money creates stress for all involved.

Are adult children expected to support elderly parents? Answers vary from family to family and are often influenced by culture. An American man wrote on a relationship finance blog, "I have friends that are Mexican and they regularly send money home to their parents, regardless of their own

---

[38]www.youtube.com/watch?v=KM5qLPR1X_Q.

[39]Richard Eisenberg, "Parents' Support to Adult Kids: A Stunning $500 Billion a Year: Are boomers and Gen Xers harming their retirement due to their generosity?" Next Avenue (2 October 2018). www.nextavenue.org/parents-support-adult-kids/.

[40]Gena Kaufman, "Apparently THIS Is the Age Most People Feel Like Adults...(Do You Feel Like a Grownup Yet?), *Glamour* (2 August 2012). www.glamour.com/story/apparently-this-is-the-age-mos.

[41]Rozina Sini, "At What Age Do You Feel You Have Reached Adulthood?" BBC News (27 April 2017). www.bbc.com/news/education-39694563.

struggles. They help pay for events [such as parties] as well, which I don't understand. Paying bills is one thing, paying for parties is another."[42]

A woman wrote, "I'm Taiwanese American and have no problem helping out my parents financially. They worked hard to put my younger sibling and I through college and it's only fair to pay some of that back. It's definitely common (and expected) in Asian culture for children to give money on a regular basis to parents. And when I was growing up, my dad used to joke about waiting for me to buy him a Mercedes Benz, etc. Unfortunately, I don't have that much money to buy my parents such lavish gifts but if I did, I would."[43]

## We Want to Stay True to Our Values

A commercial for the Ave Maria Catholic Values mutual fund shows white pills forming a nest egg, then a question mark, and finally a skull and bones. The announcer says, "You worked hard to build a nest egg, but do your investments match your values? Many mutual funds invest in companies that support abortion, Planned Parenthood, and pornography. We screen out these companies so you can put your money where your faith is." Then, we see white clouds against a blue sky and an image of a cross and an open book, as the announcer says, "Ave Maria Mutual Funds—Smart investing and Catholic values."

We encounter such terms as socially responsible investing (SRI); environmental, social, and governance (ESG) investing; sustainability investing; green investing; and impact investing. But perhaps "values-based investing" is better because it is more inclusive. Values-based investors want to stay true to their values, but values differ. SRI investors likely exclude "sin" companies producing tobacco, alcohol, and weapons. But they are less likely to exclude companies supporting Planned Parenthood, abortions, and even pornography, as Ave Maria investors do.

Investors rooted in standard finance prefer to separate values from investments and separate the utilitarian benefits of investments from the expressive and emotional benefits of staying true to values. But investors rooted in second-generation behavioral finance accept that investments and values are commingled, as are utilitarian, expressive, and emotional benefits. That was true years ago and remains true today.

---

[42]MOMM, "I'm Native American," comment on *Make Love, Not Debt*, "Raise Your Children to Rely on Them—Asian Culture and Finances" (8 May 2007). www.makelovenotdebt. com/2007/05/raise_your_children_to_rely_on_them_asian_culture_and_finances.php.

[43]Clovestar, "I'm Taiwanese American," comment on *Make Love, Not Debt*, "Raise Your Children to Rely on Them—Asian Culture and Finances" (8 May 2007). www.makelovenotdebt. com/2007/05/raise_your_children_to_rely_on_them_asian_culture_and_finances.php.

In 1996, Vanguard phone representatives were told to deliver a blunt message to investors who raised concerns about tobacco holdings or other potentially objectionable investments: The funds' "sole purpose" is to pursue the maximum return possible within their investment objectives, so funds "cannot be constrained by any special interest group's definition of acceptable investments." In 2000, however, Vanguard reversed its 1996 position and added the Vanguard Calvert Social Index Fund to its lineup of funds.[44]

The message of a 2018 editorial in *Pensions & Investments* is equally blunt: "Don't shut out the Saudi market." The editorial noted the murder of the journalist Jamal Khashoggi, "allegedly by Saudi operatives," but argued that the attractiveness of the Saudi market should not be guided by "moral outrage," because the responsibility of fiduciaries is "to evaluate the country's suitability as a long-term investment."[45]

But the same issue of *Pensions & Investments* carries an announcement of a *Pensions & Investments* webinar called "ESG Investing: Momentum Build toward the Mainstream" and articles with such titles as "More Fund Execs Look at ESG Investing as a Logical Extension of Their Mission" and "SRI Investing Jumps 38% to $12 Trillion in U.S."[46]

Many investors care about staying true to their values. This fact is evident in the proliferation of values-based mutual funds and investor reaction to a new Morningstar sustainability rating. High sustainability ratings brought net mutual fund inflows of more than $24 billion, whereas low sustainability ratings caused net mutual fund outflows of more than $12 billion.[47]

The desire to stay true to values extends to investment professionals. Mutual fund managers who make campaign contributions to Democrats in the United States hold less in stocks of companies deemed socially irresponsible, such as tobacco, guns, or defense companies, and companies with bad employee relations or diversity records. This is true even for funds not classified explicitly as socially responsible.[48]

---

[44]Meir Statman, "The Religions of Social Responsibility," *Journal of Investing* 14, no. 3 (Fall 2005): 14–21.

[45]"Don't Shut Out the Saudi Market," editorial, *Pensions & Investments* (12 November 2018). www.pionline.com/article/20181112/PRINT/181119998/don-t-shut-out-the-saudi-market.

[46]"Don't Shut Out the Saudi Market."

[47]Samuel M. Hartzmark and Abigail B. Sussman, "Do Investors Value Sustainability? A Natural Experiment Examining Ranking and Fund Flows," *Journal of Finance* (9 August). doi:10.1111/jofi.12841.

[48]Harrison Hong and Leonard Kostovetsky, "Red and Blue Investing: Values and Finance," *Journal of Financial Economics* 103, no. 1 (January 2012): 1–19.

Public pension plans are more constrained by social norms than mutual or hedge funds, and they are more likely to shun stocks of "sin" companies, such as alcohol, tobacco, and gaming companies. "Sin" stocks have had higher returns than other stocks, consistent with being shunned by values-based investors.[49]

## We Want High Social Status

Virtue and adherence to values provide expressive and emotional benefits, and they are easy to proclaim even when not followed. Indeed, the virtuous "Help for the less fortunate" is listed fourth among the benefits of wealth, just after "Financial security," "Help children become successful," and "Educate children." And the virtuous "Have an impact on personal causes I care about" is not much lower. But the status-seeking "Increase my social status" comes next to last, just above "Other."[50] Yet wants for high social status are common, even if not easy to admit, let alone proclaim.

A commercial shows a man sitting in the economy class section of an airplane, where a young boy keeps kicking the back of his seat. The man rises and walks toward first class, as a song plays: "Fly . . . me . . . to . . . the . . . moon. . . ." A smiling first-class flight attendant walks toward the man, only to snap the curtain shut in his face as the song is interrupted abruptly. The caption that follows says, "First class is to remind you that you're not in first class," followed by "Don't get mad, get [name of brokerage firm]."

Few places display social status more nakedly than airports and airplanes. Are we standing in boarding line 1, 2, or the dreaded 5? Better yet, are we standing among the "special services" passengers who board even before those in line 1? Are we sitting in first class, sipping orange juice or champagne, watching economy-class passengers trundle by, hoping for a sliver of overhead space for their luggage? Our places in airport lines and on airplanes convey the utilitarian benefits of comfort, the expressive benefits of high social status, and the emotional benefits of pride.

We do not assess our social status by comparisons to everyone. Instead, we assess it by comparison to our relevant comparison groups. As the celebrated philosopher Bertrand Russell quipped decades ago, "Beggars do not envy millionaires, though of course they will envy other beggars who are more successful" (p. 85).[51] A more recent survey found that people define "rich" by comparison groups. People with incomes under $30,000 define rich

[49]Harrison Hong and Marcin Kacperczyk, "The Price of Sin: The Effects of Social Norms on Markets," *Journal of Financial Economics* 93, no. 1 (2009): 15–36.
[50]SEI Private Wealth Management, "The Generation Gap."
[51]Bertrand Russell, *The Conquest of Happiness* (London: George Allen & Unwin, 1930).

as incomes over \$100,000, but people with incomes over \$100,000 define rich as incomes over \$500,000.[52]

Neighbors are our relevant comparison group for social status if we socialize with them. An increase in neighbors' income imposes expressive and emotional costs on a person as great as an equal reduction in that person's own income.[53] And lottery winnings increase borrowing and bankruptcy rates among winners' neighbors as they try to catch up to the social status of the winners.[54]

Transparency, as in boarding lines at airports, classes on airplanes, or salary disclosures, exacerbates the expressive and emotional costs of low social status. A subset of University of California employees was informed about a new website listing the salaries of university employees. Subsequently, all employees were surveyed about their job satisfaction and job search intentions. Workers who learned from the website that their salaries are below the median of their group and occupation reported lower satisfaction with their jobs and salaries and significant increases in the likelihood of looking for a new job.[55]

Exclusivity enhances the social status of investors in hedge funds because these funds are available only to "accredited" investors, qualified by high income and wealth. "Exclusivity and secrecy were crucial to hedge funds from

---

[52]Danielle Kurtzleben, "How Americans Define 'Rich,' in One Chart," Vox (2 March 2015). www.vox.com/2015/3/2/8125629/middle-class-rich-US.

[53]Erzo F. P. Luttmer, "Neighbors as Negatives: Relative Earnings and Well-Being," *Quarterly Journal of Economics* 120, no. 3 (August 2005): 963–1002.

[54]Sumit Agarwal, Vyacheslav Mikhed, and Barry Scholnick, "Does the Relative Income of Peers Cause Financial Distress? Evidence from Lottery Winners and Neighboring Bankruptcies," FRB of Philadelphia Working Paper No. 18-16 (24 May 2018), available at SSRN: https://ssrn.com/abstract=3192154 or http://dx.doi.org/10.21799/frbp.wp.2018.16; Richard A. Easterlin, "Does Money Buy Happiness?" *The Public Interest* 30 (Winter 1973): 3–10; Russell, *The Conquest of Happiness*; Luttmer, "Neighbors as Negatives"; Ayesha Venkataraman and Nida Najar, "Here Comes the Bride. Now Count the Rest," *New York Times* (22 February 2017), www.nytimes.com/2017/02/22/world/asia/india-weddings-law-inequality.html; Shlomit Tsur, "Billionaires Want Billionaire Neighbors," *Globes* (20 March 2017), www.globes.co.il/en/article-billionaires-want-billionaire-neighbors-1001181577; John Brooks, *The Go-Go Years: The Drama and Crashing Finale of Wall Street's Bullish 60s* (New York: Wiley Investment Classics, 1999); Carol Vogel, "Works by Johns and de Kooning Sell for \$143.5 Million," *New York Times* (12 October 2006), www.nytimes.com/2006/10/12/arts/design/12geff.html; James S. Ang, Gregory Leo Nagel, and Jun Yang, "The Effect of Social Pressures on CEO Compensation" (17 November 2014), available at SSRN: https://ssrn.com/abstract=1107280 or http://dx.doi.org/10.2139/ssrn.1107280; Konrad Raff and Linus Siming, "Knighthoods, Damehoods, and CEO Behaviour," *Journal of Corporate Finance* (11 October 2016).

[55]David Card, Alexandre Mas, Enrico Moretti, and Emmanuel Saez, "Inequality at Work: The Effect of Peer Salaries on Job Satisfaction," *American Economic Review* 102, no. 6 (October 2012): 2981–3003.

the first," wrote John Brooks in 1973, describing the go-go 1960s. "It certified one's affluence while attesting to one's astuteness" (p. 144).[56]

A private equity manager told me about asking advisers for reasons to include private equity in their clients' portfolios. Some advisers were candid enough to admit that the exclusivity of private equity elevates the social status of their clients as well as their own. "A client who had a 'liquidity event' of $10 or $20 million," he said, "does not want to be lumped together with clients who can only scrape together the $3,000 minimum of a mutual fund."

Exclusivity enhances the social status of hedge fund managers who acquire paintings costing tens of millions of dollars. Steven Cohen, the founder and manager of SAC Capital Advisors, bought Willem de Kooning's *Police Gazette*, an abstract 1955 landscape, for $63.5 million, and Kenneth Griffin, managing director and chief executive of Citadel Investment Group, bought *False Start*, a seminal 1959 painting by Jasper Johns, for $80 million.[57]

Status competitions are common among corporate managers. CEOs whose comparison groups include many wealthy people earn a pay premium relative to other CEOs. Managers in the Commonwealth of Nations compete for the social status of knighthood and damehood honors, recognizing charitable work. Knighthoods and damehoods in New Zealand were abolished in April 2000 but reinstated in August 2009. Availability of honors diverted managers' time and corporate resources from the task of increasing stock prices as they strove for higher status.[58]

Many try to restrain status competitions, aware of their expressive and emotional costs. Weddings in India might include days-long celebrations, elephants covered in finery, and brides adorned in gold. The Indian state of Jammu and Kashmir tried to restrain status competition using rules that cap the number of guests at 400 or 500 and the number of dishes served at 14— no more than 7 vegetarian and 7 nonvegetarian dishes.[59]

## We Want Inclusion and Respect

A commercial begins with a young woman displaying a large round placard with "$65,000" printed on it. As she walks, she passes by other people, each displaying a similar placard printed with a dollar amount. She enters the door of "Brokerage LLC" and takes a seat. Soon, a man whose placard is

---

[56]Brooks, *The Go-Go Years*.
[57]Vogel, "Works by Johns and de Kooning."
[58]Raff and Siming, "Knighthoods, Damehoods, and CEO Behaviour."
[59]Venkataraman and Najar, "Here Comes the Bride."

printed with $262,000 arrives. A broker appears and greets that man, who follows him to his office. Next, an older woman whose placard is printed with $526,000 arrives. The broker greets her, and she follows him to his office. Finally, the young woman leaves in disgust, tossing her placard in a garbage bin.

The announcer says, "Everyone deserves attention, whether you saved a lot or just a little. We [at this investment company] believe that you're more than just a number. So we provide personal financial advice for every retirement investor."[60]

Demonstration of inclusion and respect likely underlies placing a woman, not a man, at the center of this commercial. Today's investment companies are aware of women's perceptions of exclusion and disrespect. British women in a focus group described investment companies as "unwelcoming, patronizing, untrustworthy, male-dominated, complicated, and full of jargon."[61] The following quotes come from a survey of American women:[62]

"First and foremost, many financial planners talk down to me. I ask a lot of questions because I want to understand their investment strategies."

"I hate being stereotyped because of my gender and age, and I don't appreciate being talked to like an infant."

"As a single woman, I often feel that financial services institutions aren't looking for my business. They want people who are preparing for kids. While I'd love to have kids, I don't want another reminder that kids aren't in my near-term future."

"Advisors are almost afraid to let the woman make the decision. They tend to defer to the male, no matter who is asking the questions or doing the investing."

An investigation by Henriette Prast, Jose Sanders, and Olga Leonhard found that investment language adds to women's sense of exclusion. Such words as "building" in "building your portfolio" are metaphors: The investor does not literally pile up assets as bricks. It would have been just as easy to say "cooking," "sewing," or "weaving" your portfolio. A study of metaphors in newspaper articles on the stock market found that they are predominantly masculine. These metaphors may create positive affect among men, not

---

[60]PNC Investments, "Numbers." www.youtube.com/watch?v=u5gNNUsG2EI.

[61]Claer Barrett, "Best of Money: Why Do Most Women Fear the Stock Market?" *Financial Times* (3 June 2016). www.ft.com/content/b681b8e6-2705-11e6-8b18-91555f2f4fde.

[62]Michael J. Silverstein, Kosuke Kato, and Pia Tischhauser, "Women Want More (in Financial Services)," Boston Consulting Group (October 2009). http://image-src.bcg.com/Images/BCG_Women_Want_More_in_Financial_Services_Oct_2009_tcm9-125088.pdf.

women, and contribute to gender differences in stated risk tolerance, financial risk taking, stock market participation, and excessive trading.[63]

Disrespect to women investors and exclusion are not new. Indeed, disrespect and exclusion, coupled with condescension, were more blatant a century ago. "A woman in Massachusetts wrote to me a little while ago, in very great distress," read a story from the *World's Work* in 1911. "Of course, it took only a little persuasion and a few cold facts to demonstrate to her that what she thought was a cyclone was merely a summer breeze. Her letter and her trouble, however, are merely types. They are an extreme illustration of the facts that make difficult the transaction of investment business with women and with constitutionally frightened men."[64]

The portrait of women investors had changed little by 1965, when women were portrayed in an Investment Company Institute brochure as maturing from nursery to wedding dress and on to leisurely retirement. "By and large," it said, "women are not followers of investment trends. Women have the savings instinct but most find little pleasure in poring over complicated charts and forecasts, and hesitate to invest."

Women pushed back in the 1970s. Patricia Carbine, then publisher and editor in chief of *Ms.* magazine, told more than 500 women packing an auditorium that money might be the root of all evil, but "the root of all evil feeds the tree of life."[65]

Yet societal norms where men are assumed to have greater financial knowledge than women continue to disadvantage women. Families with husbands who are financially knowledgeable are more likely to invest in the stock market than those with wives of equal financial knowledge. An experiment revealed that female identity hinders idea contribution by women, whereas male identity causes men to be obstinate.[66]

Single women tend to avoid choices that are likely to enhance their careers because these choices imply traits, such as ambition, that are values in men but might lessen the marriage prospects of women. Single women

---

[63]Henriette Prast, Jose Sanders, and Olga Leonhard, "Can Words Breed or Kill Investment? Metaphors, Imagery, Affect and Investor Behaviour," CentER Discussion Paper Series No. 2018-014 (17 April 2018). Available at SSRN: https://ssrn.com/abstract=3164260 or http://dx.doi.org/10.2139/ssrn.3164260.

[64]C.M. Keys, "The Nervous Investor and The News," in *The World's Work*, Vol. XXI, edited by Walter H. Page, 14081–83 (Garden City, NY: Doubleday, Page & Company, 1911).

[65]Kathryn Welling, "Women and Money '77: You've Come a Long Way, Baby—Further than Brokers Think," *Barron's* (10 October 1977): 9–12.

[66]Da Ke, "Who Wears the Pants? Gender Identity Norms and Intra-Household Financial Decision Making" (4 August 2018). Available at SSRN: https://ssrn.com/abstract=2909720 or http://dx.doi.org/10.2139/ssrn.2909720.

in an MBA program asked for lower salaries, expressed lower willingness to travel, and reported lower readiness to work long hours when they were aware that their classmates, especially single men, will observe their preferences.[67]

Today's drive for inclusion and respect encompasses women as investors and as investment professionals. A 2016 CFA Institute Research Foundation brief, "Gender Diversity in Investment Management," reported the following:[68]

> In the last year, CFA Institute, along with many professional organizations, began to look more closely at the composition of its membership. We found a surprising number: Women represent less than one in five CFA charterholders. (p. 2)

> It is most noteworthy that women represent only 1 in 10 people in the key leadership positions of CEO, chief investment officer, and chief financial officer. The occupations with the highest representation of women are performance analyst, compliance analyst/officer, and relationship manager/account manager, but even in these occupations, women represent less than one in three workers. (p. 8)

Women are few among investment professionals, but they are punished more severely for misconduct. When misconduct occurs, female advisers are more likely to lose their jobs and less likely to find new jobs than male advisers. Women face more severe penalties than men despite misconduct that is less costly and a lower propensity for repeat misconduct.[69]

The 2016 CFA Institute Research Foundation report noted that investment professionals perceive benefits in gender diversity and clients perceive these benefits even more keenly. Indeed, there is evidence that all diversity, including cultural diversity, confers benefits. A study of sell-side analysts showed that cultural diversity improves the accuracy of analysts' forecasts and mitigates excessive optimism and dispersion of forecasts. A study of

---

[67]Leonardo Bursztyn, Thomas Fujiwara, and Amanda Pallais, "'Acting Wife': Marriage Market Incentives and Labor Market Investments," *American Economic Review* 107, no. 11 (November 2017): 3288–319. https://doi.org/10.1257/aer.20170029.

[68]Rebecca Fender, Renée B. Adams, Brad M. Barber, and Terrance Odean, "Gender Diversity in Investment Management: New Research for Practitioners on How to Close the Gender Gap," CFA Institute Research Foundation 2016B-5 (1 September 2016). Available at SSRN: https://ssrn.com/abstract=2978151.

[69]Mark Egan, Gregor Matvos, and Amit Seru, "When Harry Fired Sally: The Double Standard in Punishing Misconduct," Harvard Business School Finance Working Paper No. 19-047 (8 August 2018). Available at SSRN: https://ssrn.com/abstract=2931940 or http://dx.doi.org/10.2139/ssrn.2931940.

conference calls showed that cultural diversity is associated with better inter-action, evident in a greater number of analysts asking questions.[70]

Minorities and the poor are among the people granted the least inclu-sion and respect, and they are often exploited. The most profitable American credit card consumers are those on the verge of bankruptcy.[71] People residing in low-income ZIP codes refinanced mortgages and increased spending sub-stantially when home prices rose before the 2008–09 financial crisis, whereas people in high-income ZIP codes did not.[72] Subprime lenders advertised expensive mortgages, misleading borrowers into inferior mortgage choices. Indeed, advertising was most effective when targeted at the uninformed, who tend to be less educated, members of minorities, and poor.[73]

Discrimination against minorities affects their risk perceptions and port-folio decisions. Minorities perceive greater income risk, which lowers equity ownership. The economic effects of socially amplified risk perceptions are comparable to those of other known determinants of portfolio decisions.[74]

Loan applications by African-American and Hispanic borrowers are more likely to be rejected than those of white applicants. Differences in rejec-tion rates stem from loan officers' lending discrimination by facial features. Discrimination is evident in the finding that differences in rejection rates are pronounced among small lenders and independent mortgage companies but not among fintech lenders. Fintech lenders, unlike loan officers, do not observe loan applicants in person. Instead, they use algorithms in decisions to approve or reject loan applications.[75]

[70]Kenneth J. Merkley, Roni Michaely, and Joseph Pacelli, "Cultural Diversity on Wall Street: Evidence from Sell-Side Analysts' Forecasts," Swiss Finance Institute Research Paper No. 19-07 (6 February 2019). Available at SSRN: https://ssrn.com/abstract=3068232 or http://dx.doi.org/10.2139/ssrn.3068232.

[71]Andrea Freeman, "Payback: A Structural Analysis of the Credit Card Problem," *Arizona Law Review* 55, no. 151 (March 2013). Available at SSRN: http://ssrn.com/abstract=2231738.

[72]Atif Mian and Amir Sufi, "House Price Gains and U.S. Household Spending from 2002 to 2006," National Bureau of Economic Research Working Paper No. 20152 (2014).

[73]Umit G. Gurun, Gregor Matvos, and Amit Seru, "Advertising Expensive Mortgages," *Journal of Finance* 71, no. 5 (October 2016): 2371–416.

[74]William J. Bazley, Yosef Bonaparte, George M. Korniotis, and Alok Kumar, "Social Risk and Portfolio Choice," 7th Miami Behavioral Finance Conference 2016 (4 December 2018). Available at SSRN: https://ssrn.com/abstract=2863351 or http://dx.doi.org/10.2139/ssrn.2863351.

[75]Robert P. Bartlett, Adair Morse, Richard H. Stanton, and Nancy E. Wallace, "Consumer Lending Discrimination in the FinTech Era," UC Berkeley Public Law Research Paper (7 December 2017). Available at SSRN: https://ssrn.com/abstract=3063448 or http://dx.doi.org/10.2139/ssrn.3063448.

People who experience banking early in life exhibit better credit behavior through greater financial literacy and trust in financial institutions. In contrast, people who grow up in financially underdeveloped Native American reservations suffer lower credit scores and are more likely to have delinquent accounts. The effects of growing up in financially underdeveloped areas are persistent, dissipating only slowly after people move to more developed areas.[76]

## We Want Fairness

As I discussed in "Financial Advertising in the Second Generation of Behavioral Finance,"[77] an ad addressed investors' wants for fairness by emphasizing the "golden rule" philosophy that "led us to remove the noise of Wall Street and make our clients' interest the only interests. Naming you not just a client, but a client-owner. Providing at-cost funds rather than low-cost funds."[78]

Another ad quoted an investor: "Nickeled and dimed? I feel like I'm being quartered." It responded, "We prefer to focus our energy on making your portfolio bigger, not smaller. . . . There are no account service fees, no hidden fees. . . . In fact, our pricing is completely simple, transparent and completely laid out—so you always know how much, when and why."[79]

The stock market is often compared with a game. But which game is it, and what are its fairness rules? Is it a game of luck, such as craps, where the rules of fairness entitle players to fair dice? Or is it a game that combines luck with skill, like poker, where the rules of fairness entitle players to see the cards before the winner takes the pot but not to equal information about winning strategies? Or is it a game like golf played among amateurs, where stronger players are assigned a "handicap" to lessen their advantage over weak ones?

Students and investment professionals indicate that community rules of fairness correspond best to the rules of golf played by amateurs. The rules allow one trader to gain advantage over another with information gained through research, skill, or even luck but not with information, stolen or not, that another cannot gain through research or skill.

---

[76]James R. Brown, J. Anthony Cookson, and Rawley Heimer, "Growing Up Without Finance," 7th Miami Behavioral Finance Conference 2016 (8 September 2016). Available at SSRN: https://ssrn.com/abstract=2809164 or http://dx.doi.org/10.2139/ssrn.2809164.
[77]Statman, "Financial Advertising."
[78]Advertisement for Vanguard, *Money* (May 2010).
[79]Advertisement for Charles Schwab, *Money* (September 2007).

The kind of trade that is considered to be fair is one by "John Burr." He is a shareholder of the Beta Corporation, and he used just his research and skill for making his sell decision:

> The stock of the Beta Corporation went up in price from $30 last year to $50 recently. John Burr, a shareholder who owns 1,000 shares, analyzed Beta's financial prospects and thinks that the stock is worth no more than $40. John decided to sell his shares at the current $50 price. Please rate John's behavior as Acceptable or Unfair. (p. 49)[80]

John Burr's behavior was rated "Acceptable" by 99% of investment professionals and 94% of students.

Insiders, such as corporate executives, are more powerful than other members of the community because they are wealthier and their inside information often insulates them from trading losses. Both students and investment professionals consider transactions by powerful insiders especially unfair.

Consider a pair of vignettes about "Larry Wood," who trades on inside information. In the first vignette, Larry Wood is an executive who earns $150,000 per year and trades $50,000 worth of stock, whereas in the second, he is a summer intern who earns $10 per hour and trades $500 worth of stocks.

Most investment professionals and students rated the behavior of Larry Wood unfair, whether an executive or intern, but larger proportions of both groups rated the behavior of Larry Wood the executive unfair than rated that of Larry Wood the intern unfair.

Law scholar Donald Langevoort noted that there is an "emotional component" to the assessment of trading by powerful insiders, "in which envy and frustration at the wealth and power of economic elites, and resulting mistrust, also play a role" (p. 1329). He added, "One reason why insider trading regulation takes on such prominence in contemporary securities enforcement is its seemingly unique ability to interest the public and hence operate as a vehicle for the SEC to seek both visibility and support for its mission. Insider trading stories are wonderful drama: When they involve the rich and famous like Ivan Boesky and Michael Milken, they tap into images of power, greed, and hubris."[81]

We see the importance of wants for fairness in the annuity puzzle, which is the puzzle of low demand for life annuities despite their benefits in assuring

---

[80]Meir Statman, "Is It Fair? Judging the Fairness of Insider Trading," *Journal of Investment Consulting* 12, no. 1 (2011): 47–59.

[81]Donald Langevoort, "Rereading Cady, Roberts: The Ideology and Practice of Insider Trading Regulation," *Columbia Law Review* 99 (1999): 1319–41.

income throughout life. The widest differences in preferences for annuities are in perceptions of their fairness.[82]

And we see subversion of fairness by companies in the selection of arbitrators in securities disputes. Companies can identify arbitrators as systematically friendly to industry or systematically friendly to consumers. Companies use this information in the process to select industry-friendly arbitrators. Competition between arbitrators exacerbates the informational advantage of companies, leading all arbitrators to lean toward industry.[83]

## Conclusion

We share a broad set of wants. We all want to obtain financial security, to nurture our children and families, to stay true to our values, and to gain social status, respect, inclusion, and fairness. But we vary in wants by such personality traits as openness; such values as environmentalism and patriotism; religion, such as Christianity or Islam; such circumstances as life in a city or in a rural area; and education, such as college or high school.

The rational investors of standard finance separate their roles as investors from their roles as consumers. As investors, they care only about maximizing wealth. As consumers, they care about all the benefits of wealth—utilitarian, expressive, and emotional. But the normal people described in the second generation of behavioral finance commingle their roles as investors and consumers. Houses we own are investments—parts of our wealth—but they are also the providers of the utilitarian benefits of roofs over our heads and the expressive and emotional benefits of high social status and pride.

Wants are different from errors. The utilitarian benefits of renting a house might well exceed those of owning one, but owning a house is not necessarily an error. The expressive and emotional benefits of owning a house compensate some homeowners for lower utilitarian benefits.

Rational people are free of conflicts between wants and "shoulds," whereas normal investors are not. The voice of wants says, "I want to watch a movie now," but the voice of shoulds says, "You should study for tomorrow's exam." Investment advice is full of shoulds: save more, spend less, diversify, buy and hold.

---

[82]Suzanne B. Shu, Robert Zeithammer, and John W. Payne, "The Pivotal Role of Fairness: Which Consumers Like Annuities?" National Bureau of Economic Research Working Paper No. w25067 (September 2018). Available at SSRN: https://ssrn.com/abstract=3254042.

[83]Mark Egan, Gregor Matvos, and Amit Seru, "Arbitration with Uninformed Consumers," Harvard Business School Finance Working Paper No. 19-046 (June 2019). Available at SSRN: https://ssrn.com/abstract=3260442 or http://dx.doi.org/10.2139/ssrn.3260442.

We face conflicts and trade-offs between utilitarian, expressive, and emotional benefits. We stay true to our values by making socially responsible investments or through contributions to charity, but in doing so, we sacrifice some of the utilitarian, expressive, and emotional benefits of financial security.

The first generation of behavioral finance, starting in the early 1980s, focused on people's shortcuts and errors as they make choices. The second generation of behavioral finance accepts people's wants and distinguishes wants from errors, thereby providing a truer portrait of normal people.

# 3. Cognitive Shortcuts and Errors

A married couple can use a framing shortcut by placing their money into a single joint checking account. Or they can use an alternative framing shortcut by placing their money into two separate checking accounts—one for the husband and one for the wife.

Framing is a cognitive shortcut, such as framing money into one or two actual checking accounts or into one or two mental accounts we keep in our minds. Each shortcut involves considerations of utilitarian, expressive, and emotional benefits and costs.

Utilitarian considerations include differences in bank fees for a joint checking account or two separate checking accounts and differences in the likelihood of an overdraft, such as when a wife is unaware of a check drawn by her husband on their joint checking account. Expressive and emotional considerations include openness and trust between the husband and wife sharing a joint checking account and the financial independence and power of the husband and wife each having a separate account.

Neither a joint checking account nor two separate checking accounts are necessarily errors. Sometimes, however, shortcuts turn into errors, imposing costs greater than benefits and diverting us from our wants.

Framing is one example of cognitive shortcuts, errors, and associated wants, yet there is no uniform list of cognitive shortcuts, errors, and associated wants. Many lists include hundreds of cognitive errors, are rarely explicit about cognitive shortcuts, and are never explicit about which wants they satisfy. Moreover, many lists are tainted by hindsight errors, as if we can judge the wisdom of each choice by its outcome. In hindsight, we blame optimism errors for accepting good but uncertain investments whose outcomes turned out to be poor, and in equal hindsight, we blame pessimism errors for rejecting bad but uncertain investments whose outcomes turned out to be good.

I describe here cognitive shortcuts, errors, and associated wants most relevant in the context of finance, including framing, hindsight, confirmation, anchoring and adjustment, representativeness, availability, and confidence.

## Framing

"If you have been in a poker game for a while, and you still don't know who the patsy is, you're the patsy." Vanessa Selbst, the most successful female player in the history of professional poker, needs no reminding of this old poker lesson. Instead, she is using it in her new work at Bridgewater Associates, a hedge fund.[84]

Selbst frames poker games correctly as zero-sum games. All the money on the poker table comes from the pockets of the players. If some walk away from the table with winnings, it must be that others walk away from it with losses. The sum of winnings and losses must equal zero. Based on that experience, she also frames financial market games correctly. She said, "If something's undervalued, does that mean you want to buy? Well, maybe, but if you buy it, how's it going to go up? Who are the other people who are going to buy? . . . You have to be thinking about who the other players are and what they're going to do."[85]

We use framing shortcuts when we simplify complex problems and substitute solutions to the simplified problems for solutions to the complex problems. We use framing shortcuts well when the solutions to the simplified problems are close to the solutions to the complex problems. We commit cognitive errors when the solutions to the simplified problems are far from the solutions to the complex problems.

Framing poker games correctly as zero-sum games is relatively easy. Each player sees all the other players across the poker table, and it is obvious to all that all the money on the poker table comes from the pockets of players.

Framing financial market trading games as equivalents of poker games is a simplifying framing shortcut. But this shortcut can quickly turn into a framing error, because financial market trading games are market-sum games, yet they are often described inaccurately as zero-sum games. Moreover, financial market trading games are more complex than poker games because traders do not see each other.

Competent traders frame financial market trading games correctly as market-sum games. The market return of a financial market, such as a stock market, is rarely zero. Instead, it is usually positive or negative. Financial market trading games are market-sum games because the sum of the gains and losses of traders must equal the market return. Traders are correct when they object to the description of financial market trading games as zero-sum games, noting that all traders can collect positive returns when market returns are positive. Yet not all traders can be winners. If some traders are winners, collecting returns exceeding market returns, it must be that other traders are losers, collecting returns short of market returns.

---

[84]Steve Friess, "From the Poker Table to Wall Street," *New York Times* (27 July 2018). www.nytimes.com/2018/07/27/business/vanessa-selbst-poker-bridgewater.html?smprod=nytcore-ipad&smid=nytcore-ipad-share.
[85]Friess, "From the Poker Table."

A parallel fact is that poker players with above-average skills can still be patsies in games where the skills of some other players are much above average. Indeed, it is possible that the top 1% of poker players, such as Ms. Selbst, walk away with great winnings, and almost all other players, even those with above-average skills, walk away with losses.

As in poker, traders with above-average skills are not assured of winning—walking away with above-market returns. Instead, it is possible that the top 1% of traders, those with the best skills or information, garner returns much higher than market returns, and all other traders, even those with above-average skills or information, garner below-market returns.

We see framing shortcuts and errors in many financial settings. Official US statistical agencies report monthly or quarterly numbers for GDP, industrial production, inflation, and more. In many other countries, however, statistical agencies report annual numbers.

Reporting data as monthly, quarterly, or annual makes no difference to rational investors because these data are different only in frame, not in substance. Yet financial market prices react more strongly to the most recent number placed in the headline of the press release—the monthly or quarterly number in countries that place that number in the headline and the annual number in countries that place that number in the headline.[86]

Labels are framing devices. Life insurance or annuity premiums can be labeled as a "loss," whereby the expected returns are a loss, but the policies provide protection against disaster—death in the case of life insurance and outliving your money in the case of annuities. Alternatively, these premiums can be labeled as "assurance." The loss frame turned out to be effective in motivating Dutch pension plan participants to look up information about alternatives for pension income, but the loss frame also evoked negative perceptions and evaluations. The assurance frame turned out to be better—an effective motivator to look up such information, while avoiding negative perceptions and evaluations.[87]

Another study divided Dutch pension plan participants into four pension income quantification frames: annual pension income, monthly pension income, pension income as a percentage of current income, and pension

---

[86]Jeffrey A. Frankel and Ayako Saiki, "Does It Matter If Statistical Agencies Frame the Month's CPI Report on a 1-Month or 12-Month Basis?" HKS Working Paper No. 16-011 (12 March 2016). Available at SSRN: http://ssrn.com/abstract=2749123 or http://dx.doi.org/10.2139/ssrn.2749123.

[87]Wiebke Eberhardt, Elisabeth Brüggen, Thomas Post, and Chantal Hoet, "Framing the Future: Using Investment and Assurance Frames to Encourage Retirement Information Search" (4 July 2018). Available at SSRN: https://ssrn.com/abstract=3060519 or http://dx.doi.org/10.2139/ssrn.3060519.

income as a decimal of current income. Expressing pension income as a percentage of current income significantly increased the probability that plan participants perceived their pension income as too low. In contrast, expressing pension income as a decimal of current income significantly decreased the probability that plan participants perceived their pension income as too low.[88]

Client payments to financial advisers can be made "out of pocket" (that is, by writing a check) or "out of assets" (that is, out of the investment portfolio). The two are different in frame but not in substance. Yet investors are willing to pay 25% less, on average, when payments are framed as out of pocket than when framed as out of assets.[89] It is no wonder that advisers charge their clients by the out-of-assets frame.

Hal Hershfield, Stephen Shu, and Shlomo Benartzi found that framing saving as a daily amount is more effective in encouraging people to enroll in a recurring deposit program than framing the same total amount as a monthly amount. Framing deposits as a daily amount also reduced the participation gap between lower- and higher-income people: Many in the highest-income bracket but few in the lowest-income bracket participated when the program was framed as a $150 monthly deposit, but the difference in participation was eliminated when deposits were framed as $5 per day.[90]

## Hindsight

Admonitions against hindsight errors are common, conveyed in such sayings as "Hindsight is 20/20," "Monday morning quarterbacking," or as a judge said in the 1857 Corman v. The Eastern Counties Railway decision, "Nothing is so easy as to be wise after the event."

Yet not all hindsight is about errors. Indeed, good hindsight shortcuts serve as good instructors, teaching us to repeat actions that brought good outcomes and avoid actions that brought bad ones. We studied for exams and aced them. We learned that acing exams is the likely outcome of studying for exams.

---

[88]Henriette Prast and Federica Teppa, "The Power of Percentage: Quantitative Framing of Pension Income," De Nederlandsche Bank Working Paper No. 578 (11 December 2017). Available at SSRN: https://ssrn.com/abstract=3086507 or http://dx.doi.org/10.2139/ssrn.3086507.

[89]Yevgeny Mugerman, Orly Sade, and Eyal Winter, "Out-of-Pocket vs. Out-of-Profit in Financial Advisory Fees: Evidence from the Lab," Hebrew University of Jerusalem Working Paper (21 March 2019). Available at SSRN: https://ssrn.com/abstract=3061020 or http://dx.doi.org/10.2139/ssrn.3061020.

[90]Hal Hershfield, Stephen Shu, and Shlomo Benartzi, "Temporal Reframing and Participation in a Savings Program: A Field Experiment" (2 February 2019). Available at SSRN: https://ssrn.com/abstract=3097468 or http://dx.doi.org/10.2139/ssrn.3097468.

Hindsight shortcuts are always precise when there are one-to-one associations between past events and future events, actions and outcomes, and causes and consequences. But hindsight shortcuts can easily turn into hindsight errors where randomness and luck are prominent, loosening associations between past events and future events, actions and outcomes, and causes and consequences. Hindsight errors might arise from unawareness of the influence of randomness and luck or from a desire to see the world as predictable, devoid of randomness or luck.

We ace an exam without studying when luck is good and exam questions match whatever we remember from the few classes we have attended. But when luck is bad, we fail the exam and perhaps the course. Hindsight errors can mislead lucky students into thinking that they can ace exams without studying and can mislead unlucky students into thinking that studying for exams is futile.

Hindsight errors are an obstacle to all historians, including financial market historians. Once we know historical events in hindsight, we are tempted to believe that we have known them in foresight. In hindsight, ill-considered choices with good outcomes are described as excellent choices and bad outcomes of well-considered choices are described as horrendous choices.

"Who's better for stocks: Dems or GOP?" asked a CNBC article on 7 November 2016, the day before voters elected Donald Trump as president. "As the historic 2016 U.S. presidential election approaches," it said, "major Wall Street analysts agree that the S&P 500 will likely sell off if Donald Trump wins, and at least hold gains if Hillary Clinton wins."[91]

"We believe that if Trump wins, markets are likely to fall further," said J.P. Morgan stock market strategists. "The S&P 500 could potentially fall 11 to 13 percent if Trump wins the election," said Barclays' strategists. And BMO Capital Markets' strategists said, "A Trump win would likely result in 'jittery' markets . . . while markets would likely be 'happy' with a Clinton victory."[92]

These forecasts and their refutation, only a day later, teach us once more that hindsight is much clearer than foresight. The psychologist Baruch Fischhoff, who introduced us to hindsight shortcuts and errors, wrote, "In hindsight, people consistently exaggerate what could have been anticipated in foresight. . . . People believe that others should have been able to anticipate events much better than they actually did. They even misremember their

---

[91]Evelyn Cheng, "Wall Street Reacts: Here's What the Markets Will Do After the Election," Yahoo! Finance (7 November 2016). https://finance.yahoo.com/news/wall-street-reacts-heres-markets-144110170.html.
[92]Cheng, "Wall Street Reacts."

own predictions so as to exaggerate in hindsight what they knew in foresight" (p. 428).[93]

Hindsight errors underlie consequence–cause matching. We err by inferring causes from consequences we know only in hindsight, as if we had known these consequences in foresight. People inferred that a computer crash had a large cause, such as a widespread computer virus, if it had a large consequence; for example, Adam lost his job. But they inferred that the identical failure was more likely to have a smaller cause, such as a cooling fan malfunction, if the consequence was small; for example, Adam graduated on time. Yet the consequence gave no information about what caused the crash.[94]

The famous investor Warren Buffett is proficient at distinguishing foresight from hindsight. The writer Roger Lowenstein described Buffett's reaction to the increase in the Dow Jones Industrial Index beyond 1,000 in intraday trading in early 1966 and its subsequent decline by spring. Some of Buffett's partners warned him that the market might decline further. Such warnings, said Buffett, raised two questions:

"1. If they knew in February that the Dow was going to 865 in May, why didn't they let me in on it then; and

2. If they didn't know what was going to happen during the ensuing three months back in February, how do they know in May?" (p. 97)[95]

How much is clear foresight worth? Imagine that we are transported back to 10 May 1965, investing $1,000 in shares of Warren Buffett's Berkshire Hathaway at $18 per share and another $1,000 in the S&P 500 Index. Our $1,000 investment in Berkshire Hathaway would have grown to $17 million by 31 December 2018, while our $1,000 investment in the S&P 500 Index, including dividends, would have grown to only $139,400. The value in hindsight of a share of Berkshire Hathaway on 10 May 1965 was $2,195, more than 121 times greater than its $18 price that day. A $2,195 investment in the S&P 500 on 10 May 1965 would have grown to $306,000 by 31 December 2018, if growing at the S&P 500 rate of growth. The $306,000 figure is equal to the price of a share of Berkshire Hathaway on that day. Evidently, investors, as a

---

[93]Baruch Fischhoff, "Debiasing," in *Judgment Under Uncertainty: Shortcuts and Biases*, edited by Daniel Kahneman, Paul Slovic, and Amos Tversky, 422–44 (Cambridge, UK: Cambridge University Press, 1982).

[94]Robyn A. LeBoeuf and Michael I. Norton, "Consequence-Cause Matching: Looking to the Consequences of Events to Infer Their Causes," *Journal of Consumer Research* 39, no. 1 (June 2012), 128–41.

[95]Roger Lowenstein, *Buffett: The Making of an American Capitalist* (New York: Random House, 1995).

group, did not see Berkshire Hathaway's performance in foresight on 10 May 1965 as clearly as they saw it in hindsight on 31 December 2018.

Past performance, even Berkshire Hathaway's past performance, is no guarantee of future results. The ratio of the value in hindsight of Berkshire Hathaway's share to its price was 1.06 on 31 December 2002, 0.92 on 31 December 2008, and 1.02 on 31 December 2014.

## Confirmation

"Nostradamus 2018 prediction: THE END OF THE WORLD is coming next year, warns famed prophet." This alert was issued by Express.co.uk, the digital arm of the *Daily Express* and *Sunday Express*, on 30 December 2017, above a photo montage of Nostradamus holding a globe; Kim Jong-Un, president of North Korea, with a raised arm; and an exploding earth.[96]

The world did not come to an end in 2018. But true believers in end-of-the-world predictions always dismiss evidence disconfirming their beliefs, and they are sure to dismiss it in the future.

We use confirmation shortcuts when we examine evidence to confirm or disconfirm beliefs, claims, or hypotheses. We use confirmation shortcuts well when we search for disconfirming evidence as vigorously as we search for confirming evidence and assign equal weight to disconfirming and confirming evidence. We commit confirmation errors when we search for confirming evidence while neglecting disconfirming evidence and when we assign less weight to disconfirming evidence than to confirming evidence.

We might take comfort in a belief that scientists are free of confirmation errors and that aversion to disconfirming evidence is confined to those ignorant of science. The famed astronomer Carl Sagan, inducted into the International Space Hall of Fame, took such comfort. He is quoted on the hall's website as saying, "In science it often happens that scientists say, 'You know that's a really good argument; my position is mistaken,' and then they would actually change their minds and you never hear that old view from them again. . . . When Kepler found his long-cherished belief did not agree with the most precise observation, he accepted the uncomfortable fact. He preferred the hard truth to his dearest illusions, that is the heart of science."[97]

Yet Sagan's sunny view of the power of science to free us from confirmation errors is not shared by all, surely not by all scientists. Max Planck, the

---

[96]Sebastian Kettley, "Nostradamus 2018 prediction: The END OF THE WORLD is coming next year warns famed prophet," Express.co.uk (30 December 2017). www.express.co.uk/news/weird/898132/nostradamus-2018-prediction-end-of-the-world-prophecy.

[97]"Carl Sagan," International Space Hall of Fame, New Mexico Museum of Space History (website), accessed 7 September 2019. www.nmspacemuseum.org/halloffame/detail.php?id=149.

most celebrated scientist of his era, said, "A new scientific truth does not triumph by convincing its opponents and making them see the light, but rather because its opponents eventually die." We know this view in its pithier form: "Science advances funeral by funeral" (p. 2889).[98]

Findings by Pierre Azoulay, Christian Fons-Rosen, and Joshua S. Graff Zivin confirm Max Planck's view and disconfirm Carl Sagan's. They examined entry rates of academic life scientists into fields dominated by star (outstanding) academic life scientists who passed away prematurely. They found that the flow of articles by noncollaborators of the star scientists increases once fields are less hostile to findings that disconfirm the findings of deceased star scientists.[99]

Wants, reflected in motivated reasoning, underlie much of confirmation errors. Star scientists, who have established their social status and careers on claims they believe are true, are motivated to search for evidence confirming their beliefs and to dismiss disconfirming evidence.

Psychologists Nicholas Epley and Thomas Gilovich noted that most people do not reason like impartial judges. Instead, they recruit evidence like attorneys, looking for evidence that confirms their claims while trying to steer clear of evidence that might disconfirm it.[100] When considering claims they favor, people ask, "Can I believe this?" This evidentiary standard is easy to meet; after all, there is always some confirming evidence for even dubious end-of-the-world claims. In contrast, when considering claims they disfavor, people ask, "Must I believe this?" This evidentiary standard is harder to meet; after all, some disconfirming evidence exists even for the claim that Darwin's theory of evolution is consistent with the evidence.

In one study, students were told that they would be tested for an enzyme deficiency that would lead to pancreatic disorders later in life. Students deposited saliva in a cup and then put litmus paper in the saliva. Half the students were told they would know they had the enzyme deficiency if the litmus paper changed color. The other half were told they would know they had it if the paper did not change color. The litmus paper was of a kind that it did not change color.[101]

Students who were told that the unchanged litmus paper conveyed good news did not keep the paper in the cup very long. In contrast, those who were

[98]Pierre Azoulay, Christian Fons-Rosen, and Joshua S. Graff Zivin, "Does Science Advance One Funeral at a Time?," *American Economic Review* 109, no. 8 (2019): 2889–2920.

[99]Azoulay et al., "Does Science Advance One Funeral at a Time?"

[100]Nicholas Epley and Thomas Gilovich, "The Mechanics of Motivated Reasoning," *Journal of Economic Perspectives* 30, no. 3 (Summer 2016): 133–40.

[101]Peter H. Ditto and David F. Lopez, "Motivated Skepticism: Use of Differential Decision Criteria for Preferred and Nonpreferred Conclusions," *Journal of Personality and Social Psychology* 63, no. 4 (October 1992): 568–84.

told that the unchanged color reflected bad news tried to recruit more evidence. They kept the paper in the cup longer, placed the test strip directly on their tongue, re-dipped the strip, shook it, wiped it, blew on it, and in general quite carefully scrutinized the recalcitrant test strip.[102]

The reluctance to confront disconfirming evidence has financial costs. Huntington's disease (HD), a hereditary degenerative disease, shortens lifespan. Genetic testing is perfectly predictive of HD and carries little economic cost. Yet few among those at HD risk choose to undergo presymptomatic testing, likely because evidence from the tests might disconfirm the belief that they are free of HD genes. People with confirmed HD adjust their financial choices in ways consistent with their diagnosis, but untested people express optimistic beliefs about their health and make financial decisions, such as about retirement, as if they are not at risk for HD.[103]

The association between smoking and lifespans is not as tight as between HD genes and lifespans, but evidence is clear that lifespans of smokers are, on average, shorter than those of nonsmokers. The pricing of annuities by an Israeli insurance company does not take into account smoking status or other health conditions. We might expect that smokers would prefer the lump-sum option over the annuity option because their life expectancy is shorter. Yet they do not, perhaps because confirmation errors dissuade them from looking for or accepting evidence that smokers have shorter lifespans. Indeed, a survey revealed that smokers do not believe that they have shorter lifespans.[104]

## Anchoring and Adjustment

A commercial for life insurance policies shows "Duncan" walking with his wife and daughter, who holds their dog. A $500,000 life insurance policy for Duncan will cost $27 per month, but this is not what the announcer says at first. Instead, he asks, "How much do you think it cost him? $100 a month, $75, $50? Actually, Duncan got his policy for $27 a month."

This commercial demonstrates anchoring shortcuts and perhaps anchoring errors. We likely know the approximate price of a quart of milk or a gallon of gas, but we likely do not know the approximate cost of a life insurance policy. We latch on to the $100 as our anchor. Relative to this anchor, $27 is

---

[102]Ditto and Lopez, "Motivated Skepticism."

[103]Emily Oster, E. Ray Dorsey, and Ira Shoulson, "Limited Life Expectancy, Human Capital and Health Investments," *American Economic Review* 103, no. 5 (August 2013): 1977–2002.

[104]Abigail Hurwitz and Orly Sade, "An Investigation of Time Preferences, Life Expectancy and Annuity versus Lump-Sum Choices – Can Smoking Harm Long-Term Saving Decisions?" (19 February 2017). Available at SSRN: https://ssrn.com/abstract=2742652 or http://dx.doi.org/10.2139/ssrn.2742652.

quite a bargain. If this anchoring shortcut fails to persuade us to buy a life insurance policy, perhaps a framing shortcut would persuade. The announcer makes the $27 seem even smaller by framing it as "less than a dollar a day."

We use anchoring and adjustment shortcuts well when we begin with proper anchors and adjust from them properly. We begin the process of estimating the appropriate price-to-earnings ratio (P/E) of a privately held company by identifying an anchor, such as the average P/E of public companies in the same industry. We adjust our P/E estimate upward to reflect the private company's better growth opportunities and downward to reflect the status of this company as a private, rather than public, company.

We commit anchoring and adjustment errors when we begin with faulty anchors and adjust from them improperly. The average P/E of public companies in the same industry might be a faulty anchor, for example, if P/Es in this industry are inflated in a bubble.

The anchoring and adjustment shortcut in the "Duncan" commercial is of the contrast effect form, as in the Ebbinghaus illusion. The circles at the center of the two sets are identical in size, but the one contrasted with the smaller circles seems larger.[105]

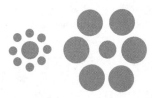

The economists Samuel Hartzmark and Kelly Shue noted that we tend to interpret information by contrasting it with what was recently observed; for example, we tend to judge crimes to be less severe after hearing stories of very serious crimes. They identified contrast effects in financial markets. Specifically, investors perceive earnings news today as positive if yesterday's earnings surprise was negative, and they perceive earnings news today as negative if yesterday's surprise was positive.[106]

We see anchoring and adjustment errors in estimates of exponential growth, as in compounding returns over long periods. We tend to estimate exponential growth as if growth is arithmetic. For example, we tend to estimate the amount of money we will have after five years to be close to $1,500,

---

[105]Nathalia Gjersoe, "The Ebbinghaus Illusion: Small, or Very Far Away?" *The Guardian* (22 August 2016). www.theguardian.com/science/head-quarters/2016/aug/22/the-ebbinghaus-illusion-small-far-away-circles-father-ted.

[106]Samuel M. Hartzmark and Kelly Shue, "A Tough Act to Follow: Contrast Effects in Financial Markets," *Journal of Finance* 73, no. 4 (August 2018): 1567–1613.

as with arithmetic growth, if our initial $1,000 grows at 10% per year, rather than $1,611, as with exponential growth.[107]

Roger Clarke and I encountered our susceptibility to anchoring and adjustment errors when we studied the Dow Jones Industrial Average (DJIA). The DJIA was introduced in 1896 at a level of 41 and reached 9,181 by the end of 1998. The DJIA, like the S&P 500 Index and almost all indexes, is a capital appreciation or price index; it does not include dividends paid to the shareholders of the companies in the index and the compounding of reinvested dividends over time. Now think of a DJIA where dividends are reinvested and compounded over time. What is your quick estimate of the level of this compounding DJIA at the end of 1998? The correct answer is 652,230.[108]

When Clarke and I first explored the compounding DJIA not long after the end of 1998, we were sure that we had made some mistake in our calculation. When doing the calculation in our minds, we started with 9,181, the level of the DJIA at the end of 1998, and multiplied it by a large number, perhaps 20, knowing that compounding works quickly and forcefully. But the number we chose was much too small. We were anchored to the 9,181 DJIA level by a short chain and failed to adjust sufficiently by multiplying it by more than 70.

The anchoring and adjustment error Clarke and I committed is one instance of a more general tendency to avoid making extreme adjustments. People shy away from making adjustments that result in apparently extreme results, even when the adjustments from anchors are warranted.[109]

Anchoring and adjustment errors are evident in many financial settings. Amateur investors tend to be anchored to 52-week stock-price highs. They tend to sell when stock prices are close to the 52-week high or place limit orders to sell at these prices. These anchoring errors are costly to amateur investors and fruitful to professional investors, who act as counterparties in these trades.[110]

---

[107]Henning Cordes, Bryan Foltice, and Thomas Langer, "Misperception of Exponential Growth: Are People Aware of Their Errors?" *Decision Analysis*, Forthcoming (2 July 2019). Available at SSRN: https://ssrn.com/abstract=3138109 or http://dx.doi.org/10.2139/ssrn.3138109.

[108]Roger G. Clarke and Meir Statman, "The DJIA Crossed 652,230," *Journal of Portfolio Management* 26, no. 2 (Winter 2000): 89–92.

[109]Joshua Lewis, Celia Gaertig, and Joseph P. Simmons, "Extremeness Aversion Is a Cause of Anchoring," *Psychological Science* 30, no. 2 (February 2019): 159–73.

[110]Josh Della Vedova, Andrew R. Grant, and P. Joakim Westerholm, "Investor Behavior at the 52 Week High," 30th Australasian Finance and Banking Conference 2017; 9th Conference on Financial Markets and Corporate Governance 2018 (20 May 2018). Available at SSRN: https://ssrn.com/abstract=3021585 or http://dx.doi.org/10.2139/ssrn.3021585.

Susceptibility to anchoring and adjustment errors places the behavior of corporate insiders closer to that of amateur investors than to professional ones. Company insiders are reluctant to buy their own companies' stocks when their prices are near their 52-week highs, but they are willing to sell them. In parallel, they are willing to buy their companies' stocks when their prices are far from the 52-week highs, but they are reluctant to sell them. This suggests that possession of private information by insiders is no barrier to the pitfalls of anchoring and adjustment errors.[111]

Sometimes two wrongs make a right, and a combination of wants and errors can *correct* other errors. People buy lottery tickets because they want riches, and people buy stocks with lottery features to satisfy the same want. Yet evidence indicates that lottery stocks (those with a small but nonzero probability of a very large gain), like lottery tickets, have low expected returns. Anchoring and adjustment errors, however, can counteract the preference for lottery stocks because they diminish the tendency to buy lottery stocks when their prices are close to the 52-week high. This is the second wrong that makes a right and is especially true for stocks held predominately by amateur investors.[112]

## Representativeness

"First to Market Play From EMS Find Inc. (EMSF)" screams the headline of a glossy brochure I received, urging me to buy the stock. "Like Uber for Ambulances!" Below the headline is a photo of a racing ambulance and a chart of an electrocardiogram. EMSF "Is Set To Shake Up $15-Billion Market With Next-Gen Breakthrough."

According to the description, EMSF's services are indeed similar to or representative of Uber's services:

"1. A nurse orders an ambulance pickup to a patient's home using EMS Find's online tools.

2. The patient is delivered safely and receives treatment.

3. After treatment the patient is loaded into an ambulance.

4. The ambulance transports the patient back home.

5. The patient is back home safely."

---

[111]Eunju Lee and Natalia Scotto Piqueira, "Behavioral Biases of Informed Traders: Evidence from Insider Trading on the 52-Week High," *Journal of Empirical Finance* 52 (June 2019): 56–75.
[112]Suk-Joon Byun and Jihoon Goh, "The Role of Psychological Barriers in Lottery-Related Anomalies" (21 November 2017). Available at SSRN: https://ssrn.com/abstract=3144907 or http://dx.doi.org/10.2139/ssrn.3144907.

But is Uber really representative of EMSF? Are we using good representativeness shortcuts or succumbing to representativeness errors when we conclude that investing in EMSF now, on its ground floor, will yield returns similar to those enjoyed by Uber ground-floor investors?

We use representativeness shortcuts when we assess the likelihood of events by their similarity to or representativeness of other events. We use representativeness shortcuts well when we consider both representativeness information and base-rate information. We commit representativeness errors when we assign too much weight to representativeness information and too little to base-rate information.

Representativeness information in the EMSF case is the company's imitation of the immensely successful Uber. Base-rate information is the information that most startups die, and very few of those that live succeed as much as Uber. It turned out that the representativeness shortcuts in this case were errors. Those who bought EMSF shares lost, unless they flipped them fast to other buyers committing bigger representativeness errors.

The price of EMSF shares almost doubled from 1 May 2015 to 12 June 2015. In 2017, EMSF changed its name to Integrated Ventures, Inc. (INTV), and launched a bitcoin mining operation. By 2 November 2018, its shares were trading at 0.3% of its 12 June 2015 price.

One manifestation of representativeness errors is the belief in the "law of small numbers," a tongue-in-cheek play on the robust law of large numbers.[113] The "law of large numbers" is an important law of science. It teaches us, for instance, that the percentage of heads in a sequence of coin tosses is likely to be closer to 50% when we toss a coin a large number of times, say, 600, than when we toss it a small number of times, say, 6.

One example of the errors introduced by the belief in the law of small numbers is that five good years of returns out of six are interpreted as a representation of the skill of a mutual fund manager rather than as a representation of luck. Therefore, we are forever chasing top funds in our quest for top returns, never pausing to ask whether the size of the sample is indeed large enough to warrant the top fund designation.

Fund managers, like the rest of us, do not hesitate to say, "no, thank you" and put down the phone when salespersons call. We do not feel obliged to listen to an entire sales pitch. As we make our decision to listen or quit, we properly take into account both representativeness information and base-rate information. We put down the phone because base-rate information tells us

---

[113]Amos Tversky and Daniel Kahneman, "Belief in the Law of Small Numbers," *Psychological Bulletin* 76 (1971): 105–10.

that most sales pitches are not worth listening to, even though the voice of this particular salesperson may be pleasant.

The same rule properly applies to mutual fund managers. If we make an error, it is in giving too much consideration to the performance of particular mutual funds and too little consideration to the average performance of all such funds relative to index funds.

The hot-hand and gambler's fallacies are reflections of the belief in the law of small numbers, whereby people identify patterns in random sequences. People who succumb to the hot-hand fallacy expect continuations of short sequences, whereas people who succumb to the gambler's fallacy expect reversals. Sellers of lottery tickets respond to buyers' hot-hand and gambler's fallacies in methods that exploit these errors. Lottery players tend to avoid buying tickets that are similar to the previous winning ticket, consistent with the gambler's fallacy. And they tend to prefer tickets acquired from sellers of previously winning tickets, consistent with the hot-hand fallacy. Ticket sellers increase their expected profits by adjusting features of the lotteries they sell. They change the number of tickets, commission rates, and ticket number combinations according to outcomes of previous lotteries, in ways consistent with exploiting both fallacies.[114]

Representativeness shortcuts are evident in the tendency of investors to form expectations about future returns by extrapolating past returns. Participants in a crowdsourcing platform ranked 10 stocks by their perceptions of future returns during the contest period, usually one week. Investors extrapolated from past returns to future returns, assigning more weight to more recent returns, especially when recent returns were negative. The tendency to extrapolate future returns from past ones was more pronounced among amateur investors than among professional ones. Representativeness shortcuts in this case turned out to be representativeness errors, as high rankings by expectations of future returns were followed by low realized returns, especially in stocks with high proportions of amateurs among their shareholders.[115]

Amateur day traders in the foreign exchange (forex) market commit representativeness errors when they conclude that they possess trading skill on the basis of trading success during short periods, despite evidence that past trading success does not predict future success. Traders react to short-term success by increasing trading and risk taking. This is especially true among

---

[114]Jaimie W. Lien and Jia Yuan, "Selling to Biased Believers: Strategies of Online Lottery Ticket Vendors," *Economic Inquiry* 53, no. 3 (July 2015): 1506–21.

[115]Zhi Da, Xing Huang, and Lawrence J. Jin, "Extrapolative Beliefs in the Cross-Section: What Can We Learn from the Crowds?" (4 May 2019). Available at SSRN: https://ssrn.com/abstract=3144849 or http://dx.doi.org/10.2139/ssrn.3144849.

novice traders who believe, in error, that they learn much from success during short periods.[116]

Amateur investors also extrapolate excessively from earnings announcements. They tend to buy stocks with recent history of high returns following earnings announcements, just before the following earnings announcements. The prices of these stocks increase predictably before these earnings announcements, as amateur investors rush to buy, but decrease soon afterwards.[117]

Each of us begins a career, and each witnesses stock market (and other) returns during that particular formative period. Yet returns during that particular period are not necessarily representative of returns during any longer period. Still, witnessing stock market returns at the beginning of a financial career leaves behind a vivid story, even though it provides almost no relevant information. Investment professionals extrapolate from returns witnessed early in their career when forming beliefs about expected returns, and early-career returns affect their expectation of future returns more than recent returns do.[118]

People also extrapolate from recent personal experiences in the housing market. Recent changes in prices of local houses affect expectations about future changes in national house prices, and higher local house price volatility causes people to expect a wider distribution of national house price changes than they rationally should. Moreover, people who suffer a bout of unemployment tend to believe that general unemployment is likely in the future, even when their personal unemployment tells nothing about future general unemployment. This tendency is more pronounced among less knowledgeable people.[119]

Pension fund managers also extrapolate from past returns in setting their expectations of future returns. Yet evidence indicates no skill underlying pension managers' expectations. Past returns in pension funds affect return

---

[116]Itzhak Ben-David, Justin Birru, and Viktor Prokopenya, "Uninformative Feedback and Risk Taking: Evidence from Retail Forex Trading," National Bureau of Economic Research Working Paper No. w22146 (April 2016). Available at SSRN: http://ssrn.com/abstract=2762097.

[117]Aytekin Ertan, Stephen A. Karolyi, Peter Kelly, and Robert C. Stoumbos, "Earnings Announcement Return Extrapolation" (25 May 2019), 7th Miami Behavioral Finance Conference 2016. Available at SSRN: https://ssrn.com/abstract=2720573 or http://dx.doi.org/10.2139/ssrn.2720573.

[118]Arvid O. I. Hoffmann, Zwetelina Iliewa, and Lena Jaroszek, "Wall Street Crosses Memory Lane: How Witnessed Returns Affect Professionals' Expected Returns," Paris December 2017 Finance Meeting EUROFIDAI – AFFI (22 January 2017). Available at SSRN: https://ssrn.com/abstract=2877366 or http://dx.doi.org/10.2139/ssrn.2877366.

[119]Theresa Kuchler and Basit Zafar, "Personal Experiences and Expectations About Aggregate Outcomes," FRB of NY Staff Report No. 748 (1 October 2015). Available at SSRN: https://ssrn.com/abstract=2677572.

expectations in all risky asset classes, including in public equities, where fund performance is known to not be persistent.[120]

## Availability

Ashley J. Thomas, P. Kyle Stanford, and Barbara W. Sarnecka described the story of 10-year-old Rafi Meitiv and his 6-year-old sister Dvora walking home from a park:

> A bystander called 911 to report a sighting of unaccompanied children. Police picked the children up and drove them home. When their father told police that Rafi and Dvora had permission to walk home from the park, the officer asked him, "Don't you realize how dangerous the world is? Don't you watch TV?" . . .
>
> The actual risk of a child being abducted by a stranger and killed or not returned is . . . one in 1.4 million annually. . . . Motor vehicle accidents, by contrast, are the most common cause of preventable death among children. Thus, by driving the Meitiv children home, . . . police actually exposed them to the much greater risk of being killed in a car accident. (p. 2)[121]

The idea that unsupervised children are in constant danger is relatively new. How have parenting norms changed so dramatically? Thomas, Stanford, and Sarnecka wrote that this change is likely due in part to availability shortcuts that turned into availability errors, magnified by wants for protecting our children and nurturing them that turn parents into "helicopter parents."[122]

We use availability shortcuts when we assess the probability of events by information that is readily available in our minds. We use availability shortcuts skillfully when all the information is available in our minds or when we are aware that not all the information is available in our minds. We commit availability errors when not all the information is available in our minds but we are not aware of its absence.

Acquiring information is mentally costly because we cannot possibly pay attention to all information. Programs such as the "Taken: Children Lost and Found" episode of CNN's *Anderson Cooper 360* reduce the cost of acquiring information, making it easier to pay attention to child abductions. But such

---

[120]Aleksandar Andonov and Joshua D. Rauh, "The Return Expectations of Institutional Investors," Stanford University Graduate School of Business Research Paper No. 18-5 (1 February 2019). Available at SSRN: https://ssrn.com/abstract=3091976 or http://dx.doi.org/10.2139/ssrn.3091976.

[121]Ashley J. Thomas, P. Kyle Stanford, and Barbara W. Sarnecka, "Correction: No Child Left Alone: Moral Judgments about Parents Affect Estimates of Risk to Children," *Collabra* 2, no. 1 (14 October 2016): 12, http://doi.org/10.1525/collabra.58.

[122]Thomas, Stanford, and Sarnecka, "Correction: No Child."

programs also distort information by making only some of it easily available to our minds. Making information about children abducted by strangers easily available to our minds leads to overestimates of the risk of child abductions, overlooking the less easily available information about the vastly greater number of children who make it safely home, as well as equally relevant information about the frequency of car accidents.

Availability shortcuts and errors are ubiquitous in investment settings. Amateur investors are frequently buyers of attention-grabbing stocks, such as those in the news, those with extreme trading volume, and those with extreme one-day returns. Attention-driven buying stems from the difficulty of searching among the thousands of stocks investors can buy. Investors do not face similar difficulty when selling because they sell only from the much smaller number of stocks they already own.[123]

Mutual funds with high returns attract investors only if the stocks in these funds have recently been featured in the media. Yet availability through the media does not help investors gain better returns. Instead, availability errors amplify the tendency of investors to flock to recently featured mutual funds containing stocks with high past returns. Mutual fund managers exploit availability errors by purchasing such stocks at times close to the dates when they report the contents of their funds, a strategy called "window dressing" that is most prevalent among poorly performing mutual funds.[124]

The SEC reduces the cost of acquiring accounting information with automated media articles of current earnings announcement news and recent stock returns. Amateur investors, however, do not incorporate value-relevant earnings information into their trading. Instead, they trade in response to recent stock returns that are vivid but offer no value-relevant information.[125]

Decision fatigue increases the cost of acquiring information and processing it. This is evident among analysts who cover many companies and often publish several forecasts in one day. The accuracy of forecasts diminishes as the number of forecasts published during the day increases. Also, when

---

[123]Brad M. Barber and Terrance Odean, "All That Glitters: The Effect of Attention and News on the Buying Behavior of Individual and Institutional Investors," *Review of Financial Studies* 21, no. 2 (April 2008): 785–818.

[124]David H. Solomon, Eugene F. Soltes, and Denis Sosyura, "Winners in the Spotlight: Media Coverage of Fund Holdings as a Driver of Flows," *Journal of Financial Economics* 113, no. 1 (July 2014): 53–72.

[125]Elizabeth Blankespoor, Ed deHaan, John Wertz, and Christina Zhu, "Why Do Individual Investors Disregard Accounting Information? The Roles of Information Awareness and Acquisition Costs," *Journal of Accounting Research*, Forthcoming (20 September 2018). Available at SSRN: https://ssrn.com/abstract=3059073 or http://dx.doi.org/10.2139/ssrn.3059073.

analysts issue more forecasts, they resort to shortcuts by herding with consensus forecasts.[126]

Absence of information makes its acquisition especially costly, because investors must begin with awareness that information is absent before proceeding to search for it. When company management does not issue forecasts, investors underestimate the magnitude of bad news implied by this lack of forecasts. As a result, management can withhold bad news without suffering significantly negative stock market consequences.[127]

## Confidence

A commercial shows a man in a lobby of an office building. "Where am I going?" he asks. "To a place where a man's success is determined not by the color of his credit card but by the position he took on the Aussie dollar in the face of rising commodity prices. I'm going where I can trade currencies on a platform that is as smart as . . . I am. I'm going to trade the world!"

The man's confident statements are followed by an announcer who says, "It's your world. Trade it at Forex.com!" The requisite warning follows: "Forex trading involves substantial risks and is not suitable to all investors."

Forex trading, presumably, is suitable for men as confident as the man in the commercial.

Confidence shortcuts and overconfidence errors are of three types, classified by psychologists Don Moore and Paul Healy: estimation, placement, and precision.[128] We use confidence shortcuts well in estimation, placement, and precision when we assess them objectively and place the objectively appropriate amount of confidence in them. We commit *overconfidence errors* when we place too much confidence in them, and we commit *underconfidence errors* when we place too little confidence in them. Overestimation, overplacement, and overprecision are not different manifestations of one underlying type of overconfidence. Instead, they are conceptually and empirically distinct.

The overconfidence of the man in the commercial is likely of the *overestimation* and *overplacement* types. We commit *overestimation errors* if we expect

---

[126]David A. Hirshleifer, Yaron Levi, Ben Lourie, and Siew Hong Teog, "Decision Fatigue and Heuristic Analyst Forecasts" (19 July 2017). Available at SSRN: https://ssrn.com/abstract=3005757 or http://dx.doi.org/10.2139/ssrn.3005757.

[127]Frank Zhou and Yuqing Zhou, "The Tale of Silent Dogs: Do Stock Prices Fully Reflect the Implication of News Withholding?" (4 August 2017). Available at SSRN: https://ssrn.com/abstract=3013757 or http://dx.doi.org/10.2139/ssrn.3013757.

[128]Don. A. Moore and Paul J. Healy, "The Trouble with Overconfidence," *Psychological Review* 115, no. 2 (April 2008): 502–17.

a 30% return on our forex trading when objective assessment indicates that we should expect a 50% loss. We commit *underestimation errors* if we expect an 80% loss.

We commit *overplacement errors* if we expect our forex trading to place us among the top 5% of traders when objective assessment would place us among the bottom 40%. We commit *underplacement errors* if we expect our forex trading to place us among the bottom 20%.

Teachers often demonstrate susceptibility to overconfidence errors by asking students to estimate confidence intervals in answers to 10 questions. For example, what is your confidence interval for the length of the Nile River such that there is a 90% probability that the true length of the Nile falls within the confidence interval—no higher than your estimated upper bound and no lower than your estimated lower bound?

Teachers delight in demonstrating that students are overconfident, evident in confidence intervals that are too narrow, such that true values fall inside confidence intervals considerably less frequently than 90% of the time. Teachers often proceed to state that this finding indicates that investors, especially men, trade too much because they are overconfident, placing themselves above average, as in *overplacement* errors. Yet the overconfidence assessed by the Nile question is not *overplacement* confidence. Instead, it is *overprecision* confidence.

We commit *overprecision errors* if we believe that there is a 90% probability that the length of the Nile falls between 4,500 and 5,000 miles. The true length of the Nile is 4,258 miles, falling outside the confidence interval. Similarly, we commit overprecision errors if we believe that there is a 90% probability our forex return would fall between 30% and 60%, when objective assessment indicates that the 90% confidence interval extends from a negative 50% return to a 50% return. We commit *underprecision errors* if we believe that there is a 90% probability that the length of the Nile falls between 1,000 miles and 8,000 miles, and we commit *underprecision errors* if we believe that our forex return extends from a negative 90% return to a 90% return.

Examination of a large group of British investors confirmed that the three kinds of overconfidence—overestimation, overplacement, and overprecision—are distinct.[129] There was substantial propensity for overprecision errors, yet there was no general propensity for overplacement errors. And there was no general propensity for overestimation, although that

---

[129]Christoph Merkle, "Financial Overconfidence Over Time: Foresight, Hindsight, and Insight of Investors," AFA 2013 San Diego Meetings Paper (10 November 2016). Available at SSRN: http://ssrn.com/abstract=2001513 or http://dx.doi.org/10.2139/ssrn.2001513.

propensity is evident in a minority of investors, including the man in the commercial and active traders polled at the 2012 Fidelity Traders Summit. The poll revealed that 62% of active traders expected to beat the market and 29% expected to match it, leaving only a handful who expected to lag the market.[130]

Moore and Healy noted further that *underconfidence* is common, even if not as common as overconfidence, and identified circumstances where people are likely to display overconfidence or underconfidence.[131] *Underestimation errors* are likely when contemplating *easy* tasks, whereas *overestimation errors* are likely when contemplating *difficult* tasks. After all, we cannot overestimate our grade of A on an easy test, but we can overestimate our C grade on a difficult test.[132] Investors who perceive investing as a *difficult* task are likely to *overestimate* their future returns.

*Overplacement errors* are likely when contemplating *easy* tasks, whereas *underplacement errors* are likely when contemplating *difficult* ones. Driving is an easy task, prompting overplacement. A frequently cited study reported that 93% of American drivers commit overplacement errors, placing themselves, on average, above average.[133] If you have tried juggling three oranges or riding a unicycle, you know that these tasks, unlike driving, are difficult. A more recent and less frequently cited study found that people on average place themselves *below* average at juggling and unicycle riding.[134] Investors who perceive investing as a *difficult* task are likely to *underplace* their future returns relative to the future returns of other people.

Another frequently cited article reported that people tend to *overplace* themselves in the likelihood of positive events, such as traveling to Europe, and tend to *underplace* themselves in the likelihood of negative events, such as getting lung cancer.[135] A more recent and less frequently cited study found, however, that our tendency to *overplace* ourselves as likely to travel

---

[130]Fidelity Investments, "Fidelity® Poll Showcases Active Investors' Confidence," Business Wire (16 May 2012). www.businesswire.com/news/home/20120516005964/en/Fidelity®-Poll-Showcases-Active-Investors'-Confidence#.VaJxbflViko.

[131]Moore and Healy, "The Trouble with Overconfidence."

[132]Ido Erev, Thomas S. Wallsten, and David V. Budescu, "Simultaneous Over- and Underconfidence: The Role of Error in Judgment Processes," *Psychological Review* 101, no. 3 (July 1994): 519–27.

[133]Ola Svenson, "Are We All Less Risky and More Skillful than Our Fellow Drivers?" *Acta Psychologica* 47, no. 2 (February 1981): 143–48.

[134]Justin Kruger, "Lake Wobegon Be Gone! The 'Below-Average Effect' and the Egocentric Nature of Comparative Ability Judgments," *Journal of Personality and Social Psychology* 77, no. 2 (August 1999): 221–32.

[135]Neil D. Weinstein, "Unrealistic Optimism about Future Life Events," *Journal of Personality and Social Psychology* 39, no. 5 (November 1980): 806–20.

to Europe and *underplace* ourselves as likely to get lung cancer is due mostly to the feature of commonness (common or rare) rather than the feature of valence (positive or negative). We commit overplacement when contemplating common events, such as traveling to Europe or living past the age of 70, but we commit underplacement when contemplating rare events, such as getting lung cancer or living past the age of 100, whether these events are positive or negative.[136] Investors who perceive above-average future returns as a *common* event are likely to *overplace* themselves relative to other investors.

## Conclusion

Wants precede cognitive shortcuts and errors. We use cognitive shortcuts and sometimes stumble into cognitive errors on our way to satisfying our wants, deriving utilitarian, expressive, and emotional benefits.

We want financial security and might believe that trading stocks is a good way to achieve it. Good framing shortcuts direct us to frame trading as, for example, tennis against a possibly better opponent on the other side of the net, rather than as playing tennis against a training wall. And good confirmation shortcuts direct us to assign equal weights to evidence confirming our trading skills and evidence disconfirming them. We commit framing errors when we frame trading as tennis against a training wall, and we commit confirmation errors when we assign greater weight to evidence confirming our trading skills than to evidence disconfirming them.

We want to nurture our children. Good availability shortcuts lead us to consider readily available information about children abducted by strangers but also information not as readily available about the miniscule probability that children will actually be abducted by strangers. Availability errors mislead us into concluding that the probability of abduction of children by strangers is high and, therefore, insisting on driving our children to school rather than letting them walk there. Availability errors also mislead us into thinking that picking the best mutual funds is easy, because mutual funds advertise five-star funds, making them available to our memory.

We want high social status. Good representativeness shortcuts guide us to consider representativeness information about friends who brag about their high status as hedge fund investors but also to consider base-rate information about the many investors in plain mutual funds who attain high social status.

---

[136]Justin Kruger and Jeremy Burrus, "Egocentrism and Focalism in Unrealistic Optimism (and Pessimism)," *Journal of Experimental Social Psychology* 40, no. 3 (May 2004): 332–40.

Representativeness errors mislead us into thinking that investment in hedge funds is a preferred path to high social status.

Knowledge of wants, cognitive shortcuts, and cognitive errors is part of human-behavior knowledge. Investment professionals can combine that knowledge with financial-facts knowledge to use helpful cognitive shortcuts and avoid cognitive errors on their way to satisfying their own wants, and they can help amateur investors do the same.

# 4. Emotional Shortcuts and Errors

Have you noticed that most movies are fiction? Of course you have. You know that Judi Dench is an actress, only pretending to be Queen Victoria. You know that the boats about to sink in a perfect ocean storm are actually floating in a studio pool. And sometimes you wear funny glasses that knowingly fool you into seeing 3D images on a flat screen. So why do we buy movie tickets, sacrificing the utilitarian benefits of money for fiction? The answer is obvious: We gain in expressive and emotional benefits more than we lose in utilitarian benefits. Movies touch our emotions and help us express our social connections in the company of dates, spouses, children, and friends. Indeed, concern about exposing ourselves as lacking social connections inhibits us from going to a movie theater alone, and these concerns also reduce the emotional benefits we derive when we watch movies alone.[137]

Advice to set emotions aside when considering investments and use reason alone is common but wrong for three reasons. First, we cannot set emotions aside even if we want to. Second, emotions are not necessarily emotional errors. Third, emotional shortcuts help more than emotional errors harm. Emotional shortcuts complement reason, and the interaction between emotions and reason is beneficial, often critically so.

A study of financial advertisements showed that compared with neutral imagery, emotionally laden imagery increases investor knowledge about important investment characteristics, such as costs, time to maturity, and dividend frequency. Emotionally laden disclosure of risk factors increases knowledge of risk factors but does not increase knowledge of other investment characteristics. Emotionally laden imagery increases average amounts invested, whereas emotionally laden disclosure of risk decreases the willingness to consider other information.[138]

Moreover, statements calling on people to set emotions aside when making financial choices deter some people from making financial choices altogether. As it is, people perceive financial choices as compatible with reason

---

[137]Rebecca K. Ratner and Rebecca W. Hamilton, "Inhibited from Bowling Alone," *Journal of Consumer Research* 42, no. 2 (August 2015): 266–83; Suresh Ramanathan and Ann L. McGill, "Consuming with Others: Social Influences on Moment-to-Moment and Retrospective Evaluations of an Experience," *Journal of Consumer Research* 34, no. 4 (December 2007): 506–24.

[138]Ruben Cox and Peter de Goeij, "What Do Investors Learn from Advertisements?" (8 September 2017). Available at SSRN: https://ssrn.com/abstract=3034144 or http://dx.doi.org/10.2139/ssrn.3034144.

and incompatible with emotions. Therefore, people who perceive themselves as making choices by emotions perceive financial choices as alien to them and, therefore, tend to avoid such choices.[139]

The famous case of Phineas Gage illustrates the crucial interaction between reason and emotion, whereby emotional shortcuts prompt reasonable choices. Gage was a thoughtful and conscientious foreman working on the construction of a railroad when an explosion propelled a tamping iron through his skull and the frontal cortex of his brain. Gage recovered physically but not emotionally, having lost all social inhibitions. A physician who treated Gage described him as "fitful, irreverent, indulging at times in the grossest profanity, . . . capricious and vacillating" and being "radically changed, so decidedly that his friends and acquaintances said he was 'no longer Gage.'"[140]

The interaction between cognition and emotion makes it difficult to attribute shortcuts, errors, and choices to one or the other. Reason tells parents that a 10-year-old child has a miniscule chance of being kidnapped when walking a few blocks from home to school, but some parents insist on driving their children to school. This choice can be made because the cognitive errors of availability exaggerate the chance of kidnapping, because the emotional errors of excessive fear exaggerate that chance, or because of a combination of cognition and emotion.

## Emotions, Mood, and Affect

There is no agreed-on list of emotions. Lists include anger, anxiety, frustration, disgust, fear, hope, joy, happiness, sadness, pride, regret, trust, envy, jealousy, grief, guilt, shame, and self-control, among others.[141]

There are also no clear lines separating emotions from moods and affect. Emotions are often described as intense but short in duration, whereas moods are less intense and longer in duration, and affect is the faint whisper of

---

[139]Jane Park and Aner Sela, "Not My Type: Why Affective Decision-Makers Are Reluctant to Make Financial Decisions," *Journal of Consumer Research* 45, no. 2 (August 2018): 298–319.
[140]http://omeka.macalester.edu/courses/russ151/exhibits/show/materials-of-the-mind/phineas-gage; www.npr.org/sections/health-shots/2017/05/21/528966102/why-brain-scientists-are-still-obsessed-with-the-curious-case-of-phineas-gage.
[141]For a model of these emotions, see Robert Plutchik, "The Nature of Emotions: Human Emotions Have Deep Evolutionary Roots, a Fact That May Explain Their Complexity and Provide Tools for Clinical Practice," *American Scientist* 89, no. 4 (July/August 2001): 344–50. For an overview of these major emotions individually (anger, fright, anxiety, guilt, shame, sadness, envy, jealousy, disgust, happiness, pride, love, and relief), see pages 217–82 of Richard S. Lazarus, *Emotion and Adaptation* (New York: Oxford University Press, 1991). See also pages 269 and 276 of Dan M. Kahan and Martha C. Nussbaum, "Two Conceptions of Emotion in Criminal Law," *Columbia Law Review* 96, no. 2 (March 1996): 269–374.

emotions or moods. Sadness is an intense emotion when we learn that a loved one has died, and it is often followed by less intense but longer-lasting grief. Fear is an intense emotion in a stock market crash, and it is often followed by less intense and longer-lasting anxiety. A house with "curb appeal" exudes positive affect, and so does a stock with "curb appeal."

The list of emotions expressed by consumers in complaints filed with the Consumer Financial Protection Bureau includes frustration, anger, sadness, fear, disgust, shame, and guilt. A consumer complaining about the practices of a financial services company wrote, "I was confused, frustrated, stressed, and upset, and at the time I did not know that I had any recourse." Frustration rose to anger in other complaints, expressed in capital letters: "I NEVER received ANY statements or cards in the mail." A consumer expressed sadness about the company's practices: "This huge corporation . . . [has become] a money hungry company. . . . Saddened and still in the Negative." Another consumer expressed fear: "I am a senior citizen and need my [$300] back! HELP!!" Yet other consumers expressed guilt, promising to pay when possible, and shame, expressed in apologies for not paying on time.[142]

## Hope and Fear

Fear is a negative emotion arising in response to danger, whereas hope is a positive one in anticipation of reward, but the two are similar in that control is in the hands of others, whether other people or situations. We fear the danger of a stock market crash but cannot control the outcome. We hope for a stock market boom but cannot control the outcome.

Terrorist attacks invoke fear, and fear increases risk aversion. An increase in the number of attacks each month by one standard deviation leads to a $75.09 million drop in aggregate flows to stock funds and a $56.81 million increase in flows to government bond funds.[143] Fear of terrorism increases people's desire for control and leads many to avoidant behaviors. In Israel, some people quit dining out because restaurants are common targets of suicide bombers, whereas others continue to eat out but ask to sit near the kitchen so they can escape a potential attack.[144]

---

[142]Pamela Foohey, "Calling on the CFPB for Help: Telling Stories and Consumer Protection," *Law and Contemporary Problems* (2017): 177–209.

[143]Yan Albert Wang and Michael Young, "Terrorist Attacks and Investor Risk Preference: Evidence from Mutual Fund Flows," *Journal of Financial Economics*, Forthcoming (14 March 2019). Available at SSRN: https://ssrn.com/abstract=3354764.

[144]Michal Herzenstein, Sharon Horsky, and Steven S. Posavac, "Living with Terrorism or Withdrawing in Terror: Perceived Control and Consumer Avoidance," *Journal of Consumer Behaviour* 14, no. 4 (July/August 2015): 228–36.

Buses are a frequent target of terrorist bombers. Yair, a 31-year-old Israeli man who drives to work in Tel Aviv every day, changed his driving strategy to feel safer by keeping his distance from buses. "I just let a few other cars get between me and the bus," he said, "and that way if something happens, I will be safe because of the buffer zone I created" (p. 231).[145]

People who believe they have no control over terrorism display the most extreme changes in behavior. Maya, a 28-year-old woman who witnessed a terrorist attack, explained, "After a while my friends realized I'm not the same person. I don't like to go out anymore. I only want to stay at home. I was really only hurt minimally but the horror I've seen with my own eyes will never leave me" (p. 231).[146]

Loan officers who have witnessed a robbery resemble people who have witnessed a terrorist act. Such loan officers adopt avoidant behavior, evident in more restrictive conditions on loans granted immediately after a bank branch robbery compared with loans granted at unaffected branches.[147]

When people desire a sense of control to reduce fear and increase hope, they become more susceptible to superstition and conspiracy theories. First-year MBA students who lack the sense of control gained by second-year students are more likely to believe in conspiracies. Athletes whose success is precarious are likely to create superstitious rituals, such as ones that link particular shirts to success. Susceptibility to superstition and conspiracy theories increases in times of economic uncertainty and precariousness.[148]

Fear inclines investors to expect low returns with high risk, whereas hope inclines them to expect high returns with low risk. A Gallup survey of investors conducted during the 1998–2007 period asked, "Do you think that now is a good time to invest in the financial markets?" Their answers revealed that high recent returns were followed by high percentages of investors who believed that now would be a good time to invest. Gallup also asked investors whether they believed the market is overvalued or undervalued. Their answers indicated that months when large proportions of investors believed the stock

---

[145]Herzenstein, Horsky, and Posavac, "Living with Terrorism."

[146]Herzenstein, Horsky, and Posavac, "Living with Terrorism."

[147]Paola Morales Acevedo and Steven Ongena, "Fear, Anger and Credit. On Bank Robberies and Loan Conditions," BAFFI CAREFIN Centre Research Paper No. 2015-10 (19 January 2016). Available at SSRN: http://ssrn.com/abstract=2653726 or http://dx.doi.org/10.2139/ssrn.2653726.

[148]Jennifer A. Whitson and Adam D. Galinsky, "Lacking Control Increases Illusory Pattern Perception," *Science* 322, no. 5898 (October 2008): 115–17.

market was *overvalued* were also months when they believed now would be a *good time to invest* in the financial markets.[149]

Fear prods investors to fly to safety. The VIX Index (Cboe Volatility Index) is a risk gauge known as the fear index. It measures expectations of future risk by measuring the expectation of future volatility of stock returns. Flight-to-safety periods coincide with increases in the VIX, bearish consumer sentiment, and bond returns that exceed stock returns.[150]

Fear increases risk aversion even among financial professionals, whose risk aversion rises after financial busts. Financial professionals who read a story about a financial bust became more fearful than those who read a story about a financial boom, and their fear led to less risky investments.[151]

Hope for great winnings drives people to buy lottery tickets and engage in stock trading.[152] Investment manager Jason Hsu noted that "investment managers are fond of telling clients that 'hope is not a strategy'; ironically, however, selling hope has turned out to be a fantastic strategy for investment managers" (p. 6).[153] And a Kauffman Foundation study of venture capital funds, echoing an old joke about second marriages, described these funds as evidence for the triumph of hope over experience and noted in 2012 that "venture capital (VC) has delivered poor returns for more than a decade. VC returns haven't significantly outperformed the public market since the late 1990s, and, since 1997, less cash has been returned to investors than has been invested in VC" (p. 3).[154]

## Happiness, Sadness, and Disgust

Happiness, sadness, and disgust can offer utilitarian, expressive, and emotional benefits, and they can impose utilitarian, expressive, and emotional costs. We sacrifice the utilitarian benefits of money when we donate to

---

[149]Meir Statman, *Finance for Normal People: How Investors and Markets Behave* (New York: Oxford University Press, 2017).

[150]Lieven Baele, Geert Bekaert, Koen Inghelbrecht, and Min Wei, "Flights to Safety," National Bureau of Economic Research Working Paper No. w19095 (May 2013).

[151]Alain Cohn, Jan Engelmann, Ernst Fehr, and Michel André Maréchal, "Evidence for Countercyclical Risk Aversion: An Experiment with Financial Professionals," *American Economic Review* 105, no. 2 (February 2015): 860–85.

[152]Meir Statman, "Lottery Players/Stock Traders," *Financial Analysts Journal* 58, no. 1 (January 2002): 14–21.

[153]Jason C. Hsu, "Selling Hope," *Rotman International Journal of Pension Management* 5, no. 2 (Fall 2012): 6–7.

[154]Diane Mulcahy, Bill Weeks, and Harold S. Bradley, "We Have Met the Enemy . . . and He Is Us: Lessons from Twenty Years of the Kauffman Foundation's Investments in Venture Capital Funds and the Triumph of Hope Over Experience" (May 2012). Available at SSRN: https://ssrn.com/abstract=2053258 or http://dx.doi.org/10.2139/ssrn.2053258.

charities, but we gain the expressive and emotional benefits of happiness. Happier people give more to charities, giving increases happiness, and the two enhance each other.[155]

Financial advisers often note that wealthy clients dislike an emphasis on the utilitarian tax benefits of charitable donations because such an emphasis suggests that utilitarian benefits to themselves underlie donations, rather than benefits to others and expressive and emotional benefits to themselves.

Sylvia Bloom was a legal secretary who retired at 96 and died not long afterward. She left $6.24 million to the Henry Street Settlement on New York City's Lower East Side, an organization that delivers a wide range of social service, arts, and health care programs to more than 50,000 New Yorkers each year. And she left an additional $2 million for scholarships at Hunter College and other educational institutions. "She never talked money and she didn't live the high life," said one of her friends. "She wasn't showy and didn't want to call attention to herself."[156]

Happiness adds utilitarian benefits by increasing productivity. In one experiment, Britons watched a 10-minute clip based on composite sketches taken from comedy routines by a well-known British comedian. Those who reported enjoying the clip had 12% greater productivity in a paid task than those who watched a neutral clip. Another study found that people affected by real-life unhappiness shocks stemming from bereavement or family illness produced less than people not similarly affected.[157]

Happiness promotes delayed gratification and increased savings. Happiness was induced in one group of Americans by a montage of standup comedy bits from Robin Williams' *Live on Broadway*. People in that group were more willing to delay gratification than people who watched a neutral clip.[158]

---

[155]Lalin Anik, Lara B. Aknin, Michael I. Norton, and Elizabeth W. Dunn, "Feeling Good About Giving: The Benefits (and Costs) of Self-Interested Charitable Behavior," Harvard Business School Marketing Unit Working Paper No. 10-012 (6 August 2009). Available at SSRN: https://ssrn.com/abstract=1444831 or http://dx.doi.org/10.2139/ssrn.1444831.

[156]Corey Kilgannon, "96-Year-Old Secretary Quietly Amasses Fortune, Then Donates $8.2 Million," *New York Times* (6 May 2018). www.nytimes.com/2018/05/06/nyregion/secretary-fortune-donates.html?hp&action=click&pgtype=Homepage&clickSource=story-heading&module=second-column-region&region=top-news&WT.nav=top-news.

[157]Andrew J. Oswald, Eugenio Proto, and Daniel Sgroi, "Happiness and Productivity," IZA Discussion Paper No. 4645 (22 December 2009). Available at SSRN: https://ssrn.com/abstract=1526075.

[158]John Ifcher and Homa Zarghamee, "Happiness and Time Preference: The Effect of Positive Affect in a Random-Assignment Experiment," *American Economic Review* 101, no. 7 (December 2011): 3109–29.

Sadness, however, created "myopic misery," increasing impatience and intensifying myopic focus on obtaining money immediately instead of later, even when waiting would have brought substantially more money.[159] Sadness is strongly associated with a sense that forces outside us control our lives. Shopping while sad—what cynics call "retail therapy"—counters these forces and restores some control over our lives.[160] Sadness among mutual fund managers following the death of a parent was associated with a 3 percentage point decline in their funds' returns. Sadness induced greater impatience, higher risk aversion, and increased sensitivity to losses.[161]

The common saying "sad but wise" is true. Sadness promotes reliance on the reflective System 2, instead of the intuitive System 1. Sadness also counters a range of cognitive and emotional errors. These include holding inflated perception of our importance, reputation, and abilities and attributing causality to other people without basis in facts.[162]

We "bank happiness" when anticipating a future sad event. Accumulated happiness serves as a resource to be drawn upon in times of sadness. Indeed, the boost from banked happiness helps people handle and overcome sad events, leaving them in a less negative mood.[163]

Disgust prompts us to expel repellent objects and keep our distance from abhorrent ideas. Disgust is intimately linked to pathogen avoidance, developed by the forces of evolution to choose what to eat, what to touch, and with whom to have sex. Disgust occurs when we perceive low expected net benefits from food consumption, contact, or sex.[164]

Consider a scale of liking ranging from "like extremely" (200 points) to "dislike immensely" (0 points). How many liking points would you assign to a glass of juice? Experiments about the effects of disgust indicate that dipping

---

[159]Jennifer S. Lerner, Ye Li, and Elke U. Weber, "The Financial Costs of Sadness," *Psychological Science* 24, no. 1 (January 2013): 72–79.

[160]Scott Rick, Beatriz Pereira, and Katherine Alicia Burson, "The Benefits of Retail Therapy: Making Purchase Decisions Reduces Residual Sadness," *Journal of Consumer Psychology* 24, no. 3 (2014): 373–80.

[161]Clark Liu, Tao Shu, Johan Sulaeman, and P. Eric Yeung, "Life Is Too Short? Bereaved Managers and Investment Decisions (1 May 2019), 27th Annual Conference on Financial Economics and Accounting Paper. Available at SSRN: https://ssrn.com/abstract=2658815 or http://dx.doi.org/10.2139/ssrn.2658815.

[162]Lerner, Li, and Weber, "The Financial Costs."

[163]Ali Faraji-Rad and Leonard Lee, "Banking Happiness" (4 February 2016). Available at SSRN: https://ssrn.com/abstract=2728061 or http://dx.doi.org/10.2139/ssrn.2728061.

[164]Debra Lieberman, Joseph Billingsley, and Carlton Patrick, "Consumption, Contact and Copulation: How Pathogens Have Shaped Human Psychological Adaptations," Philosophical Transactions of the Royal Society B, 20170203, June 2018 (6 February 2018). Available at SSRN: https://ssrn.com/abstract=3184860.

a sterilized cockroach into that glass of juice lowered average liking of that juice by more than 100 points.[165]

As part of a "lunch experiment," people were given the opportunity to buy or be paid for eating a chicken sandwich containing Evanger Super Premium for Dogs Whole Chicken Thighs. One group was placed under cognitive load by requesting that they look up and memorize the amount of calories in eight food items on a Google search. People subjected to cognitive load engaged the intuitive System 1, and the disgust arising from the dog food label caused them to offer little or ask a lot for eating the sandwich. People not subjected to cognitive load had a better opportunity to engage the reflective System 2 to balance their disgust against the nutritional value of the sandwich. They were willing to offer more or ask less for eating the sandwich.[166]

## Anger

Anger brings to mind "anger management." Indeed, chronic anger calls for anger management because it often leads to bad outcomes. Chronically angry people agree with such statements as "I am an impulsive person," "I get angry when I have to wait because of others' mistakes," and "When I am frustrated, I feel like hitting someone." Angry people have a higher than average likelihood to divorce, suffer more cardiovascular disease, and face problems at work, despite rating themselves less likely to experience these problems.[167]

Yet anger can lead to good outcomes when not chronic. Whereas fear, sadness, and disgust move us away from what seems dangerous or unpleasant, anger propels us toward them, accepting risks and confronting challenges we would otherwise flee. Anger can also counter cognitive errors, mitigating the tendency to commit confirmation errors. In one study, angry people who read an article about a controversial social issue were more likely to consider disconfirming information than sad people who read the same article.[168]

As one group of authors wrote, "Anger is a computationally complex cognitive system that evolved to bargain for better treatment. Anger coordinates facial expressions, vocal changes, verbal arguments, the withholding of benefits, the deployment of aggression, and a suite of other cognitive and

---

[165]William Schulze, Annemie Maertens, and Brian Wansink, "Eating Dogfood: Examining the Relative Roles of Reason and Emotion," *Journal of Economic Behavior & Organization* 92, issue C (August 2013), 202–13.

[166]Schulze, Maertens, and Wansink, "Eating Dogfood."

[167]Jennifer S. Lerner and Dacher Keltner, "Fear, Anger, and Risk," *Journal of Personality and Social Psychology* 81, no. 1 (July 2001): 146–59.

[168]Maia J. Young, Larissa Z. Tiedens, Heajung Jung, and Ming-Hong Tsai, "Mad Enough to See the Other Side: Anger and the Search for Disconfirming Information," *Cognition & Emotion* 25, no. 1 (2011): 10–21.

physiological variables in the service of leveraging bargaining position into better outcomes" (p. 110).[169]

Psychologist Robert Sutton described the strategic use of anger by debt collectors in an interview with Charles Duhigg. Debt collectors were trained to pretend they were angry at the debtors: "I want the payment today! Express mail!" Yet "as soon as a debtor started screaming back, the collector would switch tactics and become soothing and accommodating. The idea was, once you get them angry and aroused, you need to deliver catharsis, a sense of relief. That's going to make them more likely to pay up.'" One debt collector described how he delivered that catharsis: "Look, I know you've got a problem. I hope nothing I did set you off, because neither of us is going to benefit if we don't resolve this thing."[170]

Moral anger arises in us when we observe unfair behavior, even when that behavior has no direct effect on us. Anticipation of other people's moral anger deters homeowners considering strategic defaults on mortgages—defaults not caused by economic shocks, such as unemployment. Anger abates when economic shocks cause neighboring homeowners to default, prompting other homeowners into strategic default. Moreover, when economic shocks occur, neighbors of defaulting homeowners have a hard time distinguishing strategic from shock-based defaults and are, therefore, reluctant to punish defaulting homeowners.[171]

## Regret and Pride

Regret and pride are "cognitive emotions," the outcome of an interaction between cognition and emotion. We react instinctively when gripped by fear, recoiling from a snake or slamming the brakes. But we contemplate the regret or pride we will derive from future actions, and that contemplation affects our choice of actions.

Regret aversion and pride seeking are central in the "disposition effect" described by Hersh Shefrin and me.[172] Rational investors are quick to realize

---

[169]Aaron Sell, Daniel Sznycer, Laith Al-Shawaf, Julian Lim, Andre Krauss, Aneta Feldman, Ruxandra Rascanu, Lawrence Sugiyama, Leda Cosmides, and John Tooby, "The Grammar of Anger: Mapping the Computational Architecture of a Recalibrational Emotion," *Cognition* 168 (November 2017): 110–28.

[170]Charles Duhigg, "Why Are We So Angry?" *The Atlantic* (January/February 2019): 62–75.

[171]Martin Brown, Jan Schmitz, and Christian Zehnder, "Social Norms and Strategic Default," University of St. Gallen, School of Finance Research Paper No. 2016/08 (June 2017). Available at SSRN: http://ssrn.com/abstract=2743278 or http://dx.doi.org/10.2139/ssrn.2743278.

[172]Hersh Shefrin and Meir Statman, "The Disposition to Sell Winners Too Early and Ride Losers Too Long: Theory and Evidence," *Journal of Finance* 40, no. 3 (July 1985): 777–90.

losses and slow to realize gains on taxable investments, because realized losses reduce tax bills and their utilitarian costs, whereas realized gains add to them. Yet many normal investors are quick to realize gains (eager to enjoy the emotional benefits of pride) and slow to realize losses (reluctant to suffer the emotional costs of regret), displaying a disposition to "sell winners too early and ride losers too long."

Responsibility for choices is crucial in the emotional costs of regret and emotional benefits of pride. We experience disappointment when a broker who bears responsibility for choosing stocks for us makes a choice that results in losses. But we suffer regret when we ourselves bear responsibility for that choice. In one set of experiments, some people bore responsibility for choices whereas others did not. The disposition effect occurred only among those who bore responsibility.[173] Investors who delegate choices also delegate responsibility and blame for losses, thereby facilitating their realization.[174]

"Regret is painful while pride is pleasurable, but both are teachers, warning us against behavior likely to inflict regret and encouraging us toward behavior likely to bring pride. But sometimes the lessons of regret are overly harsh and the lessons of pride too encouraging. Stocks go up and down for many reasons and for no reason at all. We need not kick ourselves with regret every time stock prices go down, and we should not stroke ourselves with pride every time they go up" (pp. 135–136).[175]

An experiment using functional MRI showed that when people observed a positive return in a stock and chose not to buy it, a regret signal was found in an area of the brain commonly active in reward processing. People were unwilling to repurchase stocks whose prices had recently increased, even though repurchasing was optimal on the basis of the rules of the experiment. Those with high rates of repurchasing mistakes also exhibited large disposition effects: They were eager to realize gains and reluctant to realize losses.[176]

Pride seeking can make mutual fund managers eager to buy particular stocks, and regret aversion can make them reluctant to buy them. The probability of a stock being repurchased by a mutual fund is on average 17% higher if the stock was previously sold for a gain that induced pride rather than for

---

[173]Barbara Summers and Darren Duxbury, "Unraveling the Disposition Effect: The Role of Prospect Theory and Emotions" (1 August 2007). Available at SSRN: https://ssrn.com/abstract=1026915 or http://dx.doi.org/10.2139/ssrn.1026915.

[174]Tom Y. Chang, David H. Solomon, and Mark M. Westerfield, "Looking for Someone to Blame: Delegation, Cognitive Dissonance, and the Disposition Effect," *Journal of Finance* 71, no. 1 (February 2016): 267–302.

[175]Statman, "What Investors Really Want."

[176]Cary Frydman and Colin Camerer, "Neural Evidence of Regret and Its Implications for Investor Behavior," *Review of Financial Studies* 29, no. 11 (November 2016): 3108–3139.

a loss that inflicted regret. The effects of pride and regret on the behavior of fund managers persist even when they move on to work at a different fund. They still prefer to repurchase stocks that they sold for a gain at the fund they managed before. Seeking pride and avoiding regret, however, degrades investment performance: Repurchased winners underperform repurchased losers by an annual 5%.[177]

Aversion to regret inclines portfolio managers to hedge half the currency position of their portfolio to avoid the pain of regret, since a hedge of one-half is sure to make them half right; either the hedged part of the position outperforms or the unhedged part does. Either way, they have made one good decision. A William M. Mercer survey of pension funds worldwide revealed that about one-third of respondents with partially hedged currency positions believe that currency exposure should be set at one-half to minimize regret.[178]

Regret is often conflated with risk, yet the two are distinct. Indeed, people averse to risk are no more or less likely to be averse to regret.[179] Reduction of risk is commonly cited as a rationale for dollar-cost averaging. This is the practice of converting cash into stocks over a number of periods rather than all at once in a lump sum, such as converting $100,000 of cash into stocks in 10 monthly installments of $10,000. This practice does reduce risk during the 10 months because the risk of stocks is greater than the risk of cash, so the risk of $100,000 in stocks when invested in a lump sum is greater than the risk of $10,000 in stocks and $90,000 in cash when invested using dollar-cost averaging.

Yet "reverse" dollar-cost averaging is also urged when converting stocks into cash, and risk reduction cannot be the rationale for that practice. This is because $100,000 in cash received by selling stocks in a lump sum is less risky than the $90,000 in stocks and $10,000 in cash received by selling stocks using reverse dollar-cost averaging.

Risk reduction cannot be the rationale for both dollar-cost averaging and reverse dollar-cost averaging. Instead, regret reduction is the rationale for both practices. If stock prices decline after the first monthly batch of stocks

---

[177]Mengqiao Du, Alexandra Niessen-Ruenzi, and Terrance Odean, "Stock Repurchasing Bias of Mutual Funds" (10 September 2018). Available at SSRN: https://ssrn.com/abstract=3247066 or http://dx.doi.org/10.2139/ssrn.3247066.

[178]Meir Statman, "Hedging Currencies with Hindsight and Regret," *Journal of Investing* 14, no. 2 (Summer 2005): 15–19; see also Olaf Korn and Marc Oliver Rieger, "Hedging with Regret" (16 August 2017). Available at SSRN: https://ssrn.com/abstract=3020006 or http://dx.doi.org/10.2139/ssrn.3020006.

[179]Carrie Pan and Meir Statman, "Questionnaires of Risk Tolerance, Regret, Overconfidence, and Other Investor Propensities," *Journal of Investment Consulting* 13, no. 1 (March 2012): 54–63.

has been bought by dollar-cost averaging, investors can console themselves with the knowledge that now they can buy the next batch at a lower price. And if stock prices increase after the first monthly batch of stocks has been sold by reverse dollar-cost averaging, investors can console themselves with the knowledge that now they can sell the next batch at a higher price.

## Self-Control

Self-control, like pride and regret, centers on the interaction between cognition and emotion. Self-control can be insufficient, excessive, or just right. When self-control is insufficient, emotion compels us to spend too much now, while we are young, leaving too little for when we are old, and cognition does not counter that emotion sufficiently. Excessive self-control, however, is as prevalent as insufficient self-control. When self-control is excessive, emotion compels us to spend too little now—a common problem when we are old—and cognition does not counter that emotion sufficiently.

I wrote about excessive self-control in a *Wall Street Journal* article, and many readers recognized themselves in it.[180] One wrote, "I've been a dedicated saver and investor for 40 years, always practicing self-denial to the point that it's extremely difficult to spend money. I honestly get uptight about small purchases that are insignificant. The difficulty is changing a mind-set that has gripped my thinking for four decades."

Rules are self-control devices. Such rules, for example, facilitate the realization of losses. "I have a hard-and-fast rule that I never let my losses on a trade exceed ten percent," said one professional trader. "Say I buy a ten-dollar stock. As soon as it goes to nine dollars, I must sell it and take a loss. Some guys have a five per cent rule. Some may have fifteen. I'm a ten man. . . . The traders who get wiped out hope against hope, . . . they're stubborn. They refuse to take losses" (pp. 17, 18, and 30).[181]

Professional traders set rules and control systems that track trades and force the realization of losses when traders' self-control fails. One rule and associated control system mandates that traders settle their trading positions at the end of each day, realizing gains on good days and losses on bad days. The ability of control systems to force traders to realize losses is, however, only as good the ability of those systems to prevent rogue traders from thwarting them. Major trading frauds combine traders' reluctance to realize losses with their ability to thwart control systems. Reluctance to realize small losses leads

---

[180]Meir Statman, "The Mental Mistakes We Make with Retirement Spending," *Wall Street Journal* (24 April 2017). www.wsj.com/articles/the-mental-mistakes-we-make-with-retirement-spending-1492999921.
[181]Sonny Kleinfield, *The Traders* (New York: Holt, Rinehart and Winston, 1983).

to larger bets in attempts to get even by recouping losses, which then leads instead to larger losses that are impossible to hide. Control systems are useful in contexts other than trading, such as consumption of alcohol. Liquor sales decline when access to payday loans is restricted.[182]

## Trust

Trust, like regret, pride, and self-control, combines cognition with emotion. The two partners in crime in the famous prisoner's dilemma must decide whether to trust each other or not. The prisoners are told in advance that if neither confesses, each gets a one-year sentence. If one confesses, he gets off scot-free while his partner gets a five-year sentence. If both confess, each gets a three-year sentence. In the absence of trust, each confesses and gets a three-year sentence. In the presence of trust, neither confesses and each gets a one-year sentence.

"Trust is a psychological state comprising the intention to accept vulnerability based upon positive expectations of the intentions or behavior of another" (p. 1998), wrote management scholar Denise Rousseau and her coauthors.[183] A trusting partner accepts vulnerability to a five-year sentence when he confesses, if his trust is misplaced and his partner does not confess.

Risk is essential in the conceptualization of trust. Trust is unnecessary if actions can be undertaken with complete certainty about outcomes. Interdependence is essential as well, whereby the outcome for one cannot be achieved without reliance on another.

A trust question in the World Values Survey asks for one's degree of agreement with the following question: "Generally speaking, would you say that most people can be trusted or that you need to be very careful in dealing with people?" People who have a relatively high level of trust also have a high tolerance for risk and a low propensity for regret.[184]

Trust is an effective tool for limiting moral hazard. Companies in US counties where trust is greater suffer less from agency problems, are more profitable, and have higher valuations. In addition, such companies take a harsher view of ethics violations.[185]

---

[182]Harold E. Cuffe and Christopher G. Gibbs, "The Effect of Payday Lending Restrictions on Liquor Sales" (26 August 2015). Available at SSRN: http://ssrn.com/abstract=2652018 or http://dx.doi.org/10.2139/ssrn.2652018.

[183]Denise M. Rousseau, Sim B. Sitkin, Ronald S. Burt, and Colin Camerer, "Not So Different After All: A Cross-Discipline View of Trust," *Academy of Management Review* 23, no. 3 (July 1998): 393–404.

[184]Pan and Statman, "Questionnaires of Risk Tolerance."

[185]Gilles Hilary and Sterling Huang, "Trust and Contracting," INSEAD Working Paper No. 2015/42/ACC (11 May 2015). Available at SSRN: https://ssrn.com/abstract=2604974 or http://dx.doi.org/10.2139/ssrn.2604974.

We seek advice from people we trust. A change in financial regulations in Israel moved the choice of mutual funds in savings accounts from employers to individuals. Choices to switch fund were not influenced by fund performance but was strongly influenced by the choices of co-workers of the same ethnic group.[186]

Investors interacting with financially savvy people are more likely to invest in stocks, especially when trust in financially savvy people is high.[187] And trust drives reaction to information. Earnings forecasts by local Chinese analysts influence Chinese investors more than foreign investors, whereas earnings forecasts for foreign analysts influence foreign investors more than Chinese investors.[188]

Trust in banks is essential for an effective financial system, evidenced by a strong association between trust and effectiveness of banks in 52 countries. Pro-market views on economic issues are associated with a higher level of trust in banks. Women have more trust in banks than men do, and trust in banks increases with income but decreases with age and education. Access to television increases trust, whereas internet access diminishes trust.[189]

However, trust can have drawbacks when it is misplaced, as with Ponzi schemes. From a sample of 376 Ponzi schemes prosecuted by the SEC, it is evident that they occur more often in US states where people are more trusting. In addition, Ponzi scheme success—measured by duration, the total amount invested, or the percentage of money the perpetrators receive—is greater in the presence of an affinity link.[190]

Revelations of Ponzi schemes reduce trust. Investors in communities exposed to the Bernie Madoff Ponzi scheme interacted through social networks. Such investors withdrew investments from financial advisers and shifted them to cash in banks. Advisers who sustained trust suffered lower

---

[186]Yevgeny Mugerman, Orly Sade, and Moses Shayo, "Long Term Savings Decisions: Inertia, Peer Effects and Ethnicity," *Journal of Economic Behavior & Organization* 106 (2014): 235–53.

[187]Arian C.T. Borgers, Rachel A.J. Pownall, and Louis Raes, "Exposure to Bankers: Networks and Stock Market Participation" (1 October 2015). Available at SSRN: http://ssrn.com/abstract=2783360 or http://dx.doi.org/10.2139/ssrn.2783360.

[188]Chunxin Jia, Yaping Wang, and Wei Xiong, "Social Trust and Differential Reactions of Local and Foreign Investors to Public News," NBER Working Paper No. 21075 (April 2015). www.nber.org/papers/w21075.

[189]Zuzana Fungáčová, Iftekhar Hasan, and Laurent Weill, "Trust in Banks," BOFIT Discussion Paper No. 7/2016; Gabelli School of Business, Fordham University Research Paper No. 2782358 (13 May 2016). Available at SSRN: http://ssrn.com/abstract=2782358.

[190]Stephen Deason, Shivaram Rajgopal, and Gregory B. Waymire, "Who Gets Swindled in Ponzi Schemes?" (28 March 2015). Available at SSRN: http://ssrn.com/abstract=2586490 or http://dx.doi.org/10.2139/ssrn.2586490.

withdrawals, whereas advisers in a position to misappropriate the investments of their clients suffered higher withdrawals.[191]

## Mood

Mood is muted emotion—less intense but longer lasting. Sunshine induces positive mood, and sun lamps chase away winter blues. A study of credit card transactions shows that daily credit card spending is higher on sunny days than on cloudy ones. A one standard deviation decrease in abnormal cloud cover leads to an increase in daily credit card spending by around 1%.[192]

Sunshine affects decisions of lower-level financial officers by influencing their risk tolerance and subjective judgment. Sunshine is associated with more liberal credit approvals, and clouds have a large-magnitude effect in the opposite direction. The influence of sunshine on credit approvals is more pronounced when approvals involve greater discretion and reviews of approvals are not automated.[193]

Extreme temperatures affect security prices by changing the way investors acquire and process information. Increases in the mean and standard deviation of extreme temperatures—below 15 and above 85 degrees Fahrenheit— are associated with a 0.02% and 0.5% decline in stock returns, respectively. Moreover, Gallup surveys show that an increase in extreme temperatures is associated with a more negative perception of the current and future state of the economy.[194]

Shifts in clocks at the end of daylight saving time are associated with substantially lower stock returns on the day following the clock shift, especially in local, relatively small markets. This association is consistent with our knowledge of the human circadian system, which keeps us in sync with the

---

[191]Umit G. Gurun, Noah Stoffman, and Scott E. Yonker, "Trust Busting: The Effect of Fraud on Investor Behavior," Kelley School of Business Research Paper No. 15-70 (24 May 2017). Available at SSRN: http://ssrn.com/abstract=2664307 or http://dx.doi.org/10.2139/ssrn.2664307.

[192]Sumit Agarwal Souphala Chomsisengphet, Stephan Meier, and Xin Zou, "In the Mood to Consume: Effect of Sunshine on Credit Card Spending" (13 May 2019), Columbia Business School Research Paper No. 17-104. Available at SSRN: https://ssrn.com/abstract=3014541 or http://dx.doi.org/10.2139/ssrn.3014541.

[193]Kristle Romero Cortés, Ran Duchin, and Denis Sosyura, "Clouded Judgment: The Role of Sentiment in Credit Origination," *Journal of Financial Economics* 121, no. 2 (August 2016): 392–413.

[194]Christos Makridis, "Can You Feel the Heat? Extreme Temperatures, Stock Returns, and Economic Sentiment" (26 December 2018). Available at SSRN: https://ssrn.com/abstract=3095422 or http://dx.doi.org/10.2139/ssrn.3095422.

24-hour day, and suggests that the mechanism underlying the effect may be based on a loss of investors' internal clock harmony.[195]

Optimism and pessimism can be described as moods. Optimism is associated with the emotions of hope and happiness, and pessimism is associated with the emotions of fear and sadness. But optimism and pessimism are not as intense as hope, happiness, fear, or sadness. Sentiment in the context of investments often corresponds to mood. Bearish sentiment corresponds to pessimistic mood, and bullish sentiment corresponds to optimistic mood. Major terrorist attacks induce pessimism, affecting analysts' earnings forecasts. One study showed that analysts located near major terrorist attacks issued more pessimistic forecasts than analysts who were further away.[196]

Optimism enhances our life today as we contemplate an enjoyable future, but optimism has downsides. Optimism can lead to excessive debt loads. One study showed that optimistic Finns not only accumulated more debt than pessimists but were also burdened by excessive debt loads. Moreover, optimists were less attentive to forecast errors than their pessimistic brethren.[197]

Pessimism also has downsides, evident among people with low socioeconomic status, characterized by low income and a low level of education. Those with high socioeconomic status have more optimistic views on future macroeconomic trends, such as business conditions, the national unemployment rate, and equity returns. In addition, they are more likely to invest in stocks and to consider buying houses, durable goods, or automobiles. The difference between the high- and low-status groups reflects low-status people's excessive pessimism.[198]

## Affect

Affect is the faint whisper of emotion or mood, stripped down to valence, positive or negative. Psychologist Robert Zajonc, an early proponent of the

---

[195]Yevgeny Mugerman, Orr Yidov, and Zvi Wiener, "By the Light of Day: The Effect of the Switch to Winter Time on Stock Markets" (16 September 2018). Available at SSRN: https://ssrn.com/abstract=3250442 or http://dx.doi.org/10.2139/ssrn.3250442.

[196]Constantinos Antoniou, Alok Kumar, and Anastasios Maligkris, "Terrorist Attacks, Analyst Sentiment, and Earnings Forecasts" (5 April 2018). Available at SSRN: https://ssrn.com/abstract=2702051 or http://dx.doi.org/10.2139/ssrn.2702051.

[197]Ari Hyytinen and Hanna Putkuri, "Household Optimism and Borrowing," Bank of Finland Research Discussion Paper No. 21/2012 (8 May 2012). Available at SSRN: https://ssrn.com/abstract=2101025 or http://dx.doi.org/10.2139/ssrn.2101025.

[198]Sreyoshi Das, Camelia M. Kuhnen, and Stefan Nagel, "Socioeconomic Status and Macroeconomic Expectations," National Bureau of Economic Research Working Paper No. 24045; *Review of Financial Studies*, Forthcoming (13 November 2017). Available at SSRN: https://ssrn.com/abstract=3009941 or http://dx.doi.org/10.2139/ssrn.3009941.

importance of affect in making choices, wrote, "We do not just see 'a house': We see a *handsome* house, an *ugly* house, or a *pretentious* house" (p. 154).[199] Indeed, differences in the affect of houses correspond to differences in their prices.

Perceptions of luck are often related to affect. The number eight is considered lucky in Chinese culture and its affect is positive, whereas the number four is considered unlucky and its affect is negative. Singaporean Chinese are averse to apartments on floors with numbers ending in four. Such apartments sell at 1.1% below the average price, whereas apartments on floors with numbers ending in eight sell at 0.9% above the average price. There are fewer home transactions on inauspicious days of the lunar calendar, when perceptions of luck inclines Singaporean Chinese against major economic decisions. The demand for lucky addresses is also weaker on these inauspicious days.[200]

"Dragon babies" are children born in the Year of the Dragon and are preferred by Chinese parents who are concerned about luck. One study showed that from 1960 to 2007, the average number of births for the Chinese majority in Singapore increased 9.3% in Dragon years, but no such patterns were evident among non-Chinese minorities. Chinese Dragon babies have significantly lower incomes than other Chinese cohorts once they join the labor market; this adverse outcome reflects the aggregate resource implications of the substantially greater sizes of these cohorts. In addition, Dragon babies suffer lower rates of admission to national universities, which points to a limited capacity for accommodating the surge in resource demand that accompanies larger birth cohorts.[201]

Houses believed to be haunted exude negative affect, and in cities such as Hong Kong, SAR, their presence has a ripple effect on prices of nearby houses. Prices of housing units believed to be haunted drop by an average 20%. Prices drop by 5% among units on the same floor, they drop by 3% among units in the same block, and they drop by 1% among units in the same estate.[202]

---

[199]Robert B. Zajonc, "Feeling and Thinking: Preferences Need No Inferences," *American Psychologist* 35, no. 2 (February1980): 151–75.

[200]Jia He, Haoming Liu, Tien Foo Sing, Changcheng Song, and Wei-Kang Wong, "Superstition, Conspicuous Spending, and Housing Market: Evidence from Singapore" (9 February 2018). Available at SSRN: https://ssrn.com/abstract=3120932 or http://dx.doi.org/10.2139/ssrn.3120932.

[201]Sumit Agarwal, Wenlan Qian, Tien Foo Sing, and Poh Lin Tan, "Dragon Babies," Georgetown McDonough School of Business Research Paper No. 3032575 (22 November 2018). Available at SSRN: https://ssrn.com/abstract=3032575 or http://dx.doi.org/10.2139/ssrn.3032575.

[202]Utpal Bhattacharya, Daisy J. Huang, and Kasper Meisner Nielsen, "Spillovers in Asset Prices: The Curious Case of Haunted Houses," 8th Miami Behavioral Finance Conference 2017 (27 November 2017). Available at SSRN: https://ssrn.com/abstract=3077951 or http://dx.doi.org/10.2139/ssrn.3077951.

Houses in Paris and similar hot spots have great positive affect, especially among out-of-country buyers. These buyers generally purchase relatively small but high-quality properties in desirable neighborhoods and in areas with high percentages of compatriots. They pay higher prices, hold these properties longer, and realize lower capital gains.[203]

The affect of the color red is negative in financial environments where red signifies losses. Consistent with the color red causing "avoidance behavior," one study found that this color makes US investors less likely to buy equities and that the color red's effect is muted for colorblind participants and for participants in China, where red is not always used to visualize financial losses.[204]

Positive affect can have a negative effect when it acts as a comparison standard. A beautiful female mannequin had a negative effect on male and female consumers who were less physically attractive and had low self-esteem. They became threatened by its beauty standard, evaluating a product displayed by the mannequin more negatively than more attractive and higher-self-esteem consumers. That threat and its effects were mitigated by reducing the mannequin's beauty, such as by removing its hair or its head.[205]

Positive affect can also have a negative effect when it misleads investors into the belief that good stocks are stocks of good companies. Stocks of admired companies bask in the glow of positive affect, whereas stocks of spurned companies wilt in the dark of negative affect. We embrace stocks of admired companies, expecting high returns with low risk, while we keep our distance from stocks of spurned companies, expecting low returns with high risk. However, there is evidence that affect misleads investors into forgoing superior stock returns. Stocks of admired companies delivered lower returns, on average, than stocks of spurned companies.[206]

---

[203]Dragana Cvijanovic and Christophe Spaenjers, "'We'll Always Have Paris': Out-of-Country Buyers in the Housing Market," Kenan Institute of Private Enterprise Research Paper No. 18-25; HEC Paris Research Paper No. FIN-2018-1311 (3 October 2018). Available at SSRN: https://ssrn.com/abstract=3248902 or http://dx.doi.org/10.2139/ssrn.3248902.

[204]William J. Bazley, Henrik Cronqvist, and Milica Milosavljevic Mormann, "Visual Finance: The Pervasive Effects of Red on Investor Behavior" (13 March 2019), Swedish House of Finance Research Paper No. 17-16, SMU Cox School of Business Research Paper No. 18-4, University of Miami Business School Research Paper No. 2992812. Available at SSRN: https://ssrn.com/abstract=2992812 or http://dx.doi.org/10.2139/ssrn.2992812.

[205]Jennifer J. Argo and Darren W. Dahl, "Standards of Beauty: The Impact of Mannequins in the Retail Context," *Journal of Consumer Research* 44, no. 5 (February 2018): 974–90.

[206]Meir Statman, Kenneth L. Fisher, and Deniz Anginer, "Affect in a Behavioral Asset Pricing Model," *Financial Analysts Journal* 64, no. 2 (March/April 2008): 20–29.

## Conclusion

Wants precede emotional shortcuts and errors, just as they precede cognitive shortcuts and errors. We use emotional shortcuts and sometimes stumble into emotional errors on our way to satisfying our wants, deriving utilitarian, expressive, and emotional benefits.

We want financial security. Yet most of us, especially the young, do not have ample portfolios to provide financial security now and in the future by allocating them entirely to riskless money market funds. Good emotional shortcuts of hope and fear guide us to allocate some, but not all, of our portfolios to risky assets, such as stocks, to attain financial security. Yet emotional errors can imperil our financial security. Excessive hope can drive us to allocate too much of our portfolios to risky assets in boom times, and emotional errors of excessive fear can scare us into dumping all our risky assets in a crash.

Financial security also requires balancing saving and spending throughout our lifetimes through good emotional shortcuts of self-control. Yet emotional errors of insufficient self-control can drive us to save too little and spend too much when we are young, leaving too little for financial security when we are old. And emotional errors of excessive self-control can compel us to spend too little when we are old, living as if we lack financial security.

We want to nurture our children. Good emotional shortcuts of fear lead us to insist on holding the hand of our 3-year-old daughter when we cross a busy street, and good emotional shortcuts of hope lead us to establish a college savings account for her. But emotional errors of excessive fear lead us to insist on driving our 10-year-old son from school when he can be equally safe by walking that short distance, and emotional errors of excessive hope might lead us to refrain from saving, hoping that an athletic scholarship will cover all our daughter's college expenses.

We want fairness. Good emotional shortcuts of anger deter unfair behavior toward us and others and deter us from unfair behavior. Yet chronic anger is an emotional error, increasing the likelihood of divorce, cardiovascular disease, and problems at work.

Knowledge of wants, emotional shortcuts, and emotional errors is part of human-behavior knowledge. Investment professionals can combine that knowledge with financial-facts knowledge to use emotional shortcuts and avoid emotional errors on their way to satisfying their own wants, and they can help amateur investors do the same.

# 5. Balancing Wants, Acquiring Knowledge, and Correcting Errors

Knowledge of cognitive and emotional shortcuts and errors is part of human-behavior knowledge. That knowledge joins financial-facts knowledge in guiding us toward correct use of cognitive and emotional shortcuts and correction of cognitive and emotional errors on our way to satisfying our wants.

We climb three steps to correct use of shortcuts and correction of errors. The first step consists of the acquisition of financial-facts and human-behavior knowledge. This knowledge alerts us when System 1 intuition is about to mislead us into the pitfalls of cognitive and emotional errors. The second step consists of the activation of System 2 reflection when we are alerted to the pitfalls of System 1. The third step consists of outside help, such as from investment professionals, when we are unable to activate System 2 on our own.

Replacing financial-facts ignorance with knowledge is not always easy, but it can be done. For example, many amateur investors are ignorant of the financial facts of portfolio diversification. Some believe, in error, that diversification *increases* the volatility of portfolio returns; financial-facts knowledge indicates that diversification *reduces* that volatility. Investors are tripped into this error because the future volatility of the returns of familiar stocks, such as those of Facebook or Disney, seems easier to foresee than the future volatility of the returns of a portfolio, such as a total stock market portfolio, that is diversified among thousands of mostly unfamiliar stocks. Moreover, some investors believe, in error, that diversification *increases* the expected returns of portfolios; financial-facts knowledge indicates that diversification does not change expected returns. As a result, some investors choose not to diversify because they misperceive diversification as increasing volatility, and other investors choose to diversify because they misperceive diversification as offering high expected returns.[207]

Replacing human-behavior ignorance with knowledge is also not always easy, but it can be done. Framing errors mislead some investors into framing stock markets as equivalents of department stores. A stock price fall induces them to buy the stock, as it induces shoppers to buy a coat when its price falls

---

[207]Nicholas Reinholtz, Philip M. Fernbach, and Bart De Langhe, "Do People Understand the Benefit of Diversification?" (12 July 2018). Available at SSRN: http://ssrn.com/abstract=2719144 or http://dx.doi.org/10.2139/ssrn.2719144.

in a sale. This "price tag illusion" inflicts severe losses on investors who fall victim to it.[208]

## Correcting Cognitive and Emotional Errors by Acquisition of Knowledge

Financial-facts and human-behavior knowledge consists of more than financial literacy. It also includes financial comprehension and behavior demonstrating financial comprehension. Consider readers' responses to my true-or-false quiz in the 23 October 2017 issue of the *Wall Street Journal*, centering on financial comprehension and correction of cognitive and emotional errors.[209]

Is the following statement true or false? "Jane is the portfolio manager of the Alpha mutual fund, which beat its S&P 500 Index benchmark 10 years in a row. She majored in mathematics at Harvard University and received her MBA in finance at Columbia University, both with high distinction. This indicates that it is better to invest in the Alpha mutual fund rather than in an S&P 500 Index mutual fund."

I chose false as my answer, highlighting the cognitive errors of representativeness. I wrote, "Representativeness errors lead us to focus on 'representativeness' information and overlook 'base-rate' information. Some pieces of information make Jane similar to, or representative of, what we are likely to think of as excellent portfolio managers. These include her Harvard and Columbia degrees, in addition to beating the S&P 500 Index 10 years in a row. Yet base-rate information tells us that one of 1,024 people tossing a coin is likely to have 10 heads in a row, and the number of available mutual funds greatly exceeds 1,024."

Acquisition of knowledge requires a readiness for acquisition, yet not all readers were ready. One wrote, "I don't care where Jane went to school, beating the S&P 500 10 years in a row is not the result of chance. Whoever the one in 1,024 may be, it ain't because they were flipping coins."

Another wrote, "The average fund doesn't beat the indexes. True, but why would anyone invest with the average fund? Look at it this way: Start with ten funds to choose from and really get to know the people behind them, and their process, and how they have performed in various types of markets. Stick with those who invest in their own funds, have an ownership interest in their

---

[208]Fernando Chague, Rodrigo De-Losso, and Bruno Giovannetti, "The Price Tag Illusion," Department of Economics Working Paper No. 2017-31, University of Sao Paulo (16 November 2017).
[209]Meir Statman, "A Different Kind of Financial Literacy Test," *Wall Street Journal* (23 October 2017).

company, and who have strong leadership in their investment committee. Doing this you can weed out at least half of the managers as poor performers. Now select the 'average' from among those left, invest for the long term, and you'll end up in the top quartile and beat the market."

But another reader demonstrated comprehension: "There is simply no evidence to support your argument. Past performance in various markets says nothing about future performance. That is why 10 years ago Warren Buffett said he would bet any fund manager $1 million that his fund wouldn't beat the S&P over a 10-year period. Buffett recently won his bet."

Now consider the following statement: "A surgeon perfects her surgeries, and increases her rate of success as she performs surgeries more often. Likewise, an investor perfects his trading and increases his rate of success as he trades more often."

I chose false as my answer, describing those who chose true as misled by framing errors. I wrote, "The analogy between a trader and a surgeon is one that many investors make. It makes intuitive sense. But it is wrong. The human body doesn't 'compete' with the surgeon as she perfects her surgeries; it doesn't switch the heart from left to right. But two traders on the opposite side of a trade compete with each other. A trader might perfect his skills by frequent trading, but will nevertheless lose if the other trader has greater skills or possesses better information."

Some readers found it difficult to comprehend the correct frame for trading because it differs from correct frames in familiar settings, such as surgery. One reader wrote, "As you increase the number of trades, you move up in the hierarchy and trade with less skilled traders more often." Another wrote, "If I make investments in the stock market, I do not have to be better than a professional analyst to make money. Any improvements I make in those decisions has nothing to do with them."

But another reader demonstrated comprehension: "Notice how every investor this year [2017], big or small, is a 'genius'? I wonder if the economy is playing a part here. . . . Nah, we're all just geniuses."

Next, consider the following statement: "'You can beat the market by buying and holding FAANG stocks (Facebook, Amazon, Apple, Netflix, and Google). After a decade or so, it has made me stinking rich,' Paul says."

I chose false as the answer, highlighting hindsight errors. I wrote, "Hindsight errors might well be the most dangerous among the cognitive errors tripping up investors. We know, in hindsight, that FAANG stocks delivered fabulous returns in the recent past [through 2017]. Hindsight errors mislead us into thinking that our foresight is as accurate as our hindsight, but it isn't. FAANG stocks are as likely to deliver terrible returns in the future as they are likely to deliver fabulous returns."

One reader disagreed: "I got stinkin' rich on FAANG and still am. Heard the hindsight BS EVERY YEAR and never paid attention to it." Another wrote, "'You can beat the market by buying and holding FAANG stocks.' Why is this necessarily 'False'? You may not beat the market, but you most certainly CAN beat the market." But another reader responded, "You CAN also beat the market by buying GE stock. But you WON'T."

I added, "Moreover, when I hear claims such as Paul's, a voice in me struggles to come out: 'May I have an audited statement of your investments?' Is Paul really rich? Did he buy his FAANG stocks a decade ago or only recently? Did he mention all the stocks in his portfolio or just the winning stocks?"

The quiz also included questions about wants, highlighting the distinction between wants and errors. Consider the following statement: "Michael is passionate about protecting the environment and wants his investments to be true to his values. He chooses a mutual fund that excludes stocks of companies harming the environment, knowing that this fund's annual returns are likely to be 1 percentage point lower than those of a conventional fund. This choice makes sense."

I rated this statement true, writing, "It's true for Michael, that is. It is important to understand here that money is for satisfying wants, whether that means secure retirement income, nurturing children and grandchildren, gaining high social status, or being true to our values."

I went on to write, "A common way of looking at money is to separate the *production* of money from its *use* in satisfying wants—that is, produce the most money you can in a first step, and use it to satisfy wants in the second step. Yet we also properly commingle production and use—think of a choice between a career where you earn much money but are unhappy to come to work, and one where you earn less money but are happy to come to work."

I wrote further, "For some people, it makes sense to invest in a conventional fund, get the highest returns, and donate 1 percentage point of those returns to support environmental causes, being true to your values. But for some people, it makes sense to invest in an environmental fund that earns 1 percentage point less than conventional funds but is true to your values."

One reader wrote, "Nonsense. 'Don't harm the environment' is basically whatever liberals choose it to be, and this is just another pretext for punishing companies that don't conform to their totalitarian socialist agenda. Better: Let the free market decide. If the market judges a company as causing excessive environmental damage, their stock will pay the price. If not, it won't."

But another reader demonstrated comprehension: "You missed the point. The point is that for that specific individual, there is a non-financial benefit that is added to the financial benefit that makes the total benefit higher for that particular individual. That does not mean that any particular investment will have the same total benefit for any other individual, or that the non-financial benefit will accrue to anyone else."

## Correcting Cognitive and Emotional Errors by Prompting System 2

Investors we know as "chartists" search for patterns in series of past prices of stocks and other investments and use them to predict future prices. System 1 intuition might tell us that the series of Apple daily stock *prices* in **Exhibit 5.1** is representative of a "head and shoulders" pattern that could lead chartists to foresee future prices and recommend buying or selling shares. But that intuition might be nothing more than representativeness errors. We can apply System 2 reflection by presenting the same data as a series of Apple daily stock *returns* derived from these Apple stock prices, as shown in **Exhibit 5.2**. This series shows a pattern representative of randomness, correcting our System 1 intuition.

Confirmation errors are evident in assessment of the usefulness of trading rules. One rule is based on the Bearish Sentiment Index, compiled from stock market recommendations of writers of investment newsletters. The Bearish

**Exhibit 5.1. Daily *Prices* of Apple Shares Are Representative of a Pattern**

**Exhibit 5.2. Daily *Returns* of Apple Shares Are Representative of Randomness**

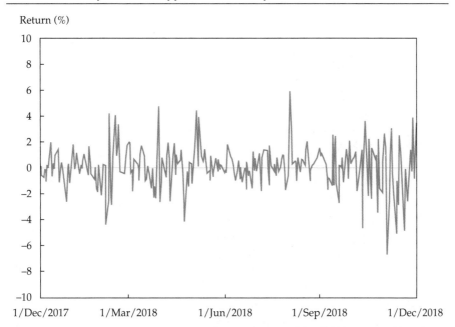

Sentiment Index is the ratio of the number of investment newsletter writers who are bearish, expecting stock market declines, to the number of writers expressing an opinion, bullish or bearish, about the stock market's future direction. A contrarian use of the Bearish Sentiment Index calls for buying stocks when bearish sentiment is high and selling when it is low.

Economist Michael Solt and I examined the usefulness of the Bearish Sentiment Index. The System 1 focus on confirming evidence is illustrated in a statement by an investment professional: "At the market high in late 1972, 75% of [writers of investment newsletters] predicted that stocks were heading skyward. Then, at the bottom of the 1974 market . . . two thirds suspected stocks would continue to free-fall; not long thereafter we had the beginning of a major bull market" (p. 45).[210]

A proper System 2 test of the hypothesis that the Bearish Sentiment Index is a useful prediction tool places observations into four boxes, depicted in **Exhibit 5.3**. The first contains "positive hits"—predictions of stock market increases followed by realized increases. The second contains "negative hits"—predictions of decreases followed by realized decreases. The third contains

---

[210]Michael E. Solt and Meir Statman, "How Useful Is the Sentiment Index?" *Financial Analysts Journal* 44, no. 5 (September/October 1988): 45–55.

**Exhibit 5.3. Predictions of Changes in Stock Prices and Their Realizations**

| | Realization | |
| --- | --- | --- |
| Prediction | Stock Prices Increased | Stock Prices Declined |
| Stock prices will increase. | Positive hits | False positives |
| Stock price will decline. | False negatives | Negative hits |

"false positives"—predictions of increases followed by realized decreases. And the fourth contains "false negatives"—predictions of decreases followed by realized increases. We commit confirmation errors when we assign much weight to the confirming evidence in the boxes of positive and negative hits while assigning little weight to the disconfirming evidence in the boxes of false positives and negatives.

In one of our tests, Solt and I set the bullish level of the index at 0.29, the mean level at DJIA market tops, and the bearish level at 0.52, the mean level at DJIA market bottoms. We examined DJIA returns during the four weeks following an index level exceeding 0.52 or falling short of 0.29. We found that the index is useless as a forecasting tool not because it fails to provide some good forecasts but because it also provides so many bad forecasts. For example, as seen in **Exhibit 5.4**, the index correctly forecast increases in the DJIA in 54 four-week periods, not much different from the 56.6 periods we would expect if there were no association between forecasts and realizations. But the index also incorrectly forecast increases in the DJIA in 55 four-week periods, not much different from the 52.4 periods we would expect if there were no association between forecasts and realizations. The persistent belief in the usefulness of the Bearish Sentiment Index is likely rooted in confirmation errors of users who focus on confirming instances and overlook disconfirming ones.[211]

Disposition for reflection, more than intelligence, prompts the use of System 2. Intelligent people are better than less intelligent people at correcting overconfidence and hindsight errors, but they are no better at correcting anchoring errors and no more successful at resisting the emotional error of excessive regret that prevents them from realizing losses.[212]

Proper framing using System 2 can correct anchoring errors. Anchors affect estimates of targets by highlighting features shared by the anchor and the target and obscuring features of the target that differ from those of

---

[211]Solt and Statman, "How Useful?"

[212]Keith E. Stanovich and Richard F. West, "On the Relative Independence of Thinking Biases and Cognitive Ability," *Journal of Personality and Social Psychology* 94, no. 4 (April 2008): 672–95.

**Exhibit 5.4. Predictions of Changes in Stock Prices by the Bearish Sentiment Index and Their Realizations**

| Forecast | Realization | | Total |
| --- | --- | --- | --- |
| | DJIA Increased in the Following 4 Weeks | DJIA Decreased in the Following 4 Weeks | |
| DJIA will increase. (Bearish Sentiment Index above 0.52) | 54 (56.6) | 55 (52.4) | 109 |
| DJIA will decrease. (Bearish Sentiment Index below 0.29) | 54 (51.4) | 45 (47.6) | 99 |
| Total | 108 | 100 | 208 |

*Notes:* Numbers in parentheses indicate the expected result if the method has no forecasting ability. Chi-square = 0.34. Level of significance = 0.56.

the anchor. Membership in the automotive industry might be highlighted as a feature shared by General Motors and Toyota, but features not shared by General Motors and Toyota might be obscured. For example, General Motors is based in the United States, whereas Toyota is based in Japan.[213] Proper framing using System 2 highlights differences between the features of anchor and target, making common membership in the automotive industry less prominent in assessments of the future prospects of General Motors and Toyota and weakening the chain that links membership in the automotive industry to assessment of the future prospects of the two companies.

We can also correct anchoring errors using System 2 by considering many anchors rather than one. Plausible anchors for the prospects of a company, such as the proportion of SUVs and trucks in the lineups of the automotive industry, exert greater influence on estimates than implausible ones, such as their dates of incorporation. When facing multiple anchors, we evaluate the plausibility of each anchor relative to the others. People facing the proportion of SUVs and trucks in the lineup as one anchor for the future prospects of each company and the date of incorporation as another choose the proportion of SUVs and trucks as an anchor because it is more plausible.[214]

---

[213]Gretchen B. Chapman and Eric J. Johnson, "Incorporating the Irrelevant: Anchors in Judgments of Belief and Value," in *Heuristics and Biases: The Psychology of Intuitive Judgment* edited by Thomas Gilovich, Dale W. Griffin, and Daniel Kahneman, 120–38 (New York: Cambridge University Press, 2002).

[214]Yan Zhang, Ye Li, and Ting Zhu, "How Multiple Anchors Affect Judgment: Evidence from the Lab and eBay," Columbia Business School Research Paper No. 14-62 (25 November 2014). Available at SSRN: http://ssrn.com/abstract=2530690 or http://dx.doi.org/10.2139/ssrn.2530690.

"Temptation bundling" can correct the emotional errors of insufficient self-control. A bundle combines a want, such as reading an attractive novel, with a "should," such as exercising at the gym. People in a temptation bundling group were granted access to iPods containing four audio novels of their choice, but they could listen to them only when exercising at the gym. People in another group were granted access to four audio novels of their choice, available at any time on their personal iPods, but they were asked to listen only while exercising. People in yet another group received a bookstore gift certificate whose value was approximately equal to the cost of borrowing four audio novels. People in the first group were most likely to exercise at the gym, followed by people in the second group and people in the third.[215]

Yet incentives, such as temptation bundling, are not always effective in correcting cognitive and emotional errors. Indeed, incentives can backfire; a study showed they could reduce performance in sports and test-taking by increasing anxiety and the propensity to replace reliable methods with unreliable ones in attempts to improve performance. The effects of accountability on performance are similar to those of incentives. Accountability improved performance in situations where effort improves performance but was not effective at correcting cognitive and emotional errors.[216]

The downside of incentives is evident among loan officers. Substantial incentives promote better screening of loans and more profitable lending choices, but incentives are less effective when compensation cannot be recovered if loans go bad. Moreover, incentives distort evaluation of the risk of loans, even among experienced professionals.[217]

## Correcting Cognitive and Emotional Errors by Investment Professionals

Investment professionals who educate and advise investment amateurs are a large subset of all investment professionals. Indeed, they constitute approximately one-third of CFA charterholders. These investment professionals carry a range of titles, including wealth manager, investment adviser, financial

---

[215]Katherine L. Milkman, Julia A. Minson, and Kevin G. M. Volpp, "Holding the Hunger Games Hostage at the Gym: An Evaluation of Temptation Bundling," *Management Science* 60, no. 2 (February 2014): 283–99.

[216]Katherine L. Milkman, John W. Payne, and Jack B. Soll, "A User's Guide to Debiasing," in *Wiley-Blackwell Handbook of Judgment and Decision Making*, edited by Gideon Keren and George Wu, 924–51 (Chichester, UK: John Wiley & Sons, Ltd, 2015).

[217]Shawn Allen Cole, Martin Kanz, and Leora F. Klapper, "Incentivizing Calculated Risk-Taking: Evidence from an Experiment with Commercial Bank Loan Officers," *Journal of Finance* 70, no. 2 (April 2015): 537–75.

adviser, financial planner, and broker. I will refer to them as "financial advisers" or simply as "advisers." Education and advice include correction of cognitive and emotional errors, but they are broader than that, encompassing education and advice about financial facts, human behavior, and the balance among various wants, such as for financial security and nurturing children.

It might well be that investors are their own worst enemies, susceptible to cognitive and emotional errors and resistant to trade-offs among wants. Indeed, there is evidence that some clients resist good adviser education and prescriptions, insisting on poor investments as some patients insist on antibiotics when medically unnecessary. Advisers do not serve clients well when they pander or condescend to them. Both attitudes get in the way of education.

A study of thousands of financial advisory sessions and corresponding clients' portfolios showed that when clients take active roles in meetings, advisers depart significantly from what they would have recommended, and such departures lead to lower portfolio diversification and worse performance.[218]

I have learned much about the many contributions of financial advisers to their clients' well-being from frequent interactions with them and their clients. An adviser spoke about balancing wants for the future with wants for the present and balancing saving with spending. He described a couple who worked hard to save for a comfortable retirement but kept a good balance between saving and spending. That balance allowed the wife to pursue her dreams of being an artist. Unfortunately, soon after she retired, she was diagnosed with ALS, a debilitating and eventually fatal disease. Fortunately, however, their savings were sufficient to sustain them, and they were grateful for her opportunity to pursue her art throughout her adult life.

Another couple spends everything they have today because "you never know what tomorrow brings." The wife worries about having enough for college expenses for their two daughters and for their own retirement. When they come to meet the adviser, the story repeats. The husband agrees they need to do something about saving because he loves his two daughters and his wife. He sees the need for saving while it is being discussed. Yet, after a few short days, they are both going on summer cruises with the daughters and other family members because that is a "tradition."

Other clients have the opposite problem, spending too little when they can spend more. An adviser described "a wonderful client who owns a good part of the known world. When he travels, he counts every nickel

---

[218]Andreas Hackethal, Christine Laudenbach, Steffen Meyer, and Annika Weber, "Client Involvement in Expert Advice: Antibiotics in Finance?" SAFE Working Paper No. 219 (23 July 2018). Available at SSRN: https://ssrn.com/abstract=3178664 or http://dx.doi.org/10.2139/ssrn.3178664.

and considers economy-class flights a luxury. As with many of our clients, my primary discussion is to encourage him to spend more; he could easily quadruple his spending and not make a dent in his estate. Haven't been successful so far."

The same adviser told me about his favorite client, a physician in his 80s. Following his analysis, the adviser explained that continuing his practice would cost the physician about $40,000 per year, factoring in his abbreviated hours, office overhead, and insurance cost. Then the adviser recommended that the physician continue to work—because retiring would cost $60,000 in psychiatry bills to deal with depression. "You've never seen a happier client leaving our office."

Wants for financial security turn into wants for high social status when people with much wealth believe that happiness will finally arrive when they have even more wealth. An adviser described a client who wanted to double his wealth because he was certain that doubled wealth would free him from worry and make him happy. Five years later, his wealth had doubled, yet he was still worried and unhappy. "Maybe if I could double it again, then I'd feel secure and be happy," he said.

Wants for wealth can mislead investors into scams. An adviser described a client who worked hard and accumulated a portfolio of nearly a million dollars. Then he received an email of the kind we are all familiar with, offering a secret opportunity. He did not tell the adviser and his staff what he was doing, but month after month, they observed increasing numbers of withdrawals from his portfolio. By the time the adviser contacted him, he had lost more than $600,000 in the scam.

Several advisers described attempts to counter clients' emotional errors of excessive fear during the 2008–09 financial crisis. Some clients abandoned their written investment policy and sold their stocks, despite advisers' attempts at education and advice. The emotional errors of excessive fear were made worse by the cognitive errors of hindsight, misleading clients into the belief that they could sell their stocks before prices dropped even lower and would have the foresight to buy them back before prices increased.

An adviser shared with me a method she uses to correct clients' hindsight errors. At the first meeting of each year, she presents clients with a list of questions about the coming year and asks them to make forecasts. The questions are along the lines of the following:

Will Bashar al-Assad cease to be president of Syria?

Will Nicolas Maduro cease to be president of Venezuela?

Will Mark Zuckerberg step down as Facebook's sole chairman or CEO?

Will domestic US stock funds outperform international stock funds?

Will a magnitude 7.0 or higher earthquake strike California?

Will Donald Trump get divorced?

Will Martha Stewart get married?

At the end-of-the-year meeting, clients might be tempted by hindsight to bring up forecasts that came true: "Why did you invest my money in stocks when it was obvious that they were destined for collapse?" At that point, the adviser will take out the list and educate her clients about the pitfalls of hindsight errors.

Framing shortcuts lead investors to separate their money into mental accounts, such as one dedicated to children's education and one dedicated to retirement income. Frames are often imbued with emotion, whether love for children or fear of poverty. Sometimes the source of money determines its mental account, such as money received as a bequest. An adviser told me of a widowed woman with substantial assets from her mother's estate, her own career, and her late husband's trust. She is risk averse, especially with the money she inherited from her mother: "I don't want to lose the money my mother gave me."

Disabilities are unfortunately common. Almost a third of families have at least one family member with a disability. One out of every nine children under the age of 18 receives special education services. And parents spend an average of approximately $4,000 per year on out-of-pocket medical expenses for each special-needs child.[219]

Disabilities affect the well-being and financial situations of disabled people and their families, and they prompt many cognitive and emotional shortcuts and errors. Parents who leave a hospital with a healthy baby might be preoccupied with getting the baby's room ready and having an adequate supply of diapers. But parents who leave a hospital with a disabled baby are likely beset by hindsight shortcuts and errors. Is the baby's disability due to genetic factors we should have known about ahead of time? Is it due to medicines I took during pregnancy or the one glass of wine I drank? Emotional shortcuts and errors follow, including regret, fear, guilt, and anger.

An adviser told the story of Gwen, a 55-year-old mother of four children. The youngest are twin girls, now in high school, afflicted by Pfeiffer

---

[219]Donald Bailey and J. William G. Chettle, *Your Legacy of Care: Providing for Your Special Needs Child Today, Tomorrow & Always* (San Jose: Loring Ward, 2017). Bailey and Chettle cited the following sources: www.census.gov/prod/2003pubs/c2kbr-17.pdf; Census Data on the 14th Anniversary of the ADA; National Organization on Disability; www.lowcountrylawofc.com.

syndrome, a genetic disorder. A month after their birth, the girls began what would be more than 50 rounds of surgery. Gwen and her husband liquidated their family farming business and, after 28 years of marriage, got divorced.

She worries about her sons and even more about her daughters. Will they be able to attend college? And how will she pay for college?

She has spoken with an attorney but has not set up a trust for her daughters yet. She needs to update her will, now that she is divorced.

She has a financial adviser who is helping her, but his plan does not include helping her children with college tuition. Yet she continues to help her son pay for college, so her finances are dwindling.[220]

Few disabilities are as devastating as mental illness, and none cause greater emotional errors. One financial adviser spoke about work with clients suffering mental illness and clients caring for family members suffering mental illness. Clients suffering bipolar disorder are apt to spend recklessly when in manic states. He keeps careful watch when such clients request to withdraw large amounts of money.

That adviser described a client admitted for psychiatric care who phoned the custodian overseeing his funds and requested that his adviser be removed. When that client's mental state improved, he was surprised at what he had done and reinstated the adviser. The client was concerned about a recurrence of his situation and has now designated a trusted person with power of attorney as a precaution against similar situations.

That financial adviser is most gratified when working with parents helping adult children suffering mental illness. These parents regularly pay for housing, food, and other expenses, keeping a close watch while allowing their children as much autonomy as possible.

## Correcting Cognitive and Emotional Errors by Families and Companies

Family members are often a first line of defense against cognitive and emotional errors and unreasonable wants of fellow family members. This is especially true of older people who are frequent victims of fraud. In interviews with 21 Canadian volunteers who provide telephone support to elderly fraud victims, the volunteers, all seniors themselves, overwhelmingly reported that fraud occurs because of the victims' loneliness and isolation.[221]

---

[220]Bailey and Chettle, *Your Legacy of Care.*
[221]Cassandra Cross, "'They're Very Lonely': Understanding the Fraud Victimisation of Seniors," *International Journal for Crime, Justice and Social Democracy* 5, no. 4 (2016): 60–75.

Angie Kennard's story is all too common. When she visited or called her 79-year-old father, he would discuss the "girlfriend" he met on the internet and sometimes sent money to. He told her she was "the love of his life" and that they planned to get married.

She was worried her father was sending all his money to the scammer, so she asked him for power of attorney, to act on his behalf and help manage his financial situation. He would not agree to it and was upset that she was trying to interfere in his personal life. The "girlfriend" made him believe his daughter only wanted his money.

Not until her father was hospitalized following a massive stroke did he give her power of attorney. At that point, she learned the extent of the scam: He essentially lost his life savings.[222]

Companies act to correct cognitive and emotional errors through education and good design of defined contribution retirement saving accounts. Employees in a large institution altered their fund allocations when the institution streamlined its fund menu by deleting nearly half of the offered funds. Employees now pay lower fees and engage in less fund turnover, leading to savings in excess of $9,400 per employee during their likely period of employment. Moreover, now employees allocate significantly less to stocks, reducing their risk.[223]

Another study found that employers are able to steer older workers to increase their contributions to supplemental savings plans through informational nudges pertaining to key features of such plans. Those who received such "nudges," in comparison to the control group, raised their contribution levels in the months that followed. In addition, those who were "nudged" reported in a follow-up survey being more likely to have set up a retirement plan and claimed to have greater confidence in their preparedness for retirement.[224]

## Conclusion

Correcting cognitive and emotional errors is not always easy, but it can be done. We must begin by admitting our propensity for errors and follow

---

[222]Veronica Dagher, "When an Elderly Parent Has Been Scammed," *Wall Street Journal* (12 June 2016). www.wsj.com/articles/when-an-elderly-parent-has-been-scammed-1465783683# comments_sector.

[223]Donald B. Keim and Olivia Mitchell, "Simplifying Choices in Defined Contribution Retirement Plan Design: A Case Study," *Journal of Pension Economics & Finance* 17, no. 3 (July 2018): 363–84.

[224]Robert L. Clark, Robert G. Hammond, Melinda Sandler Morrill, and Christelle Khalaf, "Nudging Retirement Savings: A Field Experiment on Supplemental Plans," National Bureau of Economic Research Working Paper No. 23679 (August 2017).

up by acquiring and comprehending financial-facts and human-behavior knowledge.

We can expect amateur investors to acquire and comprehend the basics of financial facts and human behavior, but we cannot expect them to be experts at it any more than we can expect patients to be experts at medicine. Patients rely on the expertise of physicians, and investment amateurs rely on the expertise of investment professionals. The reliance of amateur investors on the education and advice of investment professionals imposes a duty on investment professionals to persist in educating themselves, by reading scholarly journals, attending professional conferences, and interacting with colleagues.

It is unfortunate that some investment professionals fail to educate themselves and subsequently fail to educate their clients. This failure is evident among financial advisers who trade frequently; chase returns; prefer expensive, actively managed funds; and underdiversify. Such advisers earn, on average, negative 3% alphas, similar to their clients' alphas.[225]

It is also unfortunate that some financial advisers choose to exploit clients' ignorance and errors rather than educate clients and correct their errors. Some advisers are swayed by higher fees to recommend expensive bonds or bond funds even though cheaper versions of otherwise identical bonds or funds are available.[226] And the roughly 7% of advisers with misconduct records are five times more likely to engage in new misconduct than the average adviser. Misconduct is especially prevalent when clients are amateur investors and in locations with low education, elderly populations, and high incomes.[227] Investment professionals can do better, and financial services companies, professional associations, and regulatory agencies should help.

---

[225]Juhani T. Linnainmaa, Brian Melzer, and Alessandro Previtero, "The Misguided Beliefs of Financial Advisors," Kelley School of Business Research Paper No. 18-9 (16 May 2018). Available at SSRN: https://ssrn.com/abstract=3101426 or http://dx.doi.org/10.2139/ssrn.3101426.

[226]Mark Egan, "Brokers versus Retail Investors: Conflicting Interests and Dominated Products," *Journal of Finance* 74, no 3 (June 2019): 1217–60.

[227]Mark Egan, Gregor Matvos, and Amit Seru, "The Market for Financial Adviser Misconduct," National Bureau of Economic Research Working Paper No. w22050 (February 2016). Available at SSRN: http://ssrn.com/abstract=2739590.

# 6. Behavioral Portfolios

When speaking to investors—professionals and amateurs alike—I often say, "The biggest risks in life are not in the stock market. If you want real risk, get married. And if you want more risk, have children." The words always elicit knowing laughter because they point to what is obvious. Risk is the price we pay for a chance to satisfy our wants.

We marry and have children because we want good lifelong relationships that encompass the utilitarian benefits of mutual support and the expressive and emotional benefits of love. We know the risks of messy divorces and children who disappoint. Some choose to reject these risks and remain single or childless. Others choose to accept these risks as payment for a chance to satisfy their wants for good lifelong relationships.

Behavioral portfolios are about life, beyond money. They are about wants beyond portfolio returns. They are about expressive and emotional benefits, beyond utilitarian benefits. And they are about risk as falling short of wants, not as variance of portfolio returns.

## Behavioral Portfolios and Mean–Variance Portfolios

We can highlight the features of behavioral portfolios by placing them side by side with those of mean–variance portfolios. Harry Markowitz presented mean–variance portfolios in their initial form in 1952, and Hersh Shefrin and I presented behavioral portfolios in their initial form in 2000.[228]

The mean–variance portfolio theory offered by Markowitz in 1952 *prescribes* portfolios on *mean–variance-efficient frontiers* to investors with wants that do not extend past the utilitarian benefits of high expected returns and low risk—where risk is measured by portfolio return variances.

In contrast, behavioral portfolio theory *describes* portfolios on *behavioral-wants frontiers* and *prescribes* portfolios to investors with wants that extend past the utilitarian benefits of high expected portfolio returns and low risk, as measured by portfolio return variance. Such wants include the expressive and emotional benefits of poverty avoidance, attaining wealth, nurturing children and families, being true to one's values, and reaching high social status.

Behavioral-wants frontiers are free of ignorance and cognitive and emotional errors. Behavioral portfolio theory also describes portfolios on

---

[228]Harry Markowitz, "Portfolio Selection," *Journal of Finance* 7 (1952): 77–91; Hersh Shefrin and Meir Statman, "Behavioral Portfolio Theory," *Journal of Financial and Quantitative Analysis* 35 (2000): 127–51.

*behavioral-errors frontiers*, guiding investors away from behavioral errors by replacing ignorance with knowledge and distinguishing wants from errors.

Beginning in 1959, Markowitz revised his initial 1952 mean–variance portfolio theory by sketching "game-of-life" portfolios. This sketch brings mean–variance portfolio theory closer to behavioral portfolio theory. He wrote that "the simulated family's enjoyment for the period would depend on the size of the family, whether it lives in a large house or small apartment, whether it now has to move because someone has a new job elsewhere, etc. The approach required here is both 'behavioral' and 'rational.' It should be behavioral in that it reflects plausible human choices. It should be rational, for example, in that the rational-decision-making family understands the consequences of high-interest rate credit-card debt" (pp. 22–23).[229]

"Textbook" mean–variance portfolio theory, as presented in typical textbooks, adheres to Markowitz's initial 1952 version. This version instructs investors to begin the process of constructing portfolios by estimating the expected return and the standard deviation of the returns of each investment and the correlation between the returns of every pair of investments.

Next, the textbook version instructs investors to place these investment parameters into a mean–variance optimizer that calculates the mean–variance frontier. That frontier consists of optimal mean–variance portfolios, those with the lowest standard deviation of returns for each level of expected returns.

Finally, each investor selects an optimal portfolio on the mean–variance frontier, the one that embodies the best combination of expected returns and standard deviations of returns corresponding to that investor's specific trade-off between wants for high expected returns and wants for low standard deviations of returns.

Textbook optimal mean–variance portfolios tend to consist of few of the many available investments, and allocations to investments in the portfolios tend to be extreme, with large long positions and large short positions. Investors are averse to portfolios with few investments and extreme allocations, considering them "unpalatable."

Some have argued that extreme allocations in optimized mean–variance portfolios constructed with reasonable estimates of expected returns, standard deviations, and correlations occur because these reasonable estimates of parameters are erroneous estimates.

---

[229]Harry M. Markowitz, *Portfolio Selection: Efficient Diversification of Investments* (New York: John Wiley & Sons, 1959); Harry M. Markowitz, "Individual Versus Institutional Investing," *Financial Services Review* 1, no. 1 (1991): 1–8. Harry M. Markowitz, "Consumption, Investment and Insurance in the Game of Life," *Journal of Investment Management* 13, no. 3 (2015): 5–23.

If errors in estimates are the problem, as Fisher and I presented in a 1997 article, "then better estimation is the solution, and many people have offered better methods for estimation" (p. 41).[230] Yet extreme allocations are, in fact, inherent in optimal unconstrained mean–variance portfolios that have been constructed with proper estimates. Eliminating estimation errors would not eliminate extreme allocations, and recommendations that investors abandon their wants beyond high expected returns and low standard deviations of returns have been rejected in the past and will be rejected in the future.

In addition, estimation errors will always exist. The best we can hope for is to make them smaller. Such errors occur for two reasons: First, the nature of the equilibrium governing expected returns, standard deviations, and correlations is not known with certainty. Second, if we were willing to assume a particular equilibrium, our estimates would still deviate from the actual values because we depend only on the distribution of known past returns, not the known distribution of past returns and the unknown distribution of future returns.

If minor changes in the estimation of the parameters led to minor changes in optimized mean–variance portfolios' composition, the estimation error problem would be minor. But optimized mean–variance portfolios are very sensitive to minor parameter estimate changes, which means that attempts at obtaining better estimates are not likely to save mean–variance optimization.

To understand how sensitive mean–variance-optimized portfolios are to changes in parameters, consider two sets of mean–variance-optimized portfolios in which the estimates are based on the same indexes of US, European, and Pacific equities; bonds; and a money market fund.[231]

In the first set, the annual set, all the parameters are calculated from past annual returns. In the second set, the monthly set, expected returns are calculated from past annual returns but correlations and annualized standard deviations are calculated from past monthly returns. For example, the standard deviation of annual US stock returns during the analyzed period was 13.87% when computed from annual returns and 15.60% when computed from monthly returns. The correlation between the annual returns of US stocks and European stocks was 0.62 when computed from annual returns, and 0.65 when computed from monthly returns.

Differences between parameters estimated from annual and monthly returns lead to small differences in estimates of the expected returns of

---

[230]Kenneth L. Fisher and Meir Statman, "The Mean–Variance-Optimization Puzzle: Security Portfolios and Food Portfolios," *Financial Analysts Journal* 53, no. 4 (July/August 1997): 41–50.

[231]Fisher and Statman, "The Mean–Variance-Optimization Puzzle."

optimized mean–variance portfolios, but they lead to huge differences in the composition of the unconstrained portfolios. For example, whereas the 20% standard deviation portfolio calculated from monthly returns calls for a 24% allocation to US stocks, that 20% standard deviation portfolio calculated from annual returns calls for a 101% allocation. And whereas the 44% standard deviation portfolio calculated from annual returns calls for a zero allocation to European stocks, the 44% standard deviation portfolio calculated from monthly returns calls for a 104% short position.

Why do investors consider portfolios with extreme allocations unpalatable? We can find the answer in an analogy between investment portfolios and "food portfolios" we know as diets. Consumers' wants extend beyond high nutrition at a low cost, just as investors' wants extend beyond high expected returns and low standard deviations of returns. Consumers want diets that are also palatable, varied, and conforming to culture. The same is true for the portfolios investors want.

The history of the "diet problem" extends back to World War II, when the US military strove to identify a diet that would satisfy nutritional needs at the lowest cost. Identification of such diets continues today, made easier by fast computers. One example involves diets for people in France.[232] The French in the sample listed a total of 614 foods they consume, excluding diet beverages, tea, coffee, dietary supplements, and drinking water.

One set of low-cost diets was made consistent with macronutrient guidelines and with the recommended dietary allowance for each of the 25 nutrients in the guidelines. These diets also set safe limits on the consumption of saturated fats, added sugar and sodium, and nine other nutrients. The low-cost diet satisfying these nutritional conditions is extreme, consisting of only 12 foods out of the list of 614—porridge, pasta, semolina, mashed potatoes, wheat germ, carrots, radishes, chicken livers, grilled herring, low-fat milk, and vegetable oil.

Unsurprisingly, this diet is unappealing to typical French consumers because it departs greatly from diets that also deliver the expressive and emotional benefits of palatability, variety, and conformance to French culture. Narrowing the gap between the low-cost diet and one that is palatable, varied, and conforming to French culture calls for adding such foods as eggs, salmon, avocado, and chocolate. Adding these foods, however, more than doubles the cost of the diet. Indeed, these additions also reduce the diet's nutritional quality. The authors wrote, "It turns out that maintaining cultural

---

[232]Matthieu Maillot, Nocole Darmon, and Adam Drewnowski, "Are the Lowest-Cost Healthful Food Plans Culturally and Socially Acceptable?" *Public Health Nutrition* 13, no. 8 (August 2010): 1178–85.

norms was just as, if not more, expensive than improving the nutritional quality of the diet" (p. 1182).[233]

Textbook mean–variance consumers view foods as simply bundles of nutrients. The benefits and costs of diets besides the utilitarian nutritional benefits and the utilitarian costs are ignored because all the foods one eats mix together once ingested, thereby providing identical nutrients—whether they are from expensive food, such as salmon, or cheap food, such as herring. Similarly, textbook mean–variance investors view investments as simply bundles of expected returns, standard deviations, and correlations. The benefits and costs besides these are irrelevant because all the investments mix together once added to the portfolio—whether they are Apple shares or Con Edison shares.

The French low-cost diet appears on the *nutrition-cost frontier* of food, as shown in **Exhibit 6.1**. This diet delivers the necessary nutrition at the lowest cost. Similarly, a portfolio on the mean–variance frontier of investments delivers the necessary expected return at the lowest standard deviation of returns. However, normal consumers desire something more than a diet on

**Exhibit 6.1.   A Nutrition-Cost Frontier and a Behavioral-Wants Frontier**

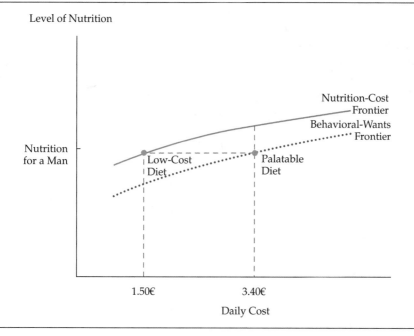

---

[233]Maillot, Darmon, and Drewnowski, "Are the Lowest-Cost?"

the nutrition-cost frontier of foods, and normal investors desire something more than a portfolio on the mean–variance frontier of investments.

One set of investor wants is for palatable portfolios—that is, portfolio asset allocations close to norms, reflected in the portfolios of peers. Professional investors, such as pension fund managers, bear the utilitarian costs of job loss when they are "wrong and alone" by deviating from the portfolios of peers and falling short of peer returns. These costs may exceed the utilitarian benefits of career advancement when they are "right and alone" by deviating from portfolios of peers and exceeding peer returns.

Keeping portfolios close to the portfolios of peers also lowers the expressive costs of a loser label when investors or portfolio managers are wrong and alone and the emotional costs of regret that accompany that label. These costs may exceed the expressive benefits of a winner label and the emotional benefits of pride when the investors are right and alone.

The effects of these wants on portfolio choices are evident among managers of a large pension fund that retained investment consultants to advise them on asset allocation in the fund's portfolio.

The consultants started their work by estimating the expected returns, standard deviations, and correlations of the returns of the fund's asset classes, including US equity, non-US equity, alternative investments, and fixed income. They estimated expected returns as equilibrium returns on the basis of the assumption that, on balance, assets are fairly priced. Some investors, however, believe that particular assets are mispriced. For example, the consultants estimated the equilibrium return of the real estate asset class at 3.99%, lower than the 6.18% estimate of the fund's managers. The consultants set aside their estimated equilibrium returns and replaced them with the estimates of the fund's managers. They proceeded by estimating standard deviations of returns and correlations as maximum-likelihood estimates.

Next, the consultants placed these estimates in a mean–variance optimizer and identified a portfolio on the mean–variance frontier, denoted as Portfolio B in **Exhibit 6.2**, with a standard deviation equal to that of the fund's existing portfolio, Portfolio A. The expected return of Portfolio B is higher than that of Portfolio A by 3.72 annual percentage points (pps).

The consultants, however, did not offer their optimized mean–variance Portfolio B to the fund's managers because they expected the managers to find that portfolio unpalatable, failing to satisfy wants beyond maximizing expected return at the existing standard deviation of returns of the fund's portfolio.

The optimized mean–variance portfolio was unpalatable because its allocations deviated greatly from allocations in the benchmark portfolio. For example, that optimized portfolio called for a zero allocation to US equity,

**Exhibit 6.2. A Mean–Variance Frontier and a Behavioral-Wants Frontier**

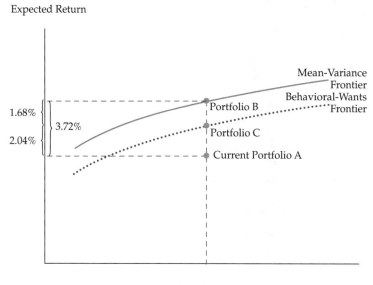

whereas the benchmark portfolio called for a 46.82% allocation. And the optimized portfolio called for a 53.92% allocation to non-US equity, whereas the benchmark portfolio called for an 18.24% allocation.

Investors apply "tracking-error optimization" to control deviations of portfolio returns from benchmark returns. In this application, risk estimates are replaced by estimates of tracking error—that is, deviation of the fund's return from the return on a benchmark portfolio. Portfolios on mean tracking error frontiers are below mean–variance frontiers, but they might well be on behavioral-wants frontiers.[234]

The expected return of Portfolio C recommended by the consultants is 2.04 pps above the expected return of the current portfolio. That portfolio is on the tracking error frontier, but it is 1.68 pps below the 3.72 pp gain offered by the optimized mean–variance portfolio.

Portfolios are made even more palatable by the applications of constraints, such as no less than 30% in US stocks and no more than 20% in non-US stocks. These constraints place portfolios closer to behavioral-wants frontiers.

[234]Richard Roll, "A Mean/Variance Analysis of Tracking Error," *Journal of Portfolio Management* 18, no. 4 (Summer 1992): 13–22. Roger G. Clarke, Scott Krase, and Meir Statman, "Tracking Errors, Regret, and Tactical Asset Allocation," *Journal of Portfolio Management* 20, no. 3 (Spring 1994): 16–24.

Markowitz described constraints as useful judgment tools for building good portfolios instead of deviations from them. He noted that estimating mean–variance parameters requires judgment. Even a purely historical estimation approach calls for judgment in selecting the estimation period—for example, the most recent or the past four decades and using monthly or annual returns. In addition, investor wants extend beyond the utilitarian benefits of high expected returns and low standard deviation of returns. Allocation constraints are a reasonable tool for incorporating judgment and wants into portfolios.[235]

Portfolios that closely track benchmark portfolios are not the only ones on behavioral-wants frontiers. So are portfolios excluding investments inconsistent with investors' values, such as in companies that pollute, exploit employees, show limited diversity in the composition of boards of directors, or act in ways incompatible with one's religious precepts.

One study compared optimized mean–variance portfolios that were limited to only socially responsible mutual funds with unconstrained optimized mean–variance portfolios that included all mutual funds.[236] The authors found that the expected annual returns of a portfolio such as Portfolio A in **Exhibit 6.3**, constrained to satisfy wants for social responsibility, fell below the expected annual returns of Portfolio B, which had an identical standard deviation of returns but was on the mean–variance frontier, by more than 3 pps. Yet constrained socially responsible portfolios may be on the behavioral-wants frontier of investors who are willing to sacrifice the utilitarian benefits of expected returns for the expressive and emotional benefits of staying true to values, as shown in Exhibit 6.3.

Portfolios appear on the behavioral-wants frontier when they fulfill investors' wants for utilitarian, expressive, and emotional benefits, without stumbling into cognitive and emotional errors. The desire to have the benefits of playing and winning illustrates the difference between wants and errors. We can illustrate this difference using the example of frequent stock trading. "Trading Is Hazardous to Your Wealth" is the title of a study that found that the returns of those who traded stocks most frequently lagged stock market returns by 6.5 pps.[237]

---

[235]Harry Markowitz, "Portfolio Theory: As I Still See It," *Annual Review of Financial Economics* 2 (December 2010): 1–23.

[236]Christopher Geczy, David Levin, and Robert Stambaugh, "Investing in Socially Responsible Mutual Funds" (October 2005). Available at SSRN: https://ssrn.com/abstract= 416380 or http://dx.doi.org/10.2139/ssrn.416380.

[237]Brad M. Barber and Terrance Odean, "Trading Is Hazardous to Your Wealth: The Common Stock Investment Performance of Individual Investors," *Journal of Finance* 55, no. 2 (April 2000): 773–806.

**Exhibit 6.3.  A Mean–Variance Frontier and a Behavioral-Wants Frontier Satisfying Wants for Social Responsibility**

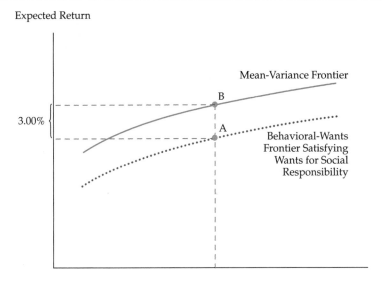

Some frequent traders may have access to exclusively or narrowly available information that lets them beat stock market returns. But the fact that, on average, the returns of frequent traders lagged market returns indicates that most frequent traders are misled into trading by ignorance or cognitive and emotional errors. Portfolios on behavioral-errors frontiers are illusory, available only in the minds of investors misled by cognitive and emotional errors into believing they are true.

We can describe portfolios of investors who trade infrequently, only for liquidity or rebalancing reasons, as on the mean–variance-efficient frontier. In contrast, the portfolios of noise traders are on behavioral-wants frontiers, behavioral-errors frontiers, or a combination of both, as illustrated in **Exhibit 6.4**.

Wants for the benefits of familiarity illustrate the effects of *changes in wants*. Wants for the expressive and emotional benefits of familiarity are evident in "home bias," the tendency to concentrate portfolios in home-country investments. Home bias places portfolios below mean–variance frontiers, but it may well place them on behavioral-wants frontiers, where the high expressive and emotional benefits of familiarity compensate for low utilitarian

**Exhibit 6.4. Behavioral-Wants Frontiers and Behavioral-Errors Frontiers**

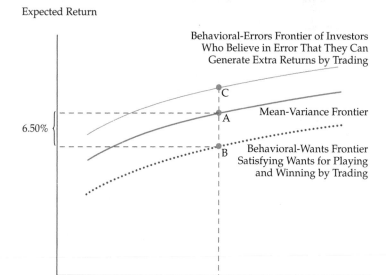

expected returns. Indeed, home bias in investment portfolios is analogous to home bias in diets or cuisines.

The cuisine wants of Americans change as they become familiar with Japanese, Thai, Ethiopian, and other foreign cuisines, and their diversification among cuisines increases. Americans who continue to frequent restaurants serving foreign cuisines indicate, in effect, that these cuisines enhance their utilitarian, expressive, and emotional benefits. The same is true for diversification among investments. Traveling to foreign countries reduces home bias in investments by increasing familiarity.[238] Increased familiarity with foreign cuisines and investments leads to changes in diets and portfolios by changing wants, replacing ignorance with knowledge, or overcoming cognitive and emotional errors.

## Nine Features of Behavioral Portfolios

In late 2018, Colin O'Brady, a 33-year-old American, and Louis Rudd, a 49-year-old Englishman, competed with each other to become the first

---

[238]Constantinos Antoniou, Alok Kumar, and Lizhengbo Yang, "Seeing Is Believing: Travel, Familiarity and International Equity Investments" (22 August 2018). Available at SSRN: https://ssrn.com/abstract=3270813 or http://dx.doi.org/10.2139/ssrn.3270813.

person ever to ski alone across Antarctica with no support from anyone. Previously, only two men had ever tried it: One gave up after 52 days, and the other died.[239]

The stories of O'Brady, Rudd, and those who preceded them illustrate nine features of behavioral portfolios. First, behavioral portfolios are about life, including stocks, bonds, real estate, and commodities, but going much beyond them. O'Brady's and Rudd's behavioral portfolios are about their lives.

Second, behavioral portfolios are built on a foundation of wants. Wants for respect and high social status are prominent among the wants of O'Brady and Rudd. O'Brady's and Rudd's choices may well place them below the mean–variance-efficient frontier, bearing high risk for low financial returns, but these choices may well place them on the behavioral-wants frontier.

Third, satisfying wants in behavioral portfolios is about gaining utilitarian, expressive, and emotional benefits and avoiding their costs. The utilitarian benefits O'Brady and Rudd will derive by being first include income from advertising deals and speaking engagements, the expressive benefits include reputations as pioneers, and the emotional benefits include pride.

Fourth, circumstances matter in behavioral portfolios. Circumstances relevant to O'Brady and Rudd include access to resources in money, knowledge, time, and physical fitness, necessary for the quest to satisfy wants. Circumstances also include culture, such as one where being first to ski across Antarctica solo with no support is valued as an accomplishment, rather than denigrated as foolishness greater than eating the most hot dogs in 12 minutes.

Fifth, behavioral portfolios account for ignorance and cognitive and emotional errors on the way to satisfying wants. The ignorance and cognitive and emotional errors of O'Brady and Rudd include possibly erroneous extrapolation from past experiences to future successes. Rudd's experiences include skiing more than 2,500 Antarctic miles, and O'Brady's experiences include a speed record for scaling the highest points in all 50 states. Cognitive and emotional errors also include misperception of benefits and costs, perhaps caused by the desire to satisfy wants. O'Brady and Rudd might overestimate the likely utilitarian, expressive, and emotional benefits of their venture and underestimate their costs.

Sixth, risk in behavioral portfolios is the probability of falling short of satisfying wants, not variance of portfolio returns. The risk facing O'Brady and Rudd is the probability of falling short of their want to be the first person to ski across Antarctica solo without any support.

---

[239]Aaron Teasdale, "Explorer Crosses South Pole in Epic Race Across Antarctica," *National Geographic* (13 December 2018). www.nationalgeographic.com/adventure/2018/12/explorers-colin-obrady-louis-rudd-race-south-pole-antarctica/.

Seventh, satisfying wants is the destination in behavioral portfolios, and risk is fuel for the vehicles we drive there. The vehicle for satisfying O'Brady's and Rudd's wants includes the right knowledge, equipment, and supply of food and other provisions, and its fuel includes high risk tolerance.

Eighth, behavioral portfolios resemble layered pyramids, where each layer is a mental account dedicated to satisfying a want. In a simple two-layer pyramid, the mental account in the bottom layer is the protection-from-poverty layer, whereas the top layer is the prospects-for-riches layer.

The protection-from-poverty layer of Rudd, at age 49, is probably composed of a military pension, such assets as a house and personal savings, and a good amount of human capital, perhaps as a guide in expeditions. The protection-from-poverty layer of O'Brady, at age 33, does not include a pension but includes even more human capital. The prospects-for-riches layers of both men include prospects for riches from advertising deals and speaking engagements that would accrue to the first person to ski across Antarctica solo with no support.

Ninth, investors rebalance behavioral portfolios when current portfolios are no longer best at satisfying wants, not when current portfolios depart from fixed proportions, such as 60% stocks and 40% bonds.

## Behavioral Portfolios as Goal-Based Portfolios

Investor wants can be described as investor goals, and behavioral portfolios can be described as goal-based portfolios. Behavioral portfolios resemble layered pyramids, where each layer is dedicated to satisfying a want, often specified as a goal. Goals are more specific than wants, as many investors have wants with no specific goals. Investors may have wants for riches, but they do not necessarily have specific dollar amounts of riches as goals.

The story of Mavis Wanczyk, the 53-year-old winner of a $758 million Powerball jackpot in 2017, illustrates a two-layer goal-based pyramid portfolio. Wanczyk's protection-from-poverty goal was a pension from Mercy Medical Center, where she had worked as a nurse for 32 years. Reaching that goal would have required 12 more years of work. Wanczyk's prospects-for-riches goal was to retire early from her work, and her means to that goal were lottery tickets she bought regularly. "I had a pipe dream," she said, "and my pipe dream finally came true." Wanczyk chuckled as she described calling Mercy Medical Center to say that she would not be coming back to work.[240]

---

[240]Travis M. Andrews and Lindsey Bever, "'My Pipe Dream Finally Came True': This Woman Won the Second-Largest Powerball Jackpot Ever," *Washington Post* (24 August 2017). www.washingtonpost.com/news/morning-mix/wp/2017/08/24/the-second-largest-jackpot-in-powerball-history-has-a-winner/?utm_term=.face2e9227ff.

Wanczyk has reached both her protection-from-poverty and prospects-for-riches goals with much to spare. Now she might add layers on top of these for supporting family, friends, and charities.

Portfolios as layered pyramids are long-standing. A 1929 portfolio recommendation placed insurance in the bottom layer of the portfolio pyramid and a cash reserve in a layer above it. Above them is a layer of safe bonds and guaranteed mortgages on real estate. Next is a layer of preferred stocks that promise higher returns than guaranteed mortgages. At the top is a layer of common stocks that promise returns exceeding those of preferred stocks.[241]

A 1952 manual of mutual funds listed the layers of portfolios from bottom to top as income, balanced, growth, and aggressive growth. Safe bonds, issued by governments and large corporations, are suitable for the income layer; other bonds as well as stocks with generous dividends, such as utility stocks, are suitable for the balanced layer; stocks that pay modest dividends but promise steady increases in their prices are for the growth layer; and stocks that pay no dividends but promise terrific increases in their prices are for the aggressive growth layer.[242]

Wants, goals, and associated pyramid portfolios vary greatly among people. An adviser described a couple who came to him for help. "Before you start planning for our retirement income," they said, "you should know that we have a disabled son. We need to establish a trust fund that will provide for him when we are gone." This couple's portfolio pyramid consists of a protection-from-poverty layer for their son, a protection-from-poverty layer for themselves, and perhaps a prospects-for-riches layer at the top.

Bonds generally belong in the protection-from-poverty layer, stocks in the prospects-for-riches layer, and houses in either, based on people's wants and perceptions of the risk of homeownership. A majority of Americans perceive houses as safe investments, belonging in protection-from-poverty layers. Indeed, many homeowners place their houses at the very bottom of protection-from-poverty layers, dedicating them as parts of their bequests to their children. Renters, however, are more likely to perceive houses as risky investments, considering them as belonging in prospects-for-riches layers or choosing not to buy them.[243]

---

[241]"No Royal Road for the Small Investor," *Literary Digest* 103, no. 11 (14 December 1929): 52–55.

[242]Arthur Wiesenberger, *Investment Companies* (New York: Arthur Wiesenberger & Company, 1952).

[243]Manuel Adelino, Antoinette Schoar, and Felipe Severino, "Perception of House Price Risk and Homeownership" (24 July 2018). Available at SSRN: https://ssrn.com/abstract=3197973 or http://dx.doi.org/10.2139/ssrn.3197973.

Behavioral portfolio rebalancing is want-based, like behavioral portfolio construction. Behavioral portfolio rebalancing is different from the risk-based mean–variance portfolio rebalancing. Mean–variance portfolio theory guides investors to gauge their trade-off between expected returns and risk, measured by the variance of returns. Investors then choose a balance of investments that gives them the expected returns they desire combined with the variance they can sleep with—say, 60% stocks and 40% bonds. If over the next few months, stock prices increase while bond prices remain the same, such that the portfolio is 70% stocks and 30% bonds, they sell stocks and buy bonds until the 60/40 proportions are restored. Such rebalancing is executed regularly, usually quarterly or annually, as stock and bond prices go up and down.

Behavioral portfolio theory, however, guides investors to reach goals and satisfy wants. Risk is measured not by the variance of portfolio returns or by losses but, rather, by falling short of reaching goals and satisfying wants. Consider an investor whose primary wants are for prospects for riches and whose secondary wants are for protection from poverty. That investor figures she can satisfy her protection-from-poverty wants with a small amount of bonds plus her income, so her portfolio is composed of a thin protection-from-poverty layer, 20%, in bonds and a fat prospects-for-riches layer, 80%, in stocks.

Next, suppose that during the following month, stock prices increase while bond prices remain the same, such that now her portfolio consists of 82% stocks and 18% bonds. Under mean–variance risk-based rebalancing, an investor would sell stocks and buy bonds. But that is not necessarily the case with want-based rebalancing of behavioral portfolios. If the investor still believes her wants for protection from poverty can be satisfied with the bonds she currently owns plus her earnings potential, then she need not rebalance at all.

Two rationales are commonly offered for the mean–variance risk-based rebalancing method. First, investors who choose a particular proportion for their portfolios have, in effect, declared that their chosen proportion reflects their optimal trade-off between portfolio returns and the variance of returns. But again, risk is not about variance; it is about failing to satisfy wants.

The second rationale centers on the claim that returns are mean reverting—that is, that above-average stock or bond returns are predictably followed by below-average returns. If so, fixed-proportion rebalancing entails selling stocks or bonds at above-average prices and buying them at below-average prices.

But stock and bond returns do not follow such predictable patterns. Yes, fixed-proportion rebalancing would have helped in 2007 as it directed us to sell stocks and buy bonds, and it would have helped again in early 2009, directing us to buy stocks and sell bonds, knowing in hindsight that stock prices decreased in 2008 and increased after March 2009. But fixed-proportion rebalancing might have also directed us to sell stocks at many points since March 2009. That would have been a costly mistake in the bull market that followed.

Moreover, mean–variance rebalancing imposes extra costs in taxable portions of portfolios. Realizing losses reduces taxes, but rebalancing is likely to involve realizing gains as we sell stocks or bonds following increases in their prices. Fixed-proportion rebalancing also imposes greater transaction costs than want-based rebalancing because it is executed more frequently. After all, rebalancing with want-based investing is executed infrequently, typically as a person goes through life's changes, whether completing a trek through Antarctica, winning the lottery, marrying, having children, or approaching retirement. Years might pass between one rebalance and the next.

## Wants, Perceptions, Circumstances, and Risk Tolerance in Behavioral Portfolios

Risk tolerance combines risk traits, wants, perceptions, and circumstances. The risk trait is a personality trait inherent in each person. We can think of it as a sixth personality trait added to the Big Five personality traits of extraversion, neuroticism, openness, conscientiousness, and agreeableness.

The Big Five personality traits are associated with one another and with the risk trait. People who rank high in the conscientiousness trait tend to rank low in the extraversion, openness, and agreeableness traits. And people who rank high in the risk trait tend to rank high in the extraversion and openness traits but low in the conscientiousness and neuroticism traits.[244]

Evidence consistent with the risk trait as a personality trait comes from its association with testosterone and cortisol. High testosterone levels are associated with high risk tolerance, whereas high cortisol levels are associated with low risk tolerance.[245] Approximately half of the relation between stock market participation and risk tolerance comes from the portion of risk tolerance associated with molecular genetic endowments affecting risk traits.[246]

---

[244]Carrie H. Pan and Meir Statman, "Investor Personality in Investor Questionnaires," *Journal of Investment Consulting* 14, no. 1 (2013): 48–56.

[245]John R. Nofsinger, Fernando Patterson, and Corey A. Shank, "Decision-Making, Financial Risk Aversion and Behavioral Biases: The Role of Testosterone and Stress" (23 November 2017). Available at SSRN: https://ssrn.com/abstract=3017977 or http://dx.doi.org/10.2139/ssrn.3017977.

[246]Richard W. Sias, Laura T. Starks, and Harry J. Turtle, "Molecular Genetics, Risk Aversion, Return Perceptions, and Stock Market Participation" (18 November 2018). Available at SSRN: https://ssrn.com/abstract=3292249 or http://dx.doi.org/10.2139/ssrn.3292249.

Evidence consistent with the risk trait as a personality trait also comes from the association between the risk taking evident in the ownership of powerful sports cars and the risk taking evident in investment behavior. Hedge fund managers who drive powerful sports cars choose riskier investments that do not yield higher returns. Moreover, sensation-seeking drives hedge fund managers into more frequent and active trading and a preference for lottery-like stocks.[247]

Stability of the risk trait, like stability of each of the Big Five traits, does not imply that risk tolerance is constant over time. Changes in wants, perceptions, and circumstances change risk tolerance. These include general changes, such as financial crises and natural catastrophes, and personal changes, such as marriage, children, employment, retirement, and emotions.[248]

Psychologist Elke Weber and investment manager Joachim Klement asked a sample of British investors each quarter, during a period that includes the 2008–09 financial crisis, to allocate GBP100,000 to UK stocks or a risk-free asset paying an annual 4% interest. They also asked investors for their degree of agreement with three statements indicating levels of the risk trait:

"It is likely I would invest a significant sum in a high-risk investment.

I am a financial risk taker.

Even if I experienced a significant loss on an investment, I would still consider making risky investments" (p. 5).[249]

Risk tolerance, assessed by the proportion invested in the UK market, changed substantially during the period, falling from an average of 56% to 46.5% in March 2009, before climbing again as the stock market recovered later in 2009. In contrast, the risk trait, measured by levels of agreement with the three statements, was nearly constant throughout the period. Circumstances, perceptions, and emotions changed substantially during the period, and risk tolerance changed with them.[250]

To see the relation between risk traits, wants, perceptions, circumstances, and risk tolerance, consider your answer to the following question:

---

[247]Stephen Brown, Yan Lu, Sugata Ray, and Melvyn Teo, "Sensation Seeking and Hedge Funds," *Journal of Finance* 73, no. 6 (December 2018): 2871–914.

[248]Andreas Oehler, Stefan Wendt, Florian Wedlich, and Matthias Horn, "Investors' Personality Influences Investment Decisions: Experimental Evidence on Extraversion and Neuroticism," *Journal of Behavioral Finance* 19, no. 1 (2018): 30–48; Pan and Statman, "Investor Personality."

[249]Elke U. Weber and Joachim Klement, "Risk Tolerance and Circumstances," *CFA Institute Research Foundation Briefs* 4, no. 2 (March 2018).

[250]Weber and Klement, "Risk Tolerance."

"Suppose that you are given an opportunity to replace your current investment portfolio with a new portfolio. The new portfolio has a 50–50 chance to increase by 50% your standard of living during your lifetime. However, the new portfolio also has a 50–50 chance to reduce by X% your standard of living during your lifetime. [What is] the maximum X% reduction in standard of living you are willing to accept?" (p. 24).[251]

The question can be interpreted as pertaining to risk aversion, measured as loss aversion. By that interpretation, people with high loss aversion offer low X% potential losses for a 50–50 chance for a 50% gain, whereas people with low loss aversion offer high X% potential losses for the same chance.

People in 23 countries answered this question. Loss aversion is common to all of them. The average X% potential losses offered by Americans was 12.61%, implying a ratio of approximately 4.0 between gains and losses.[252] This finding should not be surprising, and it surely does not indicate errors. Indeed, the notion of loss aversion as an error comes from experiments using amounts of money that are trivial relative to the usual wealth of people in developed countries, such as a 50–50 chance for a $200 gain or a $100 loss. Moreover, evidence indicates that loss aversion in small bets is hardly universal. No more than half of Americans are loss averse in such bets.[253]

The question is better interpreted, however, as being about wants. By that interpretation, answers reflect the strength of wants for protection from poverty relative to wants for prospects for riches. People whose wants for protection from poverty are relatively strong offer little reduction in their standard of living in exchange for a 50–50 chance of a 50% increase. Conversely, people whose wants for prospects for riches are relatively strong offer much reduction in standard of living in exchange for the same chance.

Loss aversion is a feature of Daniel Kahneman and Amos Tversky's prospect theory, but loss aversion is distinct from shortfall aversion, another feature of prospect theory.[254] Shortfall aversion is an aversion to falling short of "reference points" representing wants. People whose reference point is their current situation have satisfied their wants. They are shortfall averse, because their utilitarian, expressive, and emotional costs of falling short of their

---

[251]Meir Statman, "Culture in Risk, Regret, Maximization, Social Trust, and Life Satisfaction," *Journal of Investment Consulting* 16 (2015): 20–30.

[252]Statman, "Culture in Risk, Regret, Maximization, Social Trust, and Life Satisfaction."

[253]Jonathan Chapman, Erik Snowberg, Stephanie Wang, and Colin F. Camerer, "Loss Attitudes in the U.S. Population: Evidence from Dynamically Optimized Sequential Experimentation (Dose)," CESifo Working Paper No. 7262 (2018). Available at SSRN: https://ssrn.com/abstract=3275438.

[254]Daniel Kahneman and Amos Tversky, "Prospect Theory: An Analysis of Decision under Risk," *Econometrica* 47, no. 2 (March 1979): 263–92.

reference point exceed the utilitarian, expressive, and emotional benefits of exceeding it by the same magnitude. But people whose situations are short of their wants are willing to accept a chance of falling further below their wants to get a chance to satisfy their wants.

Reference points for poverty and riches vary among people. A person might be assessed by others as poor but might not consider himself poor. He is unwilling to give up protection from poverty for prospects for riches. Conversely, another person might be assessed by others as rich but might not consider herself rich. She is willing to give up protection from poverty for prospects for riches.

Shortfall aversion might seem to be risk seeking, but it is not. O'Brady and Rudd are not motivated by risk seeking as each of them skis alone across Antarctica. Instead, each is motivated by the desire to avoid shortfall from his desire to be the first person to ski across Antarctica alone without any support. Shortfall aversion is also a central feature in Lola Lopes's SP/A theory, where considerations of security (S), potential (P), and aspirations (A) combine to determine choices. Aspirations are analogous to wants, security is analogous to protection from poverty, and potential is analogous to prospects for riches.[255]

O'Brady and Rudd probably have substantial protection from poverty layers in their portfolios that will sustain them even if they fail in their Antarctica trek. Others have meager protection-from-poverty layers, which is the case of refugees from regions afflicted by poverty or war. People who choose to be refugees might well have risk traits much weaker than those of O'Brady and Rudd, but their middling risk traits combine with onerous circumstances to compel them to take a chance. The chance they are taking is of suffering an even more meager protection-from-poverty layer if they fail to make their way to Europe or the United States.

Abison Johnson is a refugee, a native of Cameroon living precariously in a forest in Morocco on the border of an enclave of Spain. He has lived there for several years now, making repeated attempts to cross the border into Spain. He has a long scar on his side, where barbed wire cut him as he attempted to climb over a border fence.[256]

Johnson comes from a poor family, and his protection-from-poverty layer is meager by the standards of developed countries. He wants a more substantial protection-from-poverty layer, perhaps as a manual laborer in Spain,

[255]Lola L. Lopes, "Between Hope and Fear: The Psychology of Risk," *Advances in Experimental Social Psychology* 20 (1987): 255–95.
[256]Leila Fadel, "Migrants Wait in Moroccan Forest for a Chance to Cross into Europe," NPR (21 April 2016). www.npr.org/2016/04/21/475079102/migrants-wait-in-a-moroccan-forest-for-a-chance-to-cross-into-europe.

sufficient for the utilitarian benefits of his living expenses and the expressive and emotional benefits of supporting his family in Cameroon.

Johnson's story ended well eventually, as he crossed into Spain. Many other stories do not end well. These include stories of people who drowned in the Mediterranean when their boats capsized and those of taxi drivers in New York City, many of whom are immigrants, who have invested their life savings in taxi medallions.

A medallion grants its owner the right to operate or lease a taxi in New York City, and its price exceeded $1 million before app-based services, such as Uber and Lyft, came along. Many taxi drivers bought these medallions with borrowed money, considering them a sure way to fill not only the protection-from-poverty layers of their portfolios but also the prospects-for-riches layers. The value of medallions plunged to fractions of their past values as competition from app-based services arrived, decimating not only the prospects-for-riches layers of the portfolios of medallion-owning taxi drivers but also the drivers' protection-from-poverty layers. Desperation drove some taxi drivers, including Yu Mein Chow, to suicide.[257]

We are likely to be different from O'Brady, Rudd, Johnson, and Chow, but they are not strangers to us. We can see analogues in our own risk traits, wants, perceptions, circumstances, and choices. It might be in choices to immigrate to a new country, relocate to another state, switch to another career, marry, or have children.

## Assessing Wants and Correcting Errors with Investor Questionnaires

Investor questionnaires offer advisers opportunities to identify and assess clients' wants, risk traits, perceptions, and circumstances; to educate them about financial facts and human behavior; and to guide them to fitting portfolios and financial plans.

The approach of typical questionnaires is risk based, but risk is not about variance of return or even losses. Instead, risk is about shortfalls relative to wants, calling for a want-based approach. Consider, again, the following question:

"Suppose that you are given an opportunity to replace your current investment portfolio with a new portfolio. The new portfolio has a 50–50 chance to increase by 50% your standard of living during your lifetime. However, the new portfolio also has a 50–50 chance to reduce by X% your standard

---

[257]Reihan Salam, "Taxi-Driver Suicides Are a Warning," *The Atlantic* (5 June 2018). www.theatlantic.com/ideas/archive/2018/06/taxi-driver-suicides-are-a-warning/561926/.

of living in during your lifetime. [What is] the maximum X% reduction in standard of living you are willing to accept?" (p. 5).[258]

Advisers who follow the want-based approach do not accept, as is, clients' stated choices of percentage decreases in standard of living for a 50–50 chance for a 50% increase. They do not proceed to construct portfolios and financial plans reflecting clients' stated choices. Instead, they probe clients' stated choices and guide them to better ones.

Does the very conservative offer of a 5% decrease in standard of living come from a man who is retired or close to retirement, with financial capital in his protection-from-poverty portfolio layer but little or no human capital in current or potential employment income? Is the man satisfied with his current standard of living? Would he be able to draw on his financial capital to maintain his standard of living throughout his life, with some margin to spare? If this is the case, then his 5% offer is reasonable, and so is a portfolio heavy in cash and bonds.

Conversely, is the client a young man with little financial capital but substantial human capital in his protection-from-poverty portfolio layer, in a steady job and promising career? The adviser might point out to his client, perhaps with the aid of simulations, that his offer of a 5% reduction in standard of living for a 50–50 chance of a 50% increase is likely to lead to a portfolio heavy in cash and bonds that would not support his current standard of living throughout his life, let alone increase it.

Or consider a woman who is willing to offer a large 50% decrease in her standard of living in exchange for a 50–50 chance of a 50% increase. An adviser would probe further. Is she a young woman with substantial human capital in her protection-from-poverty portfolio layer, who can, therefore, devote her small financial capital to her prospects-for-riches portfolio layer? If so, a reasonable choice is a portfolio heavy in stocks or even a business venture, whether a technology company or a store.

Conversely, is she an older woman like Elizabeth White, author of *Fifty-Five, Unemployed, and Faking Normal: Your Guide to a Better ~~Retirement~~ Life*, who invested her barely adequate protection-from-poverty portfolio layer in a store and lost it all?[259] Older investors with no more than adequate protection-from-poverty portfolio layers can afford to buy a few cheap lottery tickets to keep alive prospects for riches, but they have little human capital to replenish financial capital lost in business ventures.

This want-based approach to portfolio construction, where risk consists of shortfalls relative to wants, periods extend to lifetimes, and stakes are large, is

---

[258]Statman, "Culture in Risk, Regret, Maximization, Social Trust, and Life Satisfaction."

[259]Elizabeth White, *Fifty-Five, Unemployed, and Faking Normal: Your Guide to a Better ~~Retirement~~ Life* (Createspace Independent Publishing, 2016).

quite different from the risk-based approach, where risk is measured by variance of returns or losses, periods are short, and stakes are small. The risk-based approach is exemplified in a typical questionnaire by a chart of possible one-year losses or gains on a $10,000 investment, followed by this statement: "Given the potential gain and loss in any one year, I would invest my money in." The choices range from a 50–50 chance of a $164 loss or a $593 gain to a 50–50 chance of a $3,639 loss or a $4,229 gain.

However, periods and stakes matter. Investors ready to wager $10,000 on a 50–50 chance for a $3,639 loss or a $4,229 gain might not be ready to wager their entire portfolio on proportionally higher gains and losses.

Advisers following the want-based approach also ask questions that identify wants that interact with loss tolerance and possibly distort it, such as wants for winning or maximization. To what extent do you agree with the following statement: "I always want to have the best. Second best is not good enough for me"? A survey of Americans revealed that men have greater wants for maximization than women and that the young have greater such wants than the old. People who declare strong wants for maximization tend to declare high levels of loss tolerance. Yet advisers should explore whether high declared loss tolerance reflects anything more than strong wants for maximization.[260]

Maximization seeking is associated with regret aversion. To what extent do you agree with the following statement: "Whenever I make a choice, I try to get information about how the other alternatives turned out and feel bad if another alternative has done better than the alternative I have chosen"? The survey revealed that maximizers tend to be especially averse to regret, but regret is different from losses. Indeed, the correlation between regret aversion and loss aversion is close to zero.

Risk-based investor questionnaires sometimes ask, "Are you confident in your financial decisions?" The survey of Americans revealed that people who are confident in their ability to beat the market also declare high levels of loss tolerance. As with maximization, advisers should explore whether high declared loss tolerance reflects anything more than overconfidence.

Advisers should inquire about wants beyond protection from poverty, prospects for riches, maximization, and regret aversion. For example, they should inquire about wants for staying true to values.

Johann Klaassen designs client questionnaires for advisers affiliated with Horizons Sustainable Financial Services, a group that caters to investors

---

[260]Carrie Pan and Meir Statman, "Questionnaires of Risk Tolerance, Regret, Overconfidence, and Other Investor Propensities," *Journal of Investment Consulting* 13, no. 1 (March 2012): 54–63.

whose wants include staying true to their values. One part of the firm's questionnaire says the following:

> We will normally allocate approximately one third of a portfolio's bond allocation to community investments that offer a market rate of return. Some community investments offer below-market rates of return, and may be able therefore to offer greater community impact. Please indicate here how you would like to participate in community investing opportunities:
>
> 1. I/We want to opt out of all community investing vehicles in my/our portfolio.
>
> 2. I/We want to have the standard allocation to market-rate community investments.
>
> 3. I/We want to have the following percentage of my/our portfolio allocated to below-market-rate community investment opportunities: 1% to 2%, 3% to 4%, 5% to 10%.

Advisers should educate investors, replacing ignorance with knowledge and correcting cognitive and emotional errors. For example, advisers should educate investors about the benefits of global diversification before asking for their preferences.

In a questionnaire by Loring Ward, an investment company serving financial advisers who serve investors, education about global diversification comes first:

> Over time, international markets and asset classes within those markets have not always moved in unison with the US market. The graph below shows periods when US stocks have outperformed international stocks and periods when international stocks have outperformed US stocks. Historically, investing a portion of a portfolio in international stocks and bonds has demonstrated the potential to reduce volatility.

The text is followed by a figure, similar to **Exhibit 6.5**, showing that the returns of US stocks exceeded those of international stocks in some periods and fell short of them in other periods. The figure shows, moreover, that the magnitude of return gaps was substantial. Indeed, a return gap exceeding 10 pps occurred in more than half of the rolling 12-month periods. The maximum rolling 12-month gap where the return of US stocks exceeded the return of international stocks was 34.7% in the 12-month period ending in May 1983, and the maximum rolling 12-month gap where the return

**Exhibit 6.5.** **Return Gaps between US and International Stocks, 1972–2018 (rolling 12-month differences between the total returns of the S&P 500 and the returns of the MSCI EAFE Index)**

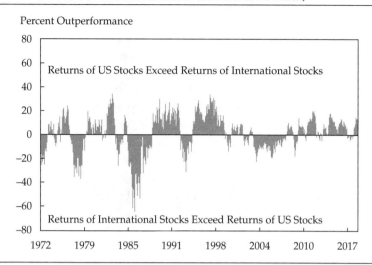

of international stocks exceeded the return of US stocks was 64.1% in the 12-month period ending in August 1986.

Next in the Loring Ward questionnaire comes exploration of investor wants:

"Which statement best reflects your view on international investing?

- I am very comfortable with international investments.

- I am comfortable with international investments.

- I am somewhat comfortable with international investments.

- I am somewhat uneasy with international investments.

- I am uneasy with international investments."

## Behavioral Portfolio Theory in Practice

The central features of behavioral portfolio theory, reflected in portfolio construction, include investors' wants, portfolios as pyramids of wants, risk as shortfalls relative to wants, and avoidance of cognitive and emotional errors in pursuit of satisfying wants. Good portfolio construction practices also include features shared by standard and behavioral portfolio theory—for example, diversification, low costs, and simplicity.[261]

Such financial advising products as those by MoneyGuidePro and Wealthcare Capital Management incorporate behavioral portfolio theory features, as do programs provided by financial services firms, such as Schwab, Fidelity, and Vanguard, and advisers who work at financial services companies or independently.

MoneyGuidePro notes that clients' wants are specified in goals that reflect hopes and dreams—education, travel, home renovating, retirement income, and bequests. Data collection turns into a conversation about investors' wants and goals.

The initial plan might place clients in the middle of a "confidence zone," with a moderately high probability of no shortfalls from goals, by trimming some goals and eliminating the bequest goal. Harold Evensky, a financial adviser who contributed to the development of MoneyGuidePro, noted that advisers should help clients identify trade-offs among goals as they consider wants and resources. For example, clients might choose to delay their retirement, thereby maintaining their travel, education, and bequest goals.[262]

Advisers using Wealthcare's program guide clients to distinguishing wants and associated "ideal goals" from "acceptable goals." The ideal retirement age for a couple might be 58, but retirement at age 65 is acceptable to them.

A stress test of a financial plan using simulations shows whether it is overfunded, underfunded, or within the confidence zone. Wants and goals of overfunded and underfunded plans are modified to bring the plan into the confidence zone. A financial adviser using Wealthcare's program described preparing for a meeting with clients, a couple, in June 2009, following the bottoming out of the stock market. After reviewing the couple's new wants and ideal goals relative to their financial resources, the adviser discovered that the wife could retire a couple of years earlier than she had planned; they could satisfy their wants for lower investment risk and for a yearly vacation, though a less expensive one.[263]

Financial services companies, such as Schwab, Vanguard, and Fidelity, like MoneyGuidePro and Wealthcare, consider investors' wants as they

---

[261]Sanjiv R. Das, Harry Markowitz, Jonathan Scheid, and Meir Statman, "Portfolios for Investors Who Want to Reach Their Goals While Staying on the Mean–Variance Efficient Frontier," *Journal of Wealth Management* 14, no. 2 (July 2011): 25–31; Sanjiv Das, Harry Markowitz, Jonathan Scheid, and Meir Statman, "Portfolio Optimization with Mental Accounts," *Journal of Financial and Quantitative Analysis* 45, no. 2 (April 2010): 311–34.
[262]www.moneyguidepro.com/ifa/.
[263]Russ Thornton, "The Levers to Financial Freedom," *Advisor Perspectives* (1 September 2009). www.advisorperspectives.com/newsletters09/pdfs/The_Levers_to_Financial_Freedom.pdf.

recommend portfolios, although they do that only implicitly. Wants for familiarity, reflected in home bias, are one example. Investors whose wants do not include familiarity might allocate half of their overall stock allocation to international stocks because international stocks make up about half of the total value of all stocks. But model portfolios of financial services companies typically allocate to international stocks only one-quarter of the overall stock allocation.

## Conclusion

Mean–variance portfolio theory prescribes portfolios on *mean–variance fron-tiers* to investors who want nothing more than the utilitarian benefits of high expected returns and low risk, measured by the variance of portfolio returns.

Behavioral portfolio theory describes portfolios on *behavioral-wants fron-tiers* and prescribes them to investors who want utilitarian benefits but also expressive and emotional benefits. These include all the benefits of protec-tion from poverty, prospects for riches, nurturing children and families, being true to values, and reaching high social status.

Behavioral portfolio theory also prescribes the avoidance of portfolios on *behavioral-errors frontiers*—tempting but illusory portfolios created by igno-rance and cognitive and emotional errors, such as the erroneous belief among amateur investors that frequent trading brings high returns.

Financial-facts and human-behavior knowledge enable investment pro-fessionals to identify wants, use cognitive and emotional shortcuts correctly, and avoid cognitive and emotional errors on the way to satisfying wants. Investment professionals need not turn themselves into psychologists to guide investors to portfolios on behavioral-wants frontiers. But investment pro-fessionals must know, teach, and use human-behavior knowledge, not only financial-facts knowledge.

Online advisers, sometimes called "robo-advisers," are an innova-tion in advising, competing with "live" advisers in guiding investors. They include Financial Engines, Betterment, Wealthfront, Personal Capital, and FutureAdvisor. Online advisers charge lower fees in doing much of the tradi-tional work of live advisers, including portfolio construction and rebalancing, loss harvesting, and even education about financial facts and human behavior. Advisers who will thrive in this new competitive environment are those who interact with their clients, explore their wants, and guide them to avoid cog-nitive and emotional errors on their way to satisfying their wants.

# 7. Behavioral Life Cycle of Saving and Spending

As I described in a 2017 article,[264] a woman offered her story about the life cycle of saving and spending:

> My husband was reared by extremely thrifty parents who survived the Great Depression and World War II, and through hard work and frugality bordering on stinginess they accumulated a very comfortable nest egg. They passed on to him their fiscal philosophies and my husband absorbed them like a sponge.
>
> My husband handled our finances. Once he died and I took over the finances, I was amazed at how much money we had. I shall have to work very hard to spend all of it, but I plan to give it my best effort. In the two and a half years since my husband died, I have been to Africa and made three trips to Europe. I have already booked trips to see lowland gorillas in Rwanda and Uganda, snow monkeys in Japan, penguins in Antarctica, and to ride a horse across the Mongolian steppes. These trips were booked after my doctor told me that based on her patients, 80 is the age at which people lose their energy and enthusiasm for traveling. I am attempting to get in as many trips as I can before hitting that mile marker.
>
> I have also made many donations to local charities and plan to set up a trust fund for a friend's grandchild who has Down syndrome and would otherwise become a ward of the state when his parents, who live a hand-to-mouth existence, die.
>
> My husband never reaped any benefits from his saving habits and only received three months of Social Security before dying. May others escape his fate. (p. 34)

Portfolio theory is about the *production* of portfolios by combining assets, such as stocks, bonds, and houses. But where do assets come from and where are they going? Life-cycle theory answers these questions, complementing portfolio theory. Life-cycle theory is about *accumulating* assets into portfolios and *decumulating* from them, as in the story of that woman and her late husband. We accumulate mostly by saving from wages and other income during our working years but also from gifts, bequests, and other receipts.

---

[264]Meir Statman, "Are Your Clients Not Spending Enough in Retirement?" *Journal of Financial Planning* (November 2017): 34–37.

We decumulate by spending during our nonworking years but also by gifts, bequests, and other outlays.

Behavioral life-cycle theory is different from standard life-cycle theory. Franco Modigliani and Richard Brumberg described standard life-cycle theory in 1954.[265] Milton Friedman offered a similar "permanent income hypothesis" in 1957.[266] Hersh Shefrin and Nobel Prize–winning economist Richard Thaler laid the foundation of behavioral life-cycle theory in 1981 and 1988.[267]

Describing Modigliani and Brumberg's theory, Nobel Prize–winning economist Angus Deaton wrote, "By building up and running down assets, working people can make provision for their retirement, and more generally, tailor their consumption patterns to their needs at different ages, independently of their incomes at each age."[268]

The focus of Modigliani and Brumberg was on the behavior of the economy as a whole, not on the behavior of individuals. Deaton explained, "This simple theory leads to important and non-obvious predictions about the economy as a whole, that national saving depends on the rate of growth of national income, not its level, and that the level of wealth in the economy bears a simple relation to the length of the retirement span."[269]

Friedman called his life-cycle theory "the permanent income hypothesis" and focused it squarely on the behavior of individuals. He recognized that consumption provides a range of benefits but chose to define consumption in terms of "purchases" rather than in terms of "value of services." Yet value of services is what matters, consisting of utilitarian, expressive, and emotional benefits.

Standard life-cycle theory predicts that people estimate their life-cycle wealth and spend "permanent income," roughly average income, each year, even as their income fluctuates from year to year. This way, they exhaust their life-cycle wealth during their lifetimes.

---

[265]Franco Modigliani and Richard Brumberg, "Utility Analysis and the Consumption Function: An Interpretation of Cross-Section Data," in *Post Keynesian Economics*, edited by K. Kurihara, 388–436 (New Brunswick, NJ: Rutgers University Press, 1954).

[266]Milton Friedman, *A Theory of the Consumption Function* (Princeton, NJ: Princeton University Press, 1957).

[267]Hersh Shefrin and Richard H. Thaler, "The Behavioral Life-Cycle Hypothesis," *Economic Inquiry* 26, no. 4 (February 1988): 609–43; Richard H. Thaler and Hersh Shefrin, "An Economic Theory of Self-Control," *Journal of Political Economy* 89, no. 2 (February 1981): 392–406.

[268]Angus Deaton, "Franco Modigliani and the Life Cycle Theory of Consumption" (March 2005). Available at SSRN: https://ssrn.com/abstract=686475 or http://dx.doi.org/10.2139/ssrn.686475.

[269]Deaton, "Franco Modigliani and the Life Cycle Theory of Consumption."

## Utilitarian, Expressive, and Emotional Benefits in Behavioral Life-Cycle Theory

Standard life-cycle theory says that our sole reason for saving during our working years is spending during our nonworking years. Behavioral life-cycle theory says that our reasons for saving and spending in all years consist of wants for the full range of utilitarian, expressive, and emotional benefits of saving and spending.

Behavioral life-cycle theory says that saving can yield expressive and emotional benefits, even as it detracts from utilitarian benefits. Reacting to a *Wall Street Journal* article I wrote about spending in retirement, one reader noted that many people believe saving is simply what responsible people do: "I'm saving now because good, admirable, upstanding people sacrifice their current standard of living to save, save, save for the future."[270]

Moreover, spending can impose expressive and emotional costs. Reacting to the same article, another reader wrote, "What if the enjoyment is in the saving, and the pain is in the spending?" And another wrote, "Every so often there are articles about people who have accumulated vast wealth relative to their lifetime income, and when they pass at an old age and people find out, they feel sad for them—that they lived frugally and never spent it on anything. I sometimes think they are missing the point. The total enjoyment for that person was in the saving and living miserly and frugally and well below one's means. To a certain degree, I am that person."

Behavioral life-cycle theory also says that mere wealth *owning*, rather than spending, yields utilitarian, expressive, and emotional benefits. A bank commercial encouraging saving shows a sequence of adult children caring about elderly parents, hugging them, dancing around them, and placing coats on their shoulders. The caption says, "Because you want your children to care about you."

Elderly parents who own wealth enjoy the utilitarian benefits of children who help in anticipation of a bequest but would not help otherwise. They enjoy the utilitarian, expressive, and emotional benefits of help from children who would help with no anticipation of a bequest. And they enjoy the expressive and emotional benefits of supporting their children with gifts from their wealth, rather than suffer expressive and emotional costs of being supported by their children. As they say, when parents give to children, all smile. When children give to parents, all cry.

---

[270]Meir Statman, "The Mental Mistakes We Make with Retirement Spending," *Wall Street Journal* (24 April 2017). www.wsj.com/articles/the-mental-mistakes-we-make-with-retirement-spending-1492999921.

# Framing, Mental Accounting, and Self-Control in Behavioral Life-Cycle Theory

We, the normal people described in behavioral life-cycle theory, find it difficult to match spending to "permanent income," even if matching is what we want. This is because we find it difficult to estimate our life-cycle wealth, longevity, and future spending needs and because we struggle to reconcile the urge for saving with the urge for spending. These problems leave us exposed to either running out of money before running out of life when we save too little or spend too much or running out of life before running out of money when we save too much or spend too little.

Behavioral life-cycle theory says that we work to overcome these difficulties through framing, mental accounting, and self-control rules. Whereas standard life-cycle theory says that we regard income and capital as mere components of life-cycle wealth, behavioral life-cycle theory says that we regard them as distinct. Current income includes current wages and current interest and dividends from bonds and stocks, among other investments. Current capital includes the current value of our portfolio of bonds, stocks, houses, and other investments and the present value of future income, including future wages, future interest and dividends, and future income from other investments.

We frame current income, current capital, and future income into separate mental accounts and set self-control rules that restrict dips into mental accounts other than those designated as permissible for dipping. One such self-control rule involves permission to spend income but prohibition to dip into capital—selling stocks, bonds, or houses and spending the proceeds. Self-control rules also restrict dips into retirement saving accounts for automobiles or home renovations or dips into children's college saving accounts for vacations or furniture.

The simplicity of mental accounting helps us face two major life challenges. One is the challenge of dividing our spending and saving between the present and the future. The other is the challenge of dividing today's spending among all we want today.

"I have a silly little system," said one woman in the 1950s, describing her tin-can mental accounting. "Whenever my husband gets paid, I take away so much for my grocery money and put it in my kitchen drawer. Then I take all the rest and I put it into a tin can. . . . If my husband doesn't have enough money for gas out of his allowance, or if we go out for some entertainment, we just take the money out of the tin can. . . . I've tried to budget with envelopes, labeling them for this and that, but we always took money out of the wrong envelope whenever we ran low. . . . Now I've found the checking account together with the tin can the best system" (p. 155).[271]

Mental accounting has migrated from the tin cans of the 1950s to the internet.

Mint.com and similar websites make it easy to track our expenses on shopping, entertainment, restaurants, gas, and groceries. We can split ATM withdrawals into spending categories and even tweet our purchases as we make them.

We can see reflections of mental accounting in distinctions we make between our own contributions to retirement saving accounts and contributions to those accounts by our employers. Money comes into defined contribution accounts of employees from two sources: employees who contribute by salary deduction and employers who match employee contributions or contribute even in the absence of employee contributions. For example, Santa Clara University, my employer, contributes 10% on top of my salary into a 401(a) account, and I contribute my voluntary amount into a 403(b) account. Employees, rather than employers, choose the investments in each account.

Employees tend to treat the two saving accounts as two distinct mental accounts. They take less risk in their employee-funded 403(b) accounts than in their employer-funded 401(a) accounts.[272]

Standard life-cycle theory does not mention self-control, assuming implicitly that people possess perfect self-control, execute their saving and spending competently, and easily overcome the temptation to spend too much or too little. Insufficient and excessive self-control, however, are central in behavioral life-cycle theory.

Self-control is not always easy to muster, and some fail to muster it at all. Deficient self-control, reflected in impulsivity, lack of organization, and preference for living for today, affects the incidence of financial distress more than differences in education or financial literacy.[273]

Online lending platforms can help people overcome financial setbacks or refinance high-interest debt, thereby decreasing bankruptcy filings. But deficient self-control leads people to overextend themselves into "debt traps," increasing bankruptcy filings. It turns out that the latter predominates.

---

[271]Lee Rainwater, Richard Coleman, and Gerald Handel, *Workingman's Wife: Her Personality, World and Life Style* (New York: Oceana Publications, 1959).

[272]Andrea Therese Anthony, Kristine Beck, and Inga Chira, "Does the Source of Money Determine Retirement Investment Choices?" (23 August 2017). Available at SSRN: https://ssrn.com/abstract=3024533 or http://dx.doi.org/10.2139/ssrn.3024533.

[273]Yvonne McCarthy, "Behavioural Characteristics and Financial Distress," ECB Working Paper No. 1303 (14 February 2011). Available at SSRN: http://ssrn.com/abstract=1761570.

One study showed that availability of the online lending platform of Lending Club increased bankruptcy filings by approximately 8%.[274]

Self-control can be replaced or augmented by outside control. Parents impose outside control over children, and marriage partners augment self-control with outside control over each other. A joint bank account induces partners to buy basic products, whereas separate bank accounts induce them to buy luxury products. These different spending patterns are driven by outside control exercised by each partner over the other, reflected in an increased need to justify spending to the partner.[275]

Overpayment of taxes followed by tax refunds are a self-control device. Recipients of tax refunds are different from those making tax payments. They tend to have lower average incomes and smaller cash buffers. Tax refunds are substantial, amounting to almost six weeks' take-home income for the average family receiving them. Expenditures on durable goods, credit card payments, and cash withdrawals increase most sharply upon receipt of a tax refund. Evidently, the tax system is a primary tool by which many families generate lump sums of cash, and tax refunds are a major financial event that resets the spending and saving patterns of families who receive them.[276]

Men in many countries view women as better budgeters, possessing greater self-control.[277] The majority of men in the Philippines say that they would be profligate in spending if their wives did not control their incomes. Men in the Philippines often keep portions of their incomes from their wives surreptitiously, a practice so common it has a name, *kupit*, which literally means to pilfer, filch, or steal in small quantities.

---

[274]Hongchang Wang and Eric M. Overby, "How Does Online Lending Influence Bankruptcy Filings?" Georgia Tech Scheller College of Business Research Paper No. 17-20 (16 November 2018). Available at SSRN: https://ssrn.com/abstract=2958916 or http://dx.doi.org/10.2139/ssrn.2958916.

[275]Emily N. Garbinsky and Joe J. Gladstone, "The Consumption Consequences of Couples Pooling Finances," *Journal of Consumer Psychology* 29, no. 3 (July 2019): 353–69.

[276]Diana Farrell, Fiona Greig, and Amar Hamoudi, "Tax Time: How Families Manage Tax Refunds and Payments" (6 March 2019). Available at SSRN: https://ssrn.com/abstract=3348019 or http://dx.doi.org/10.2139/ssrn.3348019.

[277]Villia Jefremovas, "Women Are Good with Money: The Impact of Cash Cropping on Class Relations and Gender Ideology in Northern Luzon, Philippines," in *Women Farmers and Commercial Ventures: Increasing Food Security in Developing Countries*, edited by Anita Spring, 131–50 (Boulder, CO: Lynne Reinner, 2000); Suzanne A. Brenner, "Why Women Rule the Roost: Rethinking Javanese Ideologies of Gender and Self-Control," in *Bewitching Women, Pious Men: Gender and Body Politics in Southeast Asia*, edited by Aihwa Ong and Michael G. Peletz, 19–50 (Berkeley: University of California Press, 1995); Nava Ashraf, "Spousal Control and Intra-Household Decision Making: An Experimental Study in the Philippines," *American Economic Review* 99, no. 4 (2009): 1245–77.

---

****

Female empowerment is not only a worthy goal on its own but also a road to the goal of increased saving. A study in the Philippines found that savings accounts that commit their holders to save enhance both savings and the power of women in decisions within families.[278]

Sometimes, however, even outside control fails, illustrated by Fred Schwed in *Where Are the Customers' Yachts? Or, A Good, Hard Look at Wall Street*.[279] A man, $7.5 million rich in 1929, gave his wife $1.5 million in government bonds to be placed in a protection-from-poverty mental account. The $7.5 million was a huge amount of money in 1929, equivalent to more than $100 million today. "My dearest," he said, "these securities are now yours; they are not mine. They represent quite as much income as we shall ever really need for the rest of our lives" (p. 80).

The man, aware of his self-control problem, went beyond relinquishing to his wife control over the bonds. "But if by any incredible chance I should ever come to you and ask for these bonds back again," he said, "under no circumstance give them to me, for you will know I have gone crazy" (p. 80).

The man placed the other $6 million in the prospects-for-riches mental account and kept control over it to "continue to speculate and make more money." Unfortunately for the man and his wife, his outside-control rule was not strict enough. Six months later, he needed money to recover the $6 million he had lost. "He went for the money to the wife of his bosom, who demurred. But he was a persuasive man: He got the bonds back. Temporarily"[280] (p. 80). He lost everything.

Some people are savers by nature, whereas others are not. The Big Five personality traits are conscientiousness, neuroticism, extraversion, agreeableness, and openness. Conscientiousness is the personality trait most closely associated with self-control. Conscientiousness is high among people adequately prepared for retirement, whereas neuroticism is low. Conscientious people consume more than less conscientious people, but their wealth is also higher, indicating that they save more.[281]

However, one can be too conscientious and have too much self-control. Too much self-control is as common as too little self-control. Indeed,

---

[278]Nava Ashraf, Dean Karlan, and Wesley Yin, "Female Empowerment: Further Evidence from a Commitment Savings Product in the Philippines," *World Development* 38, no. 3 (March 2010): 333–44.

[279]Fred Schwed, Jr., *Where Are the Customers' Yachts? Or, A Good, Hard Look at Wall Street* (New York: John Wiley & Sons, 1995).

[280]Schwed, *Where Are the Customers' Yachts?*

[281]Michael D. Hurd, Angela Duckworth, Susann Rohwedder, and David R. Weir, "Personality Traits and Economic Preparation for Retirement" (1 September 2012). Available at SSRN: http://ssrn.com/abstract=2239766.

proficiency at framing, mental accounting, and self-control helps people save for retirement, but the same proficiency impedes them in retirement when it is time to set these aside and enjoy the fruits of retirement savings.

Reacting to the article about spending in retirement, one wrote, "During my career I was a very conscientious saver and investor. I always maxed out my 401(k) contribution and put a large percentage of my salary and bonus into a deferred compensation program. I have had a difficult time changing my mindset from a saver to a spender. This article helped me make that mental transition. The first thing I did was to go out and get fitted for a new set of golf clubs and didn't feel guilty about it!"[282]

Another wrote, "I learned from my mom that the greatest joy in life is giving to your family. She would give something to all her six children, their spouses, the grandchildren, the great-grandchildren and all their spouses on their birthdays, anniversaries, St. Patrick's Day, Valentine's Day, and for no reason at all. If you want the closest thing to eternal life, try this."

## Spending Sources and Uses in Behavioral Life-Cycle Theory

Behavioral-life cycle theory includes "spending-sources" and "spending-uses" pyramids.

The bottom layer of the spending-sources pyramid contains "income," including wages, dividends and interest, Social Security benefits, and payments from pension plans. Above it is a layer that contains "dips into regular capital," including the proceeds from the sale of stocks, bonds, and other investments, whether in retirement accounts or outside them. Above them is a layer that contains "dips into bequest capital," including the proceeds from the sale of investments intended as bequests, usually houses. Above them is a layer of support from family, friends, government agencies, and charities, for those who must rely on them.

The bottom layer of spending-uses pyramids consists of spending on necessities, such as food, shelter, and support of minor children. However, people vary. For some, that layer also includes support of elderly parents and needy adult children. For others, these spending uses belong in the higher discretionary layer that also includes recreation, travel, gifts, and small charitable contributions. For some, savings belong in the bottom layer of necessities, whereas for others, savings belong in the higher discretionary layer. Above them is a layer of luxury and status goods, such as expensive cars, jewelry, large charitable contributions, and bequests. For some, however, luxury

---

[282]Meir Statman, "The Mental Mistakes We Make with Retirement Spending," *Wall Street Journal* (24 April 2017). www.wsj.com/articles/the-mental-mistakes-we-make-with-retirement-spending-1492999921.

cars and other status goods are necessities, not luxuries, belonging in lower layers of the pyramid.

A distinction between capital and income is a feature of behavioral life cycle theory, reflected in the spending-sources pyramid. Standard life-cycle theory predicts that we do not distinguish capital from income, because dollars of capital are different from dollars of income in form but not in substance. Behavioral life-cycle theory predicts, however, that normal investors distinguish capital from income. The evidence is consistent with behavioral life-cycle theory. American investors are more likely to spend dividends than sell shares and spend their proceeds.[283] And Finnish investors spend almost all dividends but rarely dip into capital.[284]

Consistent with the reluctance to dip into capital, investors spend little of their defined contribution (DC) retirement saving accounts in their early retirement years, let alone deplete them. One study showed that only 7% of people aged 60–69 withdrew more than 10% of their DC accounts annually, and only 18% made any withdrawals in a typical year.[285] Moreover, the proportion withdrawn averaged 1%–2% between ages 60 and 69, rising to about 5% at age 70½, when investors must withdraw money according to the required minimum distribution rules, and fluctuating around that level through age 85.

## The Annuity Puzzle

Eagerness to buy life annuities is consistent with standard life-cycle theory because annuities facilitate smoothing of spending and eliminate longevity risk by converting life-cycle wealth into permanent income for life. We refer to the reluctance to buy life annuities as the "annuity puzzle." Behavioral life-cycle theory is consistent with the reluctance to buy life annuities.

Solutions to the annuity puzzle regularly draw on behavioral finance, even when the reliance on behavioral theory is not acknowledged. It is sometimes argued that lack of annuitization reflects a bequest motive. This assertion is likely true but crosses the line into behavioral finance and its emphasis

---

[283]Malcolm Baker, Stefan Nagel, and Jeffrey Wurgler, "The Effect of Dividends on Consumption," *Brookings Papers on Economic Activity* no. 1 (Spring 2007): 231–91.

[284]Markku Kaustia and Elias Rantapuska, "Rational and Behavioral Motives to Trade: Evidence from Reinvestment of Dividends and Tender Offer Proceeds," *Journal of Banking and Finance* 36, no. 8 (August 2012): 2366–78.

[285]James M. Poterba, Steven F. Venti, and David A. Wise, "The Drawdown of Personal Retirement Assets," National Bureau of Economic Research Working Paper 16675 (January 2011, revised January 2013).

on wants beyond spending the last dollar on the day of death. Caring for children and families is prominent among the wants of normal investors.

Investors' wants include not only protection from poverty, satisfied by smoothed permanent income, but also prospects for riches. Life annuities, however, emit a "smell of death," reminding investors that they are relinquishing prospects for riches.

Wants for fairness are also prominent among the wants of normal investors. These wants are an impediment to buying life annuities. Standard finance finds nothing unfair when buyers of life annuities forfeit future payments if they die soon after purchasing a life annuity. Indeed, this forfeiture underlies the structure of life annuities, as money forfeited by annuity buyers who die early is paid to annuity buyers who live long. Yet a perception of unfairness remains, evident in the preference of some people for life annuities that pay for a "period certain"—a minimum period over which the annuity pays either the buyer or his heirs, even if the buyer dies during that period.[286]

Cognitive errors highlighted in behavioral finance are also impediments to purchasing life annuities. They include the framing errors we know as *money illusion*, which mislead investors into perceiving a lump sum as larger than its equivalent stream of annuity payments, and availability errors, where images of many kinds of early deaths are easily available. Availability errors interact with emotional errors of regret as people contemplate the possibility that their heirs would receive only a small portion of their annuity dollars when death follows soon after buying an annuity.

Aversion to dips into capital is another impediment to purchasing life annuities. Investors dip into capital when they buy annuities, converting capital into income. Aversion to dipping into capital manifests itself when investors face a choice to buy life annuities for a known lump sum but not when investors face no choice and do not know the lump sum, as in Social Security.

Behavioral life-cycle theory predicts that investors are especially reluctant to dip into "bequest capital," mostly houses. Housing equity makes up a large proportion of the wealth of older Americans, yet, on average, homes are not sold to support nonhousing consumption as people age.[287] Moreover, homeowners are reluctant to enter into reverse mortgage contracts that pay

---

[286]Suzanne B. Shu, Robert Zeithammer, and John W. Payne, "The Pivotal Role of Fairness: Which Consumers Like Annuities?" National Bureau of Economic Research Working Paper No. w25067 (September 2018). Available at SSRN: https://ssrn.com/abstract=3254042.
[287]Steven F. Venti and David A. Wise, "Aging and Housing Equity: Another Look," in *Perspectives on the Economics of Aging*, edited by David A. Wise, 127–80 (Chicago: University of Chicago Press, 2004).

homeowners while they continue to live in their homes. Only 2% of home-owners eligible for reverse mortgage contracts enter into them.[288]

## Standard and Behavioral Life-Cycle Theories in Public Policy

Public policy prescriptions for saving and spending range from libertarianism to libertarian paternalism to outright paternalism. Libertarians advocate *hands-off* policies, granting people freedom to save and spend as they wish, whether saving much when young and spending much when old or saving little when young and spending little when old. Libertarian prescriptions conform to standard life-cycle theory for people who arrange their saving and spending so as to enjoy smoothed permanent income throughout their life cycle.

Libertarian paternalists advocate policies that *nudge* people toward saving when young and toward judicious spending when old. Conventional or outright paternalists go further, advocating mandates that *shove* people into saving when young and judicious spending when old. Both conform to behavioral life-cycle theory, where people are hampered in saving and spending by conflicts between wants for saving and spending and by cognitive and emotional errors.

Standard life-cycle theory is libertarian in essence, at least implicitly. People save money for themselves during their working years and spend it on themselves before entering the labor force and in retirement. Milton Friedman discussed bequests in his permanent income hypothesis, noting that people *receiving* bequests add them to their life-cycle wealth and spend from them gradually, by the rules of permanent income, rather than regarding the bequest as current income. Yet Friedman did not discuss people who refrain from consumption to grant bequests. Moreover, there is nothing explicit in standard life-cycle theory about public policy prescriptions or the role of corporations and governments in such programs as pensions or Social Security.

But there is an explicit and prominent place for public policy prescriptions and the role of corporations and governments in behavioral life-cycle theory—in policies that protect us from our own cognitive and emotional errors and nudge, shove, and educate us to reconcile internal conflicts between saving and spending.

---

[288]Thomas Davidoff, "Reverse Mortgage Demographics and Collateral Performance" (25 February 2014). Available at SSRN: http://ssrn.com/abstract=2399942 or http://dx.doi.org/10.2139/ssrn.2399942.

Public policy prescriptions and the role of government are evident in all of investing, saving, and spending. These include direct government provisions, such as Social Security, Medicare, and Medicaid, and indirect government provisions, such as the laws and regulations that defer taxes on DC accounts and require minimum distributions from these accounts when reaching age 70½.

Social Security is paternalistic. Its compulsory nature counters inadequate self-control by shoving people into saving, curtailing today's spending. The paternalistic nature of Social Security is also evident in the absence of an option to receive a lump-sum payment in place of monthly payments.

Defined benefit (DB) pension plans are also paternalistic because they are mandatory for employees in companies and government entities that provide them. But most corporate DB plans permit lump-sum payments at retirement, tempting retirees with insufficient self-control. Combined corporate and government paternalism is evident in the Pension Benefit Guaranty Corporation, which insures workers who would otherwise lose corporate pension benefits if their pension funds default.

Many financial regulations seek to protect investors from their own cognitive and emotional errors. Margin regulations limit leverage. Stock buyers cannot borrow more than 50% of the value of their stock purchases. The paternalistic nature of margin regulations is reflected in deliberations preceding the passage of the Securities Exchange Act of 1934. These deliberations noted that a large proportion of business failures, embezzlements, and even suicides were directly attributable to losses incurred in speculative transactions made possible by lenient margin regulations.

Suitability regulations are also paternalistic, designed to counter cognitive and emotional errors. These regulations require brokers to recommend securities to customers only if they have reasonable grounds for believing that their recommendations are suitable for their customers' financial situation and needs.

Suitability standards are paternalistic, but they set a low paternalism bar. For example, suitability standards permit a broker to recommend to a client a high-cost mutual fund, paying him a high commission, over an identical low-cost fund that pays him a low commission—as long as both funds are "suitable" for that investor. Fiduciary standards set a higher paternalism bar, requiring brokers to place the interests of investors ahead of their own: They do not allow a broker to recommend a high-cost mutual fund over an identical low-cost fund.

The most prominent libertarian paternalistic nudge in the context of savings is automatic enrollment into DC retirement saving plans, such as 401(k) plans, discussed by the economist Richard Thaler and the legal scholar Cass Sunstein in their book *Nudge: Improving Decisions About Health, Wealth, and Happiness*.[289] Making enrollment in a company's retirement savings plan the default choice is a nudge that counters the tendency to procrastinate in saving and place wants for spending over wants for saving.

Congress incorporated nudges into the Pension Protection Act of 2006, and corporations apply nudges as they implement the act. It authorizes corporations to establish programs for automatic enrollment of employees into DC plans at specified contribution levels and to increase these levels automatically over time.

A study of the nudges incorporated into the choice architecture of the Swedish Premium Pension Plan—consisting of all initial choices and subsequent rebalancing activities by the entire population of 7.3 million retirement savers in Sweden from 2000 to 2016—concluded that the effects of nudges were persistent, lasting nearly two decades, if not forever.[290]

Automatic enrollment in DC plans increases the proportion of employees who enroll. Enrollment of new employees in one plan increased from 37% to 86% following the introduction of automatic enrollment.[291] Approximately 27% of 401(k) plans, especially those of large employers, offered automatic enrollment in 2014.[292] As of a year later, however, a substantial proportion of employees had stayed at the automatic or default level of salary contribution, 3% per year, despite a 50% employer match on contributions up to 6%. Employees seem anchored to the default contribution level, considering it the level recommended by the company. Increasing the contribution default rate to 6% did not decrease participation, though default contribution rates higher than 6% were accompanied by decreases.[293]

---

[289]Richard H. Thaler and Cass R. Sunstein, *Nudge: Improving Decisions About Health, Wealth, and Happiness* (New Haven, CT: Yale University Press, 2008).

[290]Henrik Cronqvist, Richard H. Thaler, and Fang Yu, "When Nudges Are Forever: Inertia in the Swedish Premium Pension Plan," AEA Papers and Proceedings, Vol. 108 May 2018 (10 January 2018). Available at SSRN: https://ssrn.com/abstract=3099886 or http://dx.doi.org/10.2139/ssrn.3099886.

[291]Brigitte C. Madrian and Dennis F. Shea, "The Power of Suggestion: Inertia in 401(k) Participation and Savings Behavior," *Quarterly Journal of Economics* 116, no. 4 (November 2001): 1149–87.

[292]David Blanchett, "Save More Today: Improving Retirement Savings Rates with Carrots, Advice, and Nudges," *Journal of Retirement* 5, no. 1 (Summer 2017): 69–95.

[293]James J. Choi, David Laibson, Brigitte C. Madrian, and Andrew Metrick, "Defined Contribution Pensions: Plan Rules, Participant Decisions, and The Path of Least Resistance," in *Tax Policy and the Economy*, vol. 16, edited by James M. Poterba, 67–114 (Cambridge, MA: MIT Press, 2002).

Mandatory DC plans are paternalistic shoves into saving, going beyond libertarian paternalistic nudges. They complement the shoves of Social Security and substitute for the shoves of increasingly rare DB plans. Mandatory DC plans exist in a number of countries, Australia being prominent among them. Australian employers are required to contribute a specified percentage of employee earnings into employees' retirement saving accounts. This percentage is scheduled to increase gradually to 12% by 2019–2020. Employees can contribute voluntarily beyond the mandatory amount. Tax provisions encourage people to withdraw their money gradually, rather than in a lump sum.

## Wealthy, Steady Middle, Precarious Middle, and Poor

Discussions about public policies that are best at promoting adequate life-cycle spending and saving, whether libertarian hands-off approaches, libertarian paternalistic nudges, or paternalistic shoves, are unfocused when we fail to distinguish among people by wealth, income, and personal characteristics, especially self-control.

We can focus discussions about life-cycle saving and spending policies by distinguishing among four groups: the *wealthy, steady middle, precarious middle*, and *poor*. The *wealthy* receive incomes in their working years that are more than sufficient, and they accumulate enough savings to ensure no retirement fears. The *steady middle* steadily receive sufficient incomes during their working years, and they save enough for sufficient retirement spending. The *poor* recieve insufficient income during their working years, preventing them from saving much for adequate retirement spending. The *precarious middle* comprises two groups—*low earners* and *high spenders*. Low earners attempt to save from their low incomes throughout their working years, but their small savings cause them to be precariously close to poverty and inadequate retirement spending. High spenders earn sufficient incomes in their working years but spend them, neglecting to save a sufficient amount for retirement spending.

Retirement saving and spending solutions often address one group's problems but neglect those of the other groups. Many solutions address longevity risk by offering life annuities. Annuities, however, offer nothing to the wealthy, given that these individuals are not exposed to longevity risk because their savings greatly surpass their rates of spending. And annuity solutions mock the precarious middle and the poor, whose meager savings render buying an annuity impractical or impossible.

An analysis of retirement transitions in four countries by economists Anna Madamba and Stephen Utkus indicated that some but not all groups face a retirement crisis. Moreover, their analysis suggested that the drumbeat of "retirement crisis" scares too many among the stable middle and the wealthy, likely subtracting from their well-being by pressing them into exaggerated worries, excessive saving, and inadequate spending.

In the United States, 59% of pre-retirees said they "believe there is a national retirement crisis," but only 10% said they "would describe [their] own retirement situation as a crisis." The corresponding percentages among retirees are even more striking: 54% believe there is a national retirement crisis, but only 4% describe their own retirement situation as a crisis. Findings among people in Canada, the United Kingdom, and Australia are generally similar to those in the United States.

In the United States, 66% of recent retirees described themselves as highly satisfied with their financial situation, and 53% of pre-retirees described themselves so. At the other end of the spectrum, 16% of recent retirees described themselves as poorly satisfied with their financial situation, and 21% of pre-retirees described themselves so. Here, too, findings among people in Canada, the United Kingdom, and Australia are generally similar to those in the United States.

A mandatory DC savings plan would do much for the high-spending segment of the precarious middle, by replacing weak self-control with strong outside control. But mandatory DC savings plans would be insufficient for the low-earning segment of the precarious middle and the poor, who have little or nothing from which to save. Financial security solutions for the precarious middle and poor require measures beyond nudges into saving.

## Conclusion

Standard life-cycle theory is the theory of standard finance, centered on the hypothesis that people want smooth spending during their entire life cycle and can do so easily, balancing spending and saving from life-cycle wealth. Behavioral life-cycle theory invokes behavioral finance, focusing on the hypothesis that even people who want smooth spending during their entire life cycle find it difficult to avoid cognitive and emotional errors and balance wants for spending now against wants for saving for tomorrow.

Behavioral life-cycle theory says that we reconcile the conflict between our wants using devices such as framing, mental accounting, and self-control rules that prohibit dips into other than designated mental accounts. In contrast, standard life-cycle theory says that we have no need for framing, mental accounting, or self-control rules for resolving such conflicts. Evidence favors behavioral life-cycle theory.

Behavioral life-cycle theory also says that we derive expressive and emotional benefits from saving, not only from spending. We gain the expressive benefits of high social status when our savings amount to considerable wealth, and we gain a benefit from expressing ourselves as responsible people who care about the future, not only the present. And the emotional benefits we gain from saving include pride and peace of mind. Yet for many the habit of saving becomes a compulsion, turning savers into misers. Investment professionals serve their clients well by helping them to calibrate saving and spending throughout their lives, so clients find utilitarian, expressive, and emotional benefits in both saving and spending, neither running out of money before running out of life nor running out of life before running out of money.

# 8. Behavioral Asset Pricing

Consider the example of economists being asked to develop an "asset pricing model" of watches. The watch asset pricing model will account for differences in the prices of watches, ranging from less than $10 to more than $1 million.

The economists would begin by identifying characteristics that can potentially account for differences between watch prices. These include watch buyers' wants for the full range of watch benefits and costs—utilitarian, expressive, and emotional. The utilitarian benefits of watches include accuracy and reliability, the expressive benefits include display of high social status and discerning taste, and the emotional benefits include pride and enjoyment of aesthetics. A $35,000 watch has the same utilitarian benefits as a $60 watch, which is likely as accurate and reliable, but we are not surprised by the wide range of watch prices. We know that the expressive and emotional benefits of some watches are greater than others, as is true for restaurant meals with equal utilitarian nutrition and cars with equal utilitarian ability to take us from home to work and back.

Scott Feinstein, a financial adviser to young athletes and actors, sets outside-control boundaries when clients with insufficient self-control are tempted by expressive and emotional benefits. One client called to say that he wanted to buy a $35,000 watch. "What time does it say?" asked Feinstein. "Ten minutes after three," answered the client. "Mine says ten after three too, and it cost me 60 bucks," said Feinstein. "Put the watch down." The client said that his adviser "really knew how to ruin a good time."[294]

Behavioral asset pricing theory, which I outlined in a 1999 article,[295] draws on economist Kelvin Lancaster's 1966 article "A New Approach to Consumer Theory."[296] Lancaster shifted his focus from products to their characteristics. We derive benefits from a meal, he wrote, as it "possesses nutritional characteristics but it also possesses aesthetic characteristics, and different meals will possess these characteristics in different relative proportions" (p. 133). The same feature, such as aesthetics, may be included in many products "so that goods which are apparently unrelated in certain of their characteristics may

---

[294]Warren St. John, "Making Sure Hollywood's Nouveau Riche Stay Riche," *New York Times* (22 August 2004). www.nytimes.com/2004/08/22/fashion/22SPEN.html.

[295]Meir Statman, "Behavioral Finance: Past Battles and Future Engagements," *Financial Analysts Journal* 55, no. 6 (November 1999): 18–27.

[296]Kelvin J. Lancaster, "A New Approach to Consumer Theory," *Journal of Political Economy* 74, no. 2 (April 1966): 132–57.

be related in others" (p. 133).[297] The utilitarian benefits of a gift in the form of a luxury watch to a high school graduate do not substitute for the utilitarian benefits of a gift in the form of a deposit into her college saving account. But the two gifts substitute for each other in expressing the good wishes of a grandfather to his granddaughter and the emotion of love.

Investments are like watches, meals, and cars, and so are their investment asset pricing models. Behavioral investment asset pricing models include all the benefits and costs of investments—utilitarian, expressive, and emotional—and also cognitive and emotional errors. In contrast, standard investment asset pricing models include utilitarian benefits and costs but exclude expressive and emotional benefits and costs and also cognitive and emotional errors.

Indeed, it is odd that the promoters of standard investment asset pricing models insist on investment risk as the only characteristic in their models, because risk incorporates not only utilitarian costs but also expressive and emotional benefits and costs and cognitive and emotional errors. Think of the emotional benefits of risk as thrills, whether in fast driving or day trading. Think of the expressive benefits of risk as a display of courage, rejecting timidity. Think of the utilitarian, expressive, and emotional benefits and costs of buying lottery tickets or lottery stocks. Think of the cognitive and emotional errors of risk perceived as volatility and the fear, described as risk, that urges investors to sell stocks in a stock market crash.

We can present the association between the characteristics of a watch and its expected price in a watch asset pricing model as follows:

The expected price of a watch is a function of

1. wants for utilitarian benefits of high accuracy and great reliability,

2. wants for expressive and emotional benefits of high social status and aesthetics, and

3. cognitive and emotional errors, such as inferring watch quality from its price.

Similarly, we can present the association between the characteristics of an investment and its expected price or expected return in an investment asset pricing model as follows:

The expected return of an investment asset is a function of

1. wants for utilitarian benefits, such as low risk,

---

[297]Meir Statman, "Behavioral Finance: Finance with Normal People," *Borsa Istanbul Review* 14, no. 2 (June 2014): 65–73.

2. wants for expressive and emotional benefits, such as staying true to values by holding socially responsible funds, acquiring high social status by investing in hedge funds, or enjoying thrills by stock trading, and

3. cognitive and emotional errors, such as a belief that stocks of "good" companies are "good" stocks and overreaction by fear following an airplane crash.

## Arbitrage in Watch Markets and Investment Asset Markets

Some watch buyers and some investors are "normal-ignorant," susceptible to cognitive and emotional errors. Others are "normal-knowledgeable," able to overcome cognitive and emotional errors but sometimes willing to accept lower utilitarian benefits for expressive and emotional benefits that matter to them. Yet others are rational, immune to cognitive and emotional errors and concerned only with utilitarian benefits and costs. Rational and knowledgeable watch buyers can potentially nullify by arbitrage the effects of ignorant watch buyers on watch prices, and rational and knowledgeable investors can potentially nullify by arbitrage the effects of ignorant investors on investment asset prices.

Consider arbitrage in luxury watch markets. Arbitrage can be performed by producers of inexpensive watches who manufacture counterfeit luxury watches that look like genuine luxury watches but are priced at small fractions of the genuine watches' prices. Indeed, such practice is widespread.

Counterfeit luxury watches offer most of the utilitarian benefits of genuine ones. They are likely as accurate, and even if not as reliable, buyers can replace faulty counterfeit luxury watches many times before their total price comes near the price of one genuine luxury watch. Moreover, unlike buyers of genuine luxury watches, buyers of counterfeit luxury watches do not bear the utilitarian cost of insuring expensive watches and the emotional cost that inhibits them from wearing their luxury watches for fear of losing or being robbed of them.

The combined force of arbitrage by producers of counterfeit luxury watches and their buyers can possibly force producers of genuine luxury watches to reduce their prices to levels not much higher than those of counterfeit ones.

Yet arbitrage is not likely to be fully effective at lowering prices of genuine luxury watches, for two reasons. First, producers of genuine luxury watches police their markets with the help of law enforcement personnel. For example, they alert Amazon and eBay to the presence of counterfeit watches on their websites, preventing their sale. Second, counterfeit products impose expressive and emotional costs on buyers, making them feel like cheats.[298] Normal-knowledgeable potential buyers might be unwilling to bear the expressive and emotional costs of feeling like cheats, even in the presence of lower utilitarian costs. These two reasons allow luxury watch manufacturers to keep their prices high, leaving the market of counterfeit luxury watches to buyers who would not buy genuine luxury watches in any event.

As we consider arbitrage in investment markets, we note that most arbitrage opportunities are not risk free, where we can buy an investment and simultaneously sell it at a higher price. Risky arbitrage entails substantial risks, deterring arbitrage and its potential effect on prices.[299]

The notorious case of Long-Term Capital Management (LTCM) illustrates risks in arbitrage and the possibilities of disastrous consequences. LTCM was a hedge fund management firm that used arbitrage trading strategies combined with high financial leverage. LTCM would identify pairs of investments, such as a pair of bonds, whose returns were highly correlated, where they estimated the value of one bond as high relative to its price and the value of the other as low relative to its price. LTCM would form arbitrage positions by buying the first and selling short the second, expecting the disparities between prices and values to narrow, thereby profiting. But when the 1997 Asian financial crisis and the 1998 Russian financial crisis occurred, the disparities widened rather than narrowed, and LTCM did not have the money necessary to wait until the disparities narrowed (which they eventually did). LTCM was bailed out by banks in 1998 and dissolved in 2000. Risks of the kind that devastated LTCM usually dissuade arbitrageurs from devoting many resources to arbitrage, thereby limiting its potential effects on prices.[300]

Capital constraints are structural impediments to arbitrage, illustrated by events in the National Stock Exchange of India. Stock prices declined substantially within 15 minutes during two stock market crashes between April and June 2006. Buying by capital-constrained traders was not sufficient,

---

[298]Francesca Gino, Michael I. Norton, and Dan Ariely, "The Counterfeit Self: The Deceptive Costs of Faking It," *Psychological Science* 21, no. 5 (March 2010): 712–20, https://doi.org/10.1177/0956797610366545.

[299]Andrei Shleifer and Robert W. Vishny, "The Limits of Arbitrage," *Journal of Finance* 52, no. 1 (March 1997): 35–55.

[300]Philippe Jorion, "Risk Management Lessons from Long-Term Capital Management," *European Financial Management* 6, no. 3 (September 2000): 277–300.

however, to halt these price declines, and domestic mutual funds were slow to buy.[301]

Inability to buy shares to cover a short position is another structural impediment to arbitrage. At the height of the global financial crisis on Monday, 27 October 2008, the stock price of Volkswagen (VW) started skyrocketing and surged past EUR1,005 per share on Tuesday, 28 October 2008, from a close on the previous Friday of EUR210 per share. As a result, VW briefly became the most valuable listed company in the world by market capitalization. Franklin Allen, Marleen Haas, Eric Nowak, and Angel Tengulov showed that this price increase was the result of a press release that Porsche SE made on 26 October 2008, in which the company announced its plan to take over Volkswagen.[302]

The announcement inflicted enormous damage on investors who held short positions in VW's stock. Porsche had previously entered into option contracts with an investment bank to lock in an acquisition price for VW's shares. The investment bank, in turn, hedged its position by purchasing derivative contracts on VW shares through other banks. These other banks held VW's shares as a hedge, which implied that the free float of VW's shares was diminished significantly. Therefore, it became increasingly difficult for short sellers to acquire VW shares to cover their short positions when the share price started rising after Porsche's announcement.

This, in turn, exerted increasing price pressure on VW's stock and resulted in more than EUR20 billion losses for investors that had entered into these short-sale trades.[303]

Wants for expressive and emotional benefits and cognitive and emotional errors can affect investment asset prices and expected returns when arbitrage is impeded. For example, wants for staying true to values affect investment asset prices and returns. One study found that shari'a-compliant Malaysian bonds yielded lower returns than noncompliant bonds. Buyers of shari'a-compliant bonds sacrificed the utilitarian benefits of maximum bond returns but

---

[301]Mila Getmansky Sherman, Ravi Jagannathan, Loriana Pelizzon, Ernst Schaumburg, and Darya Yuferova, "Stock Price Crashes: Role of Slow-Moving Capital," SAFE Working Paper No. 227 (16 July 2018). Available at SSRN: https://ssrn.com/abstract=3239440 or http://dx.doi.org/10.2139/ssrn.3239440.

[302]Franklin Allen, Marlene Haas, Eric Nowak, and Angel Tengulov, "Market Efficiency and Limits to Arbitrage: Evidence from the Volkswagen Short Squeeze," Swiss Finance Institute Research Paper No. 17-64 (14 April 2019). Available at SSRN: https://ssrn.com/abstract=2977019 or http://dx.doi.org/10.2139/ssrn.2977019.

[303]Allen et al., "Market Efficiency."

gained the expressive and emotional benefits of staying true to their values, and their wants affected bond prices and returns.[304]

## Theoretical and Empirical Asset Pricing Models

Asset pricing models can be categorized as theoretical or empirical in nature. Theoretical investment asset pricing models begin with reasons why characteristics of investment assets should be associated with their prices or expected returns. For example, the capital asset pricing model (CAPM), a theoretical model, begins with the rationale that investors prefer investments with low risk over ones with high risk and act under the assumption that the supposed association between the risk of investment assets and their prices or returns is true. One can then investigate empirically whether this is an accurate representation of reality.

Empirical asset pricing models begin with empirical evidence about associations between characteristics of investment assets and their prices or returns. For example, the empirical three-factor investment asset pricing model begins with the observation that small-capitalization stocks had higher returns than large-capitalization stocks and value stocks had higher returns than growth stocks over a long historical period, and it continues by asserting that the relationship is likely to persist in the future. One can then consider possible theoretical rationales for the observed associations.

Differences between rationales are at the center of differences between standard and behavioral investment asset pricing models, whether theoretical or empirical. Rationales in standard investment asset pricing models account only for wants for utilitarian benefits and avoidance of their costs, whereas rationales in behavioral asset pricing models account also for wants for expressive and emotional benefits and avoidance of their costs, as well as susceptibility to cognitive and emotional errors.

The CAPM predicts that differences between the expected returns of any two investment assets come only from differences between their risks, specifically that part of risk that is correlated with overall (cap-weighted) market movements as measured by beta. Yet much empirical evidence about realized returns varies from that prediction, showing abnormal returns when measured by the CAPM. Studies from the 1970s and 1980s found that stocks of companies with low ratios of prices to earnings had higher subsequent realized returns than predicted by the CAPM. The same was found among stocks of companies with small market capitalizations, stocks of companies with low

---

[304]Emily Shafron, "Investor Tastes: Implications for Asset Pricing in the Public Debt Market," *Journal of Corporate Finance* 55 (April 2019): 6–27.

ratios of prices to book values, and stocks of companies with low Tobin's $q$ (price to replacement cost).[305]

The empirical challenges to the CAPM persuaded Eugene Fama and Kenneth French to introduce their empirical three-factor investment asset pricing model in 1992.[306] Fama and French started with the known empirical associations between stock returns and the small–large factor, measured by the difference between the returns of small- and large-capitalization stocks, and the value–growth factor, measured by the difference between the returns of value and growth stocks. They proceeded to argue that the small–large and value–growth factor betas measure the risk of investment assets better than the single-factor or market beta used in the CAPM.

The most recent investment asset pricing model set forth by Fama and French is a five-factor model, adding two factors identified by empirical evidence to the original three in the three-factor model.[307] The robust–weak factor is the difference in returns between a portfolio of stocks of the most profitable companies and a portfolio of stocks of the least profitable companies, and the conservative–aggressive factor is the difference in returns between a portfolio of stocks of companies that invest conservatively and a portfolio of stocks of companies that invest aggressively. Yet empirical evidence about factors cannot substitute for theoretical rationales for them when constructing investment asset pricing models. It is possible, in the absence of a theoretical explanation or reason, that the observed factors are statistical artifacts or one-time occurrences.

Consider once again a watch pricing model. Theoretical rationales exist for associations between watch prices and such characteristics as quality of materials and workmanship and such "complications" as perpetual calendars and moon phases. But what can the rationale be for the higher prices of watches made in Switzerland? It might be the role of the label "Made in Switzerland" as a proxy for utilitarian benefits, such as those provided by

---

[305]Sanjoy Basu, "Investment Performance of Common Stocks in Relation to Their Price-Earnings Ratios: A Test of the Efficient Market Hypothesis," *Journal of Finance* 32, no. 3 (June 1977): 663–82; Barr Rosenberg, Kenneth Reid, and Ronald Lanstein, "Persuasive Evidence of Market Inefficiency," *Journal of Portfolio Management* 11, no. 3 (Spring 1985): 9–16; Rolf W. Banz, "The Relationship Between Return and Market Value of Common Stocks," *Journal of Financial Economics* 9, no. 1 (March 1981): 3–18; Michael E. Solt and Meir Statman, "Good Companies, Bad Stocks," *Journal of Portfolio Management* 15, no. 4 (Summer 1989): 39–44.
[306]Eugene F. Fama and Kenneth R. French, "The Cross-Section of Expected Stock Returns," *Journal of Finance* 47, no. 2 (June 1992): 427–65.
[307]Eugene F. Fama and Kenneth R. French, "A Five-Factor Asset Pricing Model," *Journal of Financial Economics* 116, no. 1 (April 2015): 1–22.

reliability, or its role as a carrier of expressive and emotional benefits, whereby watches made in Switzerland confer higher social status than watches made elsewhere. We can possibly find tests that would distinguish one rationale from another. Meanwhile, we might include country of origin in the watch pricing model while we study its theoretical rationale.

Turning to investment asset pricing models, consider the perverse empirical association between returns, market (single-factor) betas, and the variance of returns. US stocks with high variance of returns and high betas have yielded substantially *lower* returns than stocks with low variance of returns and low betas. One possible theoretical rationale combines individual investors' preference for risk, reflected in purchasing lottery tickets, with institutional investors' mandates that proscribe leverage and thus force portfolio managers to buy higher-beta stocks (instead of leveraging the portfolio) if they want to take more risk.[308] This pushes the prices of high-beta stocks up and their future returns down relative to low-beta stocks.

## Standard and Behavioral Rationales

We know from empirical studies that small-capitalization stocks had higher returns than large-capitalization stocks over long periods and that value stocks had higher returns than growth stocks. But why? What theoretical rationales underlie these empirical associations? Are they standard rationales or behavioral ones? Two streams of my research, one with Hersh Shefrin and the other with economist Deniz Anginer and investment manager Kenneth Fisher, explored five hypotheses about theoretical rationales that underlie these empirical associations, illustrating how inquiries in standard finance and behavioral finance differ. The first two rationales are standard, and the last three are behavioral.[309]

1. Data mining hypothesis: The empirical associations come from "data mining" among an unlimited number of possible factors, including the small–large and value–growth factors.

---

[308]Malcolm P. Baker, Jeffrey Wurgler, and Brendan Bradley, "A Behavioral Finance Explanation for the Success of Low Volatility Portfolios," NYU Working Paper No. 2451/29537 (January 2010). Available at SSRN: http://ssrn.com/abstract=2284643.

[309]Meir Statman, "Investor Sentiment, Stock Characteristics, and Returns," *Journal of Portfolio Management* 37, no. 3 (Spring 2011): 54–61; Meir Statman, Kenneth L. Fisher, and Deniz Anginer, "Affect in a Behavioral Asset Pricing Model," *Financial Analysts Journal* 64, no. 2 (March/April 2008): 20–29; Hersh Shefrin, *A Behavioral Approach to Asset Pricing*, Second Edition (Burlington, MA: Elsevier Academic Press, 2008); Hersh Shefrin and Meir Statman, "The Style of Investor Expectations," in *The Handbook of Equity Style Management*, 3rd ed., edited by T. Daniel Coggin and Frank J. Fabozzi, 195–218 (New York: Wiley, 2003).

2. Risk hypothesis: The empirical associations come from the role of the small–large and value–growth factors as indicators of risk, whereby the risk of stocks of small and value companies is higher than the risk of stocks of large and growth companies.

3. Cognitive-errors hypothesis: The empirical associations come from cognitive errors, such as representativeness, whereby investors incorrectly extrapolate high past returns, sales, earnings, and other measures into the future.

4. Emotional-errors hypothesis: The empirical associations come from emotional errors, such as the misleading positive affect of admired companies and the equally misleading negative affect of disliked companies.

5. Wants for expressive and emotional benefits hypothesis: The empirical associations come from wants for high expressive and emotional benefits.

**1. Data Mining Hypothesis.** Fischer Black wrote that it is difficult to overcome the problem of data mining because data on realized returns are limited and noisy, adding, "I don't know how to begin designing tests that escape the data-mining trap" (p. 11).[310]

One way to escape the data mining trap is to examine out-of-sample data from periods before or after the period from which factors were identified. This is what economists Juhani Linnainmaa and Michael Roberts did in their exploration of the history of the cross section of stock returns.[311] Examining factors out of sample, they found that most factors identified earlier are, in fact, nothing more than outcomes of data mining. In particular, they found that the abnormal returns associated with the investment aggressiveness and profitability (robustness) factors that Fama and French used to turn their three-factor model into their five-factor model are largely absent in out-of-sample data. These two factors always lacked theoretical foundation, and Linnainmaa and Roberts found that they also lack empirical foundation.

An alternative route to escape the data mining trap is by examining investors' *expectations of returns* in addition to examining *realized returns*. This is what Hersh Shefrin and I did.[312] Think of a survey in which investors are given only names of companies and their industries and are asked for their expectations of the future returns of these companies' stocks. This, in essence, is one part of the *Fortune* surveys of company reputations by attributes,

---

[310]Fischer Black, "Beta and Return," *Journal of Portfolio Management* 20, no. 1 (Fall 1993): 8–18.

[311]Juhani T. Linnainmaa and Michael R. Roberts, "The History of the Cross-Section of Stock Returns," *Review of Financial Studies* 31, no. 7 (July 2018): 2606–49.

[312]Shefrin and Statman, "The Style of Investment Expectation."

conducted annually since 1983. The attribute of long-term investment value is a proxy for expectations of the returns of companies' stocks.[313]

The data mining hypothesis is the claim that there is no true association between expectations of stock returns and book-to-market ratios, which distinguish value stocks from growth ones, or market capitalization, which distinguishes small stocks from large ones. It is also the claim that the strong empirical associations between realized returns and price-to-book ratios and market capitalizations are accidental, the outcome of data mining. If these claims are true, we should find weak associations, at best, between expectations of stock returns and book-to-market ratios and market capitalizations.

This, however, is not what we find. A regression of expectations of stock returns on book-to-market ratios, market capitalizations, and market (single-factor) betas shows statistically significant associations between expectations of stock returns and book-to-market ratios and market capitalizations. This finding is not consistent with the data mining hypothesis, which predicts weak associations at best.

**2. Risk Hypothesis.** If expectations about returns conform to risk as defined by the CAPM, we should find strong associations between expectations of returns and market betas but no associations between expectations of returns and book-to-market ratios and market capitalization. This, however, is not what we find. Instead, we find no association between expectations of returns and market betas and, as noted earlier, strong associations between expectations of returns and book-to-market ratios and market capitalizations. Therefore, if differences in expectations of returns are due to differences in risk, that risk is not indicated by market beta as predicted by the CAPM.

Fama and French argued that high book-to-market ratios and low market capitalizations in the three-factor model indicate high risk. If true, we should find that expectations of returns are high for value stocks, which have high book-to-market ratios, and low for large stocks, which have large market capitalizations. Yet we find that expectations of returns are *low* for stocks with high book-to-market ratios and *high* for stocks with large market capitalizations. Therefore, if differences in expectations of returns are due to differences in risk, that risk is not indicated by high book-to-market ratios or small market capitalizations, as in Fama and French's notion of risk in the three-factor model.

**3. Cognitive-Errors Hypothesis.** The cognitive-errors hypothesis in this case is better called the "characteristics hypothesis" because it claims that

---

[313]Clark, Martire & Bartolomeo, the marketing and opinion research firm that conducted the *Fortune* surveys, stated that this attribute stands for expectations of the future return of the company's stock.

investors consider but misinterpret characteristics, such as by observing the characteristic of value—a high book-to-market ratio—and misinterpreting it as an indication of low, rather than high, expected stock returns.

To examine the characteristics hypothesis, I conducted an experiment in which high-net-worth investors completed a questionnaire that provided only characteristics of companies and their stocks, not their names or industries. The three characteristics were price-to-book ratio, market capitalization, and past stock returns. The last characteristic is associated with the momentum factor. The price-to-book ratio was used rather than its book-to-market inverse because it is more familiar to investors. Characteristics scores that combine the three characteristics are mean scores by the surveyed investors.

If investors consider characteristics as they estimate expected future returns, we should find strong associations between characteristics scores and expectations of returns. But this is not what we find. Instead, we find weak associations, indicating weak support, at best, for the cognitive errors hypothesis.[314]

**4. Emotional-Errors Hypothesis.** The emotional-errors hypothesis is the claim that affect creates halos over companies and their stocks, misleading investors into the belief that stocks of admired companies, those with positive affect, offer higher expected returns and lower risk than stocks of companies with negative affect. Indeed, the opposite is true. In a study I carried out, stocks of admired companies yielded *lower* returns than stocks of disliked companies. In other words, stocks of good companies are, on average, bad stocks. This finding is consistent with the emotional-errors hypothesis.[315]

Other studies provide further support for the emotional-errors hypothesis. In one study, two groups looked at a list of 30 countries. One group was asked for its expectations of the future return of the stock index of each country, whereas the other was asked for its assessment of the risk of the stock index of each country. The risk hypothesis predicts that expectations of high returns would be accompanied by assessments of high risk, but this is not what was found. Instead, countries where future returns were expected to be high were also countries where the risk of stocks was assessed as *low*.[316] Similar evidence comes from experiments with students and investment professionals.[317]

---

[314]Statman, "Investor Sentiment."

[315]Statman, "Investor Sentiment."

[316]Yoav Ganzach, "Judging Risk and Return of Financial Assets," *Organizational Behavior and Human Decision Processes* 83, no. 2 (November 2000): 353–70.

[317]Hersh Shefrin, "Do Investors Expect Higher Returns from Safer Stocks Than from Riskier Stocks? *Journal of Psychology & Financial Markets* 2, no. 4 (2001): 176–81.

**5. Wants for Expressive and Emotional Benefits Hypothesis.** The wants hypothesis is the claim that the empirical associations between stock returns, book-to-market ratios, and market capitalizations is due to investors' desire for the expressive and emotional benefits of stocks of admired companies. Those tend to be large growth companies, with large capitalization and low book-to-market ratios.

Wants are not always easy to distinguish from errors because some wants are implicit and we are reluctant to admit them to others or even to ourselves. Admitting our wants for socially responsible investing is easy and, therefore, likely explicit. Admitting our wants for high social status—or just the feel-good effect of investing in a high-quality company that makes great products—is difficult and, therefore, likely implicit.

Yet, as noted earlier, investors conclude nothing about expected returns from the characteristics of market capitalizations and book-to-market ratios. This finding is not consistent with the characteristics version of the cognitive-errors hypothesis, but it is consistent with the emotional-errors and wants hypotheses.

Further evidence consistent with the emotional-errors and wants hypotheses comes from a study that identified very few active mutual funds with high book-to-market ratios, among all active funds, whereas it identified many low book-to-market ratios. Indeed, most funds describing themselves as value funds hold a higher proportion of their portfolios in stocks with low book-to-market ratios—growth stocks—than in high book-to-market stocks—value stocks. The characteristics distributions of exchange-traded funds (ETFs) and hedge funds are similar to those of mutual funds.[318]

In sum, the evidence favors the emotional-errors and wants hypotheses over the data mining, risk, and cognitive-errors hypotheses in explaining the empirical association between stock returns, book-to-market ratios, and market capitalizations.

## Fleeting and Sustained Factors in Asset Pricing Models

Associations between factors and investment asset prices in standard and behavioral investment asset pricing models can change over time. A factor may have a place in an investment asset pricing model at one time but not necessarily at another time.

---

[318]Martin Lettau, Sydney C. Ludvigson, and Paulo Manoel, "Characteristics of Mutual Fund Portfolios: Where Are the Value Funds?" National Bureau of Economic Research Working Paper No. w25381 (December 2018). Available at SSRN: https://ssrn.com/abstract=3306086.

The story of watch prices offers an example. Watches have been manufactured for more than three centuries, and utilitarian benefits were at the center of the watch pricing model. These benefits include accuracy and reliability. Horological historian David Christianson noted that England and Switzerland each produced 200,000 watches in 1800, but by 1850, the Swiss were producing 2,200,000 watches, whereas the British did not increase their production. "The Swiss were able to produce 'fake watches' that looked like English or French watches but were of lower quality," he said.[319]

Competition from Japanese companies and the introduction of digital watches in the 1970s seemed to signal the end of Swiss watch manufacturing. Indeed, many Swiss watch factories closed. Swiss watch manufacturing was saved, however, by adding expressive and emotional benefits to the utilitarian benefits of watches. The Swiss restyled watches as luxuries, with high prices signifying high social status.[320]

Jean-Marie Brucker is training salespeople in the craft of selling luxury watches. "We sell luxury," he says, "It's an emotion." Brucker urges salespeople to sell "romance" rather than "products." He recommends the "macaron technique" for selling watches, named after the sandwich-like French pastry, where the pesky price of the watch is sandwiched between its romantic benefits.[321]

Associations between factors and returns in standard and behavioral asset pricing models range in duration from fleeting to sustained. A fleeting association is eliminated in a short amount of time. A sustained association remains for long periods and is not eliminated even if known. We know that stocks are riskier than bonds and yielded higher returns over periods as long as centuries. We are reasonable in claiming that the factor of risk explains the difference in returns, so this factor is a sustained one.

Economists David McLean and Jeffrey Pontiff explored the sustainability of 82 factors identified by empirical evidence. Their list includes the well-known factors of small–large, value–growth, and momentum, as well as many lesser-known characteristics, such as levels of stock prices and maximum daily return during a month. They explored returns during (1) the period studied in a working paper identifying a factor, (2) the period following the posting of

---

[319]Victoria Gomelsky, "How Switzerland Came to Dominate Watchmaking," *New York Times* (20 November 2014). www.nytimes.com/2014/11/21/style/international/what-enabled-switzerland-to-dominate-watchmaking.html.

[320]Gomelsky, "How Switzerland Came to Dominate Watchmaking."

[321]Christina Binkley, "How to Sell a $35,000 Watch in a Recession: Salespeople Study Distracting the Wife, Avoiding Talk of 'Price' and Other Tactics," *Wall Street Journal* (23 July 2009). www.wsj.com/articles/SB10001424052970203517304574304322707126380.

that working paper but preceding publication in a journal, and (3) the period following publication.[322]

If the association between a factor and future returns disappears subsequent to the study period with no evidence of arbitrage, we can conclude that the observed association reflects nothing more than data mining. If the association disappears with evidence of arbitrage, we can conclude that the association was real but fleeting, perhaps reflecting wants or cognitive and emotional errors of some investors but eliminated by arbitrage. If the association does not disappear despite evidence of arbitrage, we can conclude that the association is sustained, reflecting wants or cognitive and emotional errors of some investors that were not eliminated by arbitrage.

McLean and Pontiff found that abnormal returns associated with a factor usually decline subsequent to availability of information about the factor in working papers. Abnormal returns decline further once working papers are published in journals.

It is often hard to tell whether an association between a factor and returns is fleeting or sustained. Fama and French noted that the average monthly difference between stock returns and one-month T-bill returns is substantial, and so are the average differences between the returns of value stocks and growth stocks and between the returns of small stocks and large stocks. Yet even if associations between returns and the factors of value–growth and small–large are sustained, they are not necessarily evident in the three- or five-year periods commonly used to evaluate investment performance. There are high probabilities that the returns of growth stocks would exceed those of value stocks and the returns of large stocks would exceed those of small stocks over periods of three or five years. And there are nontrivial probabilities of these occurrences over 10 or 20 years.[323]

## Behavioral Investment Asset Pricing Models

Behavioral investment asset pricing models, like standard investment asset pricing models, begin with theoretical rationales for factors and characteristics or else identify factors and characteristics empirically and then strive to identify theoretical rationales for them.

Behavioral investment asset pricing models differ, however, in the breadth of the theoretical rationales. Theoretical rationales in behavioral investment asset pricing models encompass wants for utilitarian, expressive,

---

[322]R. David McLean and Jeffrey Pontiff, "Does Academic Research Destroy Stock Return Predictability?" *Journal of Finance* 71, no. 1 (February 2016): 5–32.
[323]Eugene F. Fama and Kenneth R. French, "Volatility Lessons," *Financial Analysts Journal* 74, no. 3 (July 2018): 42–53.

and emotional benefits and susceptibility to cognitive and emotional errors, whereas theoretical rationales in standard investment asset pricing models assume that investors' wants are limited to utilitarian benefits and that they are immune to cognitive and emotional errors.

The behavioral asset pricing model introduced by Hersh Shefrin and me in 1994 was motivated by the same challenges to the CAPM that motivated Fama and French to introduce their three-factor model. These include a weak association between realized stock returns and market betas and strong associations between realized stock returns and market capitalization and between realized stock returns and book-to-market ratios.[324]

The model uses a steering wheel metaphor whereby two kinds of traders act as drivers, "information drivers" and "noise drivers." The two kinds of drivers struggle to control a steering wheel that forms investment asset prices. Information drivers are rational drivers, free of cognitive errors, whereas noise drivers are normal drivers, susceptible to "sentiment" consisting of cognitive and emotional errors. The Shefrin–Statman model focuses on representativeness errors, which are cognitive errors whereby investors either extrapolate past returns into the future or expect their reversals.

Prices of investment assets equal their intrinsic values in markets where all drivers are information drivers. But prices deviate from intrinsic values in markets where some drivers are noise drivers who steer prices in directions corresponding to their sentiment and the forces of arbitrage are too weak to eliminate the drivers' effects on prices.

The Shefrin–Statman model resides within the first generation of behavioral finance, accounting for investors' cognitive and emotional errors. Behavioral investment asset pricing models in the second generation of behavioral finance, however, also account for investors' wants for expressive and emotional benefits, beyond utilitarian benefits.

We can illustrate behavioral investment asset pricing models by a "behaviorally augmented" asset pricing model that adds two social responsibility factors to the one-factor asset pricing model (CAPM), the three-factor asset pricing model, and the five-factor asset pricing model. I hasten to emphasize at the outset that these "behaviorally augmented" models are only illustrations of what behavioral asset pricing models would look like.

The first social responsibility factor, reflecting cognitive errors, is a "top–bottom" factor, consisting of the difference between the returns of stocks of companies ranked high and low on five social responsibility criteria. They are community (e.g., generous giving, support for housing), diversity (e.g.,

---

[324]Hersh Shefrin and Meir Statman, "Behavioral Capital Asset Pricing Theory," *Journal of Financial and Quantitative Analysis* 29, no. 3 (September 1994): 323–49.

promotion of women and minorities, outstanding family benefits), employee relations (e.g., strong union relations, cash profit sharing), environment (e.g., pollution prevention, recycling), and products (e.g., product quality and safety, provision of products for the economically disadvantaged).[325]

The association between employee satisfaction and stock returns is a case in point. A value-weighted portfolio of the "100 Best Companies to Work For in America" earned an annual abnormal return of 3.5% from 1984 to 2009 and 2.1% above industry benchmarks.[326] This statistic suggests that many investors commit cognitive errors, failing to fully value intangibles, such as employee satisfaction, and that arbitrage actions by investors free of cognitive errors are insufficient to nullify the effects on prices exerted by investors committing cognitive errors.

The second social responsibility factor, reflecting wants for expressive and emotional benefits, is an "accepted–shunned" factor, consisting of the difference between the returns of stocks of companies commonly accepted by socially responsible investors and the returns of company stocks commonly shunned by them because they conflict with their values, imposing expressive and emotional costs. These are companies in the alcohol, tobacco, gambling, firearms, military, and nuclear industries.

Investors are aware of trade-offs among wants. Some, but not all, are willing to trade utilitarian expected returns for the expressive and emotional benefits of avoiding stocks of shunned companies. The story of the Timothy Plan mutual funds is a case in point. The Timothy funds take their name from a letter written by the apostle Paul. They cater to conservative Christians. The flagship Timothy Plan Small Cap Value Fund performed poorly for several years, and many investors lost faith and abandoned it. "There were those that thought if they invested in Timothy they'd have top returns, the Lord would bless them," said Arthur Ally, the funds' founder. "When that didn't happen, some of them went to better-performing funds."[327]

The construction of the two social responsibility factors begins by calculating for each company, as of the end of each year, its top–bottom and accepted–shunned scores. These scores are matched with monthly stock returns in the subsequent 12 months. The "top" portfolio is a portfolio of

---

[325]Meir Statman and Denys Glushkov, "Classifying and Measuring the Performance of Socially Responsible Funds," *Journal of Portfolio Management* 42, no. 2 (Winter 2016): 140–51.

[326]Alex Edmans, "Does the Stock Market Fully Value Intangibles? Employee Satisfaction and Equity Prices," *Journal of Financial Economics* 101, no. 3 (2011): 621–40.

[327]Danny Hakim, "On Wall St., More Investors Push Social Goals," *New York Times* (11 February 2001). www.nytimes.com/2001/02/11/business/on-wall-st-more-investors-push-social-goals.html.

stocks of companies rated in the top third by the five social responsibility criteria—community, diversity, employee relations, environment, and products. The "bottom" portfolio is a portfolio of stocks of companies rated in the bottom third by the five social responsibility criteria. The top–bottom factor is the difference between the monthly returns of the two portfolios.

Similarly, the "accepted" portfolio is a portfolio of stocks of accepted companies, and the "shunned" portfolio is a portfolio of stocks of shunned companies—those in the alcohol, tobacco, gambling, firearms, military, and nuclear industries. The accepted–shunned factor is the difference between the monthly returns of the two portfolios.

The two social responsibility factors are added as Factors 2 and 3, in a "behaviorally augmented" CAPM, Factors 4 and 5 in a "behaviorally augmented" three-factor asset pricing model, and Factors 6 and 7 in a "behaviorally augmented" five-factor asset pricing model that includes the factors of market, small–large, value–growth, robust–weak, and conservative–aggressive.

**Exhibit 8.1** presents a side-by-side comparison of the Vanguard FTSE Social Index Fund, the Vice Fund, and the Vanguard 500 Index Fund using models that include the two added social responsibility factors. The Vanguard FTSE Social Index Fund "seeks to track the investment performance of the FTSE4Good US Select Index—a benchmark of large- and mid-capitalization stocks that are screened based on social criteria such as workplace issues, environmental issues, product safety, human rights, and corporate responsibility."[328] The Vice Fund "invests in strong businesses with significant barriers to entry which should result in more predictable market correlations. We believe that fundamentally sound equities of alcohol, tobacco, gaming, and defense companies offer these characteristics to investors and deliver results that are less dependent upon the economic climate."[329]

The positive and statistically significant 0.20 coefficient of the accepted–shunned factor of the Vanguard FTSE Social Index Fund in the augmented five-factor model indicates that its selection of stocks tilts toward those of accepted companies, away from stocks of shunned companies. This finding is as expected from a socially responsible fund. In contrast, the negative and statistically significant −0.46 coefficient of the accepted–shunned factor of the Vice Fund indicates that its selection of stocks tilts toward stocks of shunned companies, away from stocks of accepted companies. The accepted–shunned coefficient of the Vanguard 500 Index Fund is not statistically significant, showing no significant tilt toward or away from stocks of shunned companies.

---

[328]https://institutional.vanguard.com/web/cf/product-details/fund/0213.
[329]https://usamutuals.com/vice-fund/.

**Exhibit 8.1. Comparison of the Vanguard FTSE Social Index Fund and Vice Fund to the Vanguard 500 Index Fund by "Behaviorally Augmented" Asset Pricing Models That Include the Two Social Responsibility Factors, 2002–2012**

| | Vanguard 500 Index Fund | Vanguard FTSE Social Index Fund | Vice Fund |
|---|---|---|---|
| *A. "Behaviorally augmented" CAPM* | | | |
| Alpha (annualized) | −0.86% | −2.74% | 1.77% |
| Beta of market factor | 0.98 | 1.10 | 0.87 |
| Top–bottom beta | 0.02 | 0.06 | −0.04 |
| Accepted–shunned beta | −0.08*** | 0.13** | −0.33** |
| *B. "Behaviorally augmented" three-factor model* | | | |
| Alpha (annualized) | −0.30% | −2.13% | 1.00% |
| Beta of market factor | 1.01 | 1.11 | 0.86 |
| Beta of small–large factor | −0.15*** | −0.12*** | 0.16 |
| Beta of value–growth factor | 0.03*** | 0.15*** | −0.17* |
| Top–bottom beta | 0.02** | 0.08** | −0.06 |
| Accepted–shunned beta | −0.01 | 0.22*** | −0.45*** |
| *C. "Behaviorally augmented" five-factor model* | | | |
| Alpha (annualized) | −0.47% | −1.49% | 0.98% |
| Market factor beta | 1.02 | 1.08 | 0.88 |
| Small–large beta | −0.15*** | −0.13*** | 0.22** |
| Value–growth beta | 0.03*** | 0.17*** | −0.07 |
| Robust–weak beta | 0.03*** | −0.11* | 0.03 |
| Conservative–aggressive beta | 0.03*** | −0.11 | −0.55*** |
| Top–bottom beta | 0.02** | 0.08** | 0.04 |
| Accepted–shunned beta | −0.01 | 0.20*** | −0.46*** |

*Statistically significant at the 0.10 level.
**Statistically significant at the 0.05 level.
***Statistically significant at the 0.01 level.

The positive and statistically significant 0.08 coefficient of the top–bottom factor of the Vanguard FTSE Social Index Fund in the augmented five-factor model indicates that its selection of stocks tilts away from bottom companies toward top companies—companies that rank at the top by the five criteria of community, diversity, employee relations, environment, and products. The 0.02 top–bottom coefficient of the Vanguard 500 Index

Fund is positive and statistically significant, though smaller than that of the Vanguard FTSE Social Index Fund. The 0.04 top–bottom coefficient of the Vice Fund is positive but not statistically significant.

Note that the Vice Fund outperformed the other funds significantly during the period. This finding is unsurprising given the sacrifice of return that socially responsible investors are willing to make for the emotional or expressive benefits they gain by staying true to their values.[330]

## Conclusion

Behavioral asset pricing models, like standard asset pricing models, are factor or characteristic models that either begin with theoretical rationales for factors and characteristics or strive to identify theoretical rationales for factors and characteristics found empirically. Behavioral asset pricing models and standard asset pricing models differ in the breadth of theoretical rationales. Theoretical rationales in behavioral asset pricing models encompass wants for utilitarian, expressive, and emotional benefits and the presence of cognitive and emotional errors, whereas theoretical rationales in standard asset pricing models are limited to wants for utilitarian benefits—mainly low risk and high expected returns—and feature an absence of cognitive and emotional errors.

Behavioral investment asset pricing models, like their standard counterparts, are works in progress, as one can see from two observations. First, the list of factors has grown as from one in the CAPM to three in the three-factor model and five in the five-factor model. Second, the identification of the theoretical rationales for factors is incomplete. The theoretical rationale for the small–large and value–growth factors might be wants for the utilitarian benefits of low risk, as in standard investment asset pricing models, or wants for expressive and emotional benefits and pitfalls of cognitive and emotional errors, as in behavioral investment asset pricing models.

---

[330]Harrison Hong and Marcin Kacperczyk, "The Price of Sin: The Effects of Social Norms on Markets," *Journal of Financial Economics* 93, no. 1 (2009): 15–36; Meir Statman and Denys Glushkov, "The Wages of Social Responsibility," *Financial Analysts Journal* 65, no. 4 (2009): 33–46.

# 9. Behavioral Efficient Markets

The efficient market hypothesis is at the center of standard finance, and as I discussed in *Finance for Normal People*, many believe that behavioral finance refutes it. Indeed, many believe that refutation of the efficient market hypothesis is the most important contribution of behavioral finance. This issue becomes confused, however, when discussants fail to distinguish between two versions of efficient markets and their corresponding efficient market hypotheses—the *price-equals-value efficient market hypothesis* and the *hard-to-beat efficient market hypothesis*. And it remains a mystery why so many investors believe that markets are easy to beat.

Both standard finance and behavioral finance provide evidence refuting the price-equals-value efficient market hypothesis, but their evidence generally supports the hard-to-beat efficient market hypothesis. Behavioral finance also explains why so many investors believe that markets are easy to beat when, in fact, they are hard to beat.

Price-equals-value efficient markets are markets where investment prices always equal their intrinsic values, and the price-equals-value efficient market hypothesis is the claim that investment prices always equal their intrinsic values. The intrinsic value of an investment is the present value of its expected future payments, such as dividends, discounted by an expected return determined by a correct asset pricing model.

Hard-to-beat efficient markets are markets wherein some investors are able to beat the market consistently, earning abnormal returns over time, but most are unable to do so. Abnormal returns are returns exceeding the returns one would expect according to a correct asset pricing model.

In what follows, I refer to "intrinsic value" as "value" and to "price-equals-value efficient" markets as "value-efficient" markets. I refer to "stock" interchangeably with "investment."

Value-efficient markets are impossible to beat because abnormal returns come from exploiting discrepancies between prices and values. Such discrepancies are absent in value-efficient markets. But hard-to-beat efficient markets are not necessarily value-efficient markets. It might be that substantial discrepancies between prices and values are common, implying markets far from value efficiency, but discrepancies are hard to identify in time or difficult to exploit for abnormal returns. As I often say, markets are crazy, but this does not make you a psychiatrist.

Direct tests of the value-efficient market hypothesis are difficult because estimating the values of investments is difficult. This problem leads to the common but usually implicit replacement of the value-efficient market hypothesis with the hard-to-beat efficient market hypothesis in discussions of the efficient market hypothesis and the implicit assumption that the two hypotheses are identical. But they are not. Value-efficient markets are impossible to beat, but hard-to-beat efficient markets are not necessarily value-efficient markets.

The rational investors described in standard finance know that markets are hard to beat, but many of the normal investors described in behavioral finance believe that markets are easy to beat. In truth, the market beats most investors who attempt to beat it. Cognitive and emotional errors mislead many investors into the belief that beating the market is easy. Other investors are able to overcome cognitive and emotional errors yet are willing to accept lower returns and their utilitarian benefits for the expressive benefits of the image of being an "active" rather than a "passive" investor and the emotional benefits arising from the hope of beating the market.

## Efficient Markets and Information

Eugene Fama introduced the term "efficient markets" in the mid-1960s. In 2013, he was awarded the Nobel Prize in Economics largely for his work on market efficiency. Fama defined market efficiency in a 1965 article, "Random Walks in Stock Market Prices."[331] He wrote, "In other words, in an efficient market at any point in time the actual price of a security will be a good estimate of its value" (p. 56). This corresponds to value-efficient markets.

The value of a stock is estimated on the basis of information about that stock. But how do we classify information? Fama classified information into three categories and defined three corresponding forms of the efficient market hypothesis.

The weak form is the claim that the price of each stock equals its value, whereby value is based on information about past prices, a subcategory of public information. The semistrong form is the claim that the price of each stock equals its value, whereby value is based on the full panoply of public information. And the strong form is the claim that the price of each stock equals its value, where value is based on the category of all information, private as well as public.

The hard-to-beat efficient market hypothesis comes in a corresponding set of three forms. The weak form is the claim that investors find it hard to beat the market consistently using information about the past prices. The semistrong form is the claim that investors find it hard to beat the market

---

[331]Eugene F. Fama, "Random Walks in Stock Market Prices," *Financial Analysts Journal* 21, no. 5 (September/October 1965): 55–59.

consistently through public information. And the strong form is the claim that investors find it hard to beat the market consistently using any information, public or private.

Later, in 1991, Fama described efficient markets as ones "in which prices always fully reflect available information" (p. 1575).[332] "Available information," however, is an ambiguous term, and so are the terms "public information" and "private information."

We can clarify distinctions by classifying information into the three groups: exclusively available information, narrowly available information, and widely available information. Gradations of information can be made finer, such as distinguishing narrowly available information from very narrowly available information.

Exclusively available information is information available to only one person, such as the CEO of a company. Narrowly available information is information available to only a few, such as members of the board of directors of a company, analysts following the company, and readers of specialized publications, such as *Grant's Interest Rate Observer*, a publication directed at a narrow audience of investment professionals. Widely available information includes, for example, information published in major newspapers, such as the *Wall Street Journal*, directed at wide audiences.

As illustrated in **Exhibit 9.1**, people who possess exclusively available information also possess narrowly available and widely available information.

**Exhibit 9.1. Three Levels of Information**

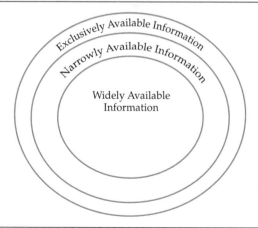

Exclusively Available Information

Narrowly Available Information

Widely Available Information

---

[332]Eugene F. Fama, "Efficient Capital Markets: II," *Journal of Finance* 46, no. 5 (December 1991): 1575–617.

People who possess narrowly available information also possess widely available information but not exclusively available information. And people who possess only widely available information possess neither exclusively available nor narrowly available information.

The boundaries between widely available, narrowly available, and exclusively available information redraw the boundary between "public information" and "private information" in Fama's classification. These boundaries also separate typical amateur investors, who possess only widely available information, from typical professional investors, who also possess narrowly available information and sometimes even exclusively available information.

We see the advantage of setting boundaries between widely available, narrowly available, and exclusively available information over setting it between public information and private information in the case of EntreMed (ENMD), a biotechnology company, explored by economists Gur Huberman and Tomer Regev. The Sunday, 3 May 1998 edition of the *New York Times* reported a breakthrough in cancer research and mentioned ENMD, a company with licensing rights to the breakthrough. The price of ENMD's shares increased greatly when the story was published in the *New York Times*, yet the information had been published in *Nature*, a specialized British journal directed at scientists, more than five months earlier.[333]

Huberman and Regev noted that information in *Nature* was public information and so was the information in the *New York Times*. The "new-news content of the *Times* story was nil" (p. 387), they wrote. Yet the information in *Nature* was narrowly available, whereas the *New York Times* made it widely available. The ENMD case also shows the boundary between amateur and professional investors. Typical amateur investors possess only widely available information, such as that published in the *New York Times*, whereas professional investors also possess narrowly available information, such as that published in *Nature*. Investment professionals were more likely to have beaten the market, buying shares of ENMD at low prices following the publication of the news in *Nature*, whereas amateur investors likely failed to beat the market, buying shares of ENMD at higher prices following publication in the *New York Times*.

## Value Efficiency, Proportional Efficiency, and Directional Efficiency

The formula for calculating the value of a stock is simple, nothing more than the formula for the present value of future dividends. Potentially, we can

---

[333]Gur Huberman and Tomer Regev, "Contagious Speculation and a Cure for Cancer: A Nonevent That Made Stock Prices Soar," *Journal of Finance* 56, no. 1 (February 2001): 387–96.

support or refute the value-efficiency hypothesis by placing, side by side, stock prices and stock values calculated using that formula and observing whether they are the same, supporting the value-efficiency hypothesis, or different, refuting that hypothesis. Yet precise calculations of value are nonexistent, because precise estimates of future dividends are nonexistent. Discrepancies between stock prices and estimates of stock values might indicate that markets are not value efficient or that calculations of value are imprecise. Alternatively, we can search for evidence refuting the value-efficiency hypothesis. Failure to find evidence refuting the value-efficiency hypothesis would constitute evidence supporting that hypothesis.

Value-efficient markets sit at the top of a three-layer pyramid, as illustrated in **Exhibit 9.2**. At the bottom of the pyramid are "directionally efficient" markets, where information indicating change in the value of a stock is consistently accompanied by change in the price of the stock in a direction consistent with that information. Positive information indicating an increase in the value of a stock is consistently accompanied by an increase in the price of the stock. Negative information indicating a decrease in the value of a stock is consistently accompanied by a decrease in the price of the stock. And absence of information indicating change in value of a stock or information not indicating a change in value of a stock is consistently accompanied by no change in the price of the stock.

Above "directionally efficient" markets are "proportionally efficient" markets, where information indicating change in the value of a stock is consistently accompanied not only by a change in the price of the stock in a direction

**Exhibit 9.2.  The Three Levels of Market Efficiency**

consistent with that information but also by a change in price equal in proportion (magnitude) to the change in value.

At the top of the pyramid, beyond proportionally efficient markets, are "value-efficient" markets, where stock prices always equal values.

Each level of the pyramid builds on the levels below. It is not possible for a market to conform to one of the higher levels of efficiency without also conforming to each lower level of efficiency. For example, a proportionally efficient market is always also a directionally efficient market. Likewise, a value-efficient market is always also both proportionally efficient and directionally efficient.

The opposite is not true. The fact that a market conforms to lower levels of efficiency does not necessarily imply that the market also conforms to higher levels of efficiency. For example, a directionally efficient market is not necessarily proportionally efficient or value efficient. Similarly, a market that is both directionally efficient and proportionally efficient is not necessarily value efficient.

Evidence showing that a stock trades in both a directionally efficient market and a proportionally efficient market *is not sufficient* to support the hypothesis that the stock also trades in a value-efficient market. Yet evidence showing that a stock does *not* trade in a directionally efficient or proportionally efficient market *is sufficient* to refute the hypothesis that the stock trades in a value-efficient market.

Consider an example where the price per share of a company exceeds its value by $20. Now imagine the arrival of information that the value per share of the company increased by $5—for example, because its new movie turned out to be an unexpected blockbuster—and the price per share increased by $5. This example is consistent with the claim that the market is both directionally and proportionally efficient, because the change in the price of shares equals the change in value in both direction and proportion, but it refutes the claim that the market is value efficient because the share price remains $20 higher than its value.

The market for the shares of IMM, the owner of the Titanic (the ship, not the movie), illustrates markets that are both directionally efficient and proportionally efficient, although not necessarily value efficient. The Titanic left Southampton, England, on its way to New York on 10 April 1912 and collided with a giant iceberg on the night of 14 April. By the morning of 15 April, the ship and 1,503 of its 2,207 passengers lay at the bottom of the Atlantic Ocean.[334]

---

[334]Arun Khanna, "The Titanic: The Untold Economic Story," *Financial Analysts Journal* 54, no. 5 (1998): 16–17.

The Titanic, built for $7,500,000, was insured by Lloyds for $5,000,000. Therefore, the net decline in the value of IMM shares following the Titanic disaster was $2,500,000. It turns out the price of all IMM's shares declined by a total of $2,604,500 during 15 and 16 April, the two days following the Titanic disaster. The change in price was somewhat greater than the change in value, but the two are close enough to support the claim that the market for IMM's shares was both directionally and proportionally efficient. The case of IMM, however, neither supports nor refutes the claim that the market for IMM was value efficient. It is possible that the value of IMM shares exceeded or fell short of their values both before and after the Titanic disaster.

Cases of aviation disasters also illustrate directional and proportional efficiency. Whereas they support directional efficiency, they refute proportional efficiency. The average decline in value of companies following an aviation disaster is no more than $1 billion, but the average decline in stock prices corresponds to a loss of more than $60 billion.[335] This finding also refutes value efficiency because, as discussed earlier, a market cannot be value efficient if it is not proportionally efficient.

If markets are proportionally efficient or even directionally efficient, we should find that either an absence of information indicating change in value or the presence of information indicating no change in value is accompanied by no change in the price of a stock or index of stocks. Yet economist Ray Fair found many instances where large changes in the level of the S&P 500 Index occurred with no information likely associated with changes in value.[336] This finding refutes directional and proportional efficiency and implies refutation of value efficiency.

For example, negative information on 22 October 1987 included an Iranian attack on a Kuwaiti oil terminal, a fall in markets overseas, and analysts predicting lower prices. This accumulation of bad news suggests a market decline and, in fact, was accompanied by a 3.92% decrease in the S&P 500. Positive information on 29 October 1987 included the beginning of deficit reduction talks, an increase in durable goods orders, and rallies in overseas markets. This parcel of good news was accompanied by a 4.46% increase in the S&P 500.

Yet Fair also found much evidence inconsistent with directional and proportional efficiency. He found many large changes in the level of the S&P 500 with no information associated with changes in value. In a proportionally

---

[335]Guy Kaplanski and Haim Levy, "Sentiment and Stock Prices: The Case of Aviation Disasters," *Journal of Financial Economics* 95, no. 2 (July 2010): 174–201.
[336]Ray Fair, "Events That Shook the Market," *Journal of Business* 75, no. 4 (October 2002): 713–31.

or even directionally efficient market, absence of information associated with changes in values would be accompanied by no changes in prices. Fair wrote, "The results . . . suggest that stock price determination is complicated. Many large price changes correspond to no obvious events, and so many large changes appear to have no easy explanation. Also, of the hundreds of fairly similar announcements that have taken place between 1982 and 1999, only a few have led to large price changes. . . . And it does not appear easy to explain why some do and some do not" (p. 722).[337]

Economist Richard Roll also found evidence refuting directional and proportional efficiency, implying refutation of value efficiency.[338] He calculated $R^2$ statistics, in this case, the proportion of the variation of stock returns that is accounted for by information about changes in their values, and concluded that the average $R^2$ is only 0.35 when monthly returns are used and only 0.20 when daily returns are used. The $R^2$ would have been 1.00 if the only cause of changes in stock prices were information about changes in values.

Direct evidence refuting the value-efficiency hypothesis comes from Palm Computing's spinoff from its parent, 3Com, as reported by economist Owen Lamont and Nobel Prize–winning economist Richard Thaler. (Palm Computing manufactured the Palm Pilot personal digital assistant.) The spinoff occurred at the height of the internet boom. Initially, only 5% of Palm Computing shares were sold to investors. The other 95% remained with 3Com. Enthusiasm for the shares of Palm Computing was so great and their price shot up so high that the total value of the 95% of Palm Computing shares still owned by 3Com greatly exceeded the total value of all 3Com shares, implying the absurd conclusion that the rest of 3Com's business had negative value. The more likely conclusion is that the price of 3Com shares was far below their value, the price of Palm Computing shares was far above their value, or both.

## Who Beats a Hard-to-Beat Market?

Hard-to-beat markets are not impossible to beat. Investors possessing exclusively or narrowly available information find it hard but not impossible to beat the market consistently. Evidence that investors possessing exclusively or narrowly available information beat the market refutes the exclusively and narrowly available information forms of the hard-to-beat efficient market hypothesis.

Investors possessing exclusively and narrowly available information are typically investment professionals. Typical investment amateurs, however,

---

[337]Fair, "Events That Shook the Market."
[338]Richard Roll, "R2," *Journal of Finance* 43, no. 3 (July 1988): 541–66.

possess nothing more than widely available information and find it impossible to beat the market consistently. Instead, investment amateurs are beaten by the market more often than they beat it. Indeed, investors possessing exclusively available and narrowly available information gain their market-beating returns by emptying the pockets of investors who attempt to beat the market with widely available information alone.

Investment professionals search for narrowly available information in many places and from far distances, as far away as space. Kayrros, a company named after the Greek deity of opportunity, collects information on oil supplies using photos from satellites, selling the information to investment professionals at a hefty price. That information is valuable because there is uncertainty about the number of barrels of oil being produced on any day; the number can range from 500,000 to 1.5 million. High production can cause oil gluts, pressing prices lower, and low production can cause oil shortages, pushing prices higher.[339]

Members of Congress used narrowly available information to beat the market. During 2004–10, the buy-minus-sell portfolios of powerful Republican members of Congress earned the highest abnormal returns, exceeding an annual 35%. Abnormal returns disappeared, however, after the Stop Trading on Congressional Knowledge Act was passed in 2012.[340]

Political connections facilitate the transfer of narrowly available information from politicians to corporate insiders. This fact was especially evident during the global financial crisis, when government interventions were major and the effects of these interventions on stock prices were substantial. A study of trades during the period uncovered strong evidence that corporate insiders with political connections earned abnormal returns. The relation was especially strong when Troubled Asset Relief Program (TARP) funds were dispersed and strongest among politically connected insiders at banks that received TARP funds.[341]

Some narrowly available information is inside information of the kind prohibited for use by law. But most narrowly available information is not prohibited. For example, analysts with work experience in the industries they

---

[339]Stanley Reed, "Satellites Aid the Chase for Better Information on Oil Supplies," *New York Times* (8 October 2018). www.nytimes.com/2018/10/08/business/search-for-better-information-on-oil-supplies.html.

[340]Serkan Karadas, "Trading on Private Information: Evidence from Members of Congress," *Financial Review* 54, no. 1 (February 2019): 85–131.

[341]Alan D. Jagolinzer, David F. Larcker, Gaizka Ormazabal, and Daniel J. Taylor, "Political Connections and the Informativeness of Insider Trades," Rock Center for Corporate Governance at Stanford University Working Paper No. 222 (29 July 2017). Available at SSRN: https://ssrn.com/abstract=2836053 or http://dx.doi.org/10.2139/ssrn.2836053.

analyze possess more narrowly available information than analysts lacking that experience, and their forecasts are more accurate.

Analysts making forecasts about companies in industries related to their pre-analyst experience issue more accurate forecasts, evoke stronger price reactions to earning revisions, and are more likely to be named *Institutional Investor* all-stars.[342] Fund managers with industry knowledge acquired before switching to the financial industry exploit this knowledge by overweighting and picking outperforming stocks from these industries.[343] And corporate insiders tend to buy stocks of companies from their own industry and earn substantial abnormal returns on these stocks. Yet these corporate insiders do not use inside information in these trades, suggesting that general knowledge of their own industry underlies their abnormal returns.[344]

## Who Is Beaten by Hard-to-Beat Markets?

Think of security markets, such as stock markets, as a game. You profit by $1,000 if you do not play. You profit by $2,000 if you play and win and zero if you play and lose. Would you play?

Investors who know financial facts and human behavior, including cognitive and emotional shortcuts and errors, frame stock markets correctly as market-sum games. The market returns of stock markets are rarely zero. Instead, they are positive more often than negative, by a margin of, say, 7% of invested capital per year. Stock market games are market-sum games because the sum of the gains and losses of investors must equal market returns.

"Passive" investors refrain from playing. Instead, they buy and hold low-cost diversified stock market index mutual funds or exchange-traded funds that match the market, collecting their 7% annual positive return, which amounts to, let's say, a $1,000 average profit in a hypothetical example. "Active" investors, however, aim to beat the market by playing, buying an undiversified handful of stocks, trading them frequently, and collecting $2,000 if they win or zero if they lose.

Divide investors into two kinds—amateurs possessing nothing but widely available information and professionals also possessing exclusively or narrowly

---

[342]Daniel Bradley, Sinan Gokkaya, and Xi Liu, "Before an Analyst Becomes an Analyst: Does Industry Experience Matter?" *Journal of Finance* 72, no. 2 (September 2017): 751–92.

[343]Gjergji Cici, Monika Gehde-Trapp, Marc-André Goericke, and Alexander Kempf, "The Investment Value of Fund Managers' Experience Outside the Financial Sector" (10 June 2017). Available at SSRN: https://ssrn.com/abstract=2498797 or http://dx.doi.org/10.2139/ssrn.2498797.

[344]Itzhak Ben-David, Justin Birru, and Andrea Rossic, "Industry Familiarity and Trading: Evidence from the Personal Portfolios of Industry Insiders," *Journal of Financial Economics* 132 (2019): 49–75.

available information—and imagine that there is an equal number of each. Professionals win half the games when facing professionals on the other side of their trades, collecting $1,000 on average in each game. Professionals always win when facing amateurs, collecting $2,000 in each game, for an overall $1,500 average.

Amateurs win half the games when facing amateurs, collecting $1,000 on average in each game. They lose all games when facing professionals, collecting zero in each game, for an overall $500 average.

Why do so many investment amateurs, possessing nothing more than widely available information, play when their average $500 falls below the $1,000 they could collect by not playing? This is the trading puzzle.

Fischer Black described the trading puzzle in "Noise," his American Finance Association presidential address delivered in 1986. He stated, "A person with information or insights about individual firms will want to trade, but will realize that only another person with information or insights will take the other side of the trade. Taking the other side's information into account, is it still worth trading? From the point of view of someone who knows what both the traders know, one side or the other must be making a mistake. If the one who is making a mistake declines to trade, there will be no trading on information" (p. 531).[345]

Black distinguished "information traders" from "noise traders." We can think of information traders as active investors possessing exclusively or narrowly available information and passive investors possessing only widely available information. We can think of noise traders as active investors possessing only widely available information. Noise can be, for example, false information offered by fraudsters in pump-and-dump schemes or truthful information, such as about oil field discoveries, presented in widely read newspapers and websites yet perceived by noise traders as exclusively or narrowly available information.

Black noted that noise trading is the key to solving the trading puzzle: "People who trade on noise are willing to trade even though from an objective point of view they would be better off not trading" (p. 531). Some noise traders are motivated to trade by ignorance about financial facts and human behavior. "Perhaps they think the noise they are trading on is information" (p. 531), stated Black. Other noise traders are motivated to trade by wants: "Or perhaps they just like to trade" (p. 531).

Much evidence points to the poor performance of active amateur investors. One study found that American investors who traded frequently earned,

---

[345]Fischer Black, "Noise," *Journal of Finance* 41, no. 3 (July 1986): 528–43.

on average, almost 7 pps less than passive investors.[346] Another study found that Swedish amateur investors who traded frequently lost, on average, almost 4% of their total financial wealth each year.[347] And fewer than 1% of Taiwanese day traders earned consistent abnormal returns, according to another study.[348]

Amateur investors who trade frequently lag further those who buy and hold because they tend to buy high and sell low. Research has shown that amateur investors who traded frequently in 19 major international stock markets lagged buy-and-hold investors by an annual average of 1.5 pps.[349] Other research found that amateur investors who switched among mutual funds frequently lagged buy-and-hold investors by an annual 0.84 pp when switching among US stock funds, 1.24 pps when switching among international stock funds, and 2.05 pps when switching among taxable bond funds.[350]

Active amateur investors possessing nothing but widely available information can be do-it-yourself investors, buying an undiversified handful of stocks and trading them frequently. Alternatively, they can hire professional investors, such as managers of active mutual funds, to invest for them. Many fund managers possess narrowly available information and possibly exclusively available information—that is, information beyond the widely available—enabling them to generate abnormal returns. Yet investors in active funds are not assured of abnormal returns unless fund managers *share* them.

Economists Jonathan Berk and Jules van Binsbergen found that active mutual fund managers do beat the market, generating abnormal returns, but, on average, they do not share their abnormal returns with their investors. Managers of active mutual funds generated an annual average of $3.2 million of abnormal returns in each fund, yet they kept the entire $3.2 million as fees,

---

[346]Brad M. Barber and Terrance Odean, "Trading Is Hazardous to Your Wealth: The Common Stock Investment Performance of Individual Investors," *Journal of Finance* 55, no. 2 (2000): 773–806.

[347]Anders Anderson, "Trading and Under-Diversification," *Review of Finance* 17, no. 5 (September 2013): 1699–1741.

[348]Brad M. Barber, Yi-Tsung Lee, Yu-Jane Liu, and Terrance Odean, "The Cross-Section of Speculator Skill: Evidence from Day Trading," *Journal of Financial Markets* 18 (March 2014): 1–24.

[349]Ilia D. Dichev, "What Are Stock Investors' Actual Historical Returns? Evidence from Dollar-Weighted Returns," *American Economic Review* 97, no. 1 (March 2007): 386–401.

[350]Christine Benz, "The Error-Proof Portfolio: OK, People—What Have We Learned? The Bull Market Is Entering Its Fifth Year, But How Have Investors Done Since the Market Recovered?" Morningstar (28 October 2013). http://news.morningstar.com/articlenet/article.aspx?id=616424.

delivering to their investors returns equal, on average, to returns earned by investors in passive index funds.[351]

Index fund investors earn market returns. So do active fund investors. Who, then, lags the market by amounts equal to the total active managers' fees? Berk and van Binsbergen said that investors who lag the market are mostly do-it-yourself active investors—those who buy handfuls of stocks and trade them frequently. The authors said they are the source of the before-fee alpha generated by professionals.

Others have concluded, however, that active fund manager fees exceed the above-market returns generated. That is, they deliver to their investors average returns lower than index fund returns. The economist Burton Malkiel wrote that "managed funds are regularly outperformed by broad index funds, with equivalent risk" (p. 78).[352] And Fama and Kenneth French found that "the high costs of active management show up intact as lower returns to investors" (p. 1915).[353]

## Why Do Amateur Investors Persist in Attempts to Beat the Market?

Why do amateur investors, possessing nothing more than widely available information, persist in their attempts to beat the market as do-it-yourself investors or as active mutual fund investors? Some do-it-yourself amateur investors may be able to earn consistent abnormal returns by luck or skill. And some managers of active mutual funds, hedge funds, and other investment vehicles share their abnormal returns with their investors.

Still, many amateur investors persist in their attempts to beat the market when they are more likely to lag the market. Some of these investors are misled by cognitive and emotional errors. Others follow their wants.

Framing errors are prominent among cognitive errors. Amateur investors regularly frame trading by analogy to surgery, driving, cabinet making, or plumbing. A plumber improves her work as she does more of it, fixing more leaks. Framed by analogy, an investor improves his performance as he trades more often, increasing his profits. Framing trading by analogy to plumbing is flawed, however, because pipes and fittings do not compete against the

---

[351]Jonathan B. Berk and Jules H. Van Binsbergen, "Measuring Managerial Skill in the Mutual Fund Industry," National Bureau of Economic Research Working Paper No. 18184 (June 2012). Available at SSRN: https://ssrn.com/abstract=2089256.

[352]Burton G. Malkiel, "The Efficient Market Hypothesis and Its Critics," *Journal of Economic Perspectives* 17, no. 1 (Winter 2003): 59–82.

[353]Eugene F. Fama and Kenneth R. French, "Luck versus Skill in the Cross-Section of Mutual Fund Returns," *Journal of Finance* 65, no. 5 (October 2010): 1915–47.

plumber, inducing her to choose the wrong fitting. But a trader always faces a competing trader on the other side of his trade, sometimes inducing him to choose the wrong trading strategy.

When luck shines, a trader possessing only widely available information faces another trader possessing only widely available information. If so, he is likely to break even (before accounting for trading costs). When luck dims, however, the trader loses to a trader with exclusively or narrowly available information. Breaking even when lucky and losing when unlucky sum to an overall loss.

Active traders possessing only widely available information often commit another framing error: framing their returns relative to zero rather than relative to the market return, the return they could have earned by investing in a low-cost diversified index fund. A 15% annual return is excellent, but it is inferior when an index fund delivers 20%.

Moreover, amateur investors tend to form general impressions of their returns rather than calculate them. Doing so leads them into the trap of confirmation errors, whereby they count gains, confirming their image as winners, while overlooking losses that disconfirm that image. Indeed, a study of amateur investors, members of the American Association of Individual Investors, found that they overestimated their investment returns on average by 3.4 pps compared with their actual returns and by 5.1 pps compared with those of the average investor.[354]

Some amateur investors commit representativeness errors of the kind we know as the belief in the law of small numbers. A sample of 10 might well be sufficient for general conclusions about the quality of meals at a particular restaurant, because there is relatively little randomness in the quality of meals at any particular restaurant. Seven bad meals out of ten or even two bad meals out of three might well be all we need for a general conclusion that it is best to forgo dining at that restaurant. Moreover, we lose little when we forgo that particular restaurant when, in truth, its meals are generally good. There are hundreds more restaurants to explore.

Yet a sample of 10 trades or even 100 is too small to reach general conclusions about the quality of a trader or the validity of a trading strategy, because there is much randomness in trading outcomes. A lucky trader possessing only widely available information might enjoy a streak of wins when trading against other traders possessing only widely available information. That lucky trader might even win sometimes when trading against traders possessing exclusively or narrowly available information. And unlike the case of

---

[354]William Goetzmann and Nadav Peles, "Cognitive Dissonance and Mutual Fund Investors," *Journal of Financial Research* 20, no. 2 (1997): 145–58.

restaurants, amateur traders are likely to forgo substantial amounts when they conclude, in error, that they can beat the market.

Amateur investors are also susceptible to availability errors, whereby they form estimates and opinions based on easily available information. Social interactions make information easily available, misleading investors into trading when fellow investors disclose their winning trades but withhold their losing ones.[355] And available fake news misleads investors who misperceive it as truthful. A study of stock promotions using fake news articles revealed that many are parts of "pump-and-dump" schemes operated by corporate insiders who profit by trading with investors ignorant of the falsity of the news.[356]

Many amateur investors are drawn into active investing by cognitive errors, but some are also drawn into it by wants for expressive and emotional benefits. A study of 421 pump-and-dump schemes in Germany and the corresponding trading records of more than 110,000 amateur investors indicated that participation in such schemes inflicted an average loss of nearly 30%. Yet roughly 11% of pump-and-dump investors participated in four or more schemes during the sample period, perhaps because they committed cognitive errors or perhaps because they derived from pump-and-dump schemes expressive and emotional benefits similar to those derived from gambles or lotteries.[357]

Wants for expressive and emotional benefits are evident among Dutch investors who agreed with the statements "I invest because I like to analyze problems, look for new constructions, and learn" and "I invest because it is a nice free-time activity" more than they agreed with the statement "I invest because I want to safeguard my retirement."[358] These wants are evident in a study of German investors who enjoy investing; they traded twice as much as other investors.[359] And these wants are evident among the one-quarter of

---

[355]Bing Han, David A. Hirshleifer, and Johan Walden, "Social Transmission Bias and Investor Behavior," Rotman School of Management Working Paper No. 3053655 (31 May 2019). Available at SSRN: https://ssrn.com/abstract=3053655 or http://dx.doi.org/10.2139/ssrn.3053655.

[356]Shimon Kogan, Tobias J. Moskowitz, and Marina Niessner, "Fake News: Evidence from Financial Markets" (15 April 2019). Available at SSRN: https://ssrn.com/abstract=3237763 or http://dx.doi.org/10.2139/ssrn.3237763.

[357]Christian Leuz, Steffen Meyer, Maximilian Muhn, Eugene F. Soltes, and Andreas Hackethal, "Who Falls Prey to the Wolf of Wall Street? Investor Participation in Market Manipulation," Center for Financial Studies Working Paper No. 609 (24 November 2018). Available at SSRN: https://ssrn.com/abstract=3289931 or http://dx.doi.org/10.2139/ssrn.3289931.

[358]Arvid O. I. Hoffmann, "Individual Investors' Needs and the Investment Professional: Lessons from Marketing," *Journal of Investment Consulting* 8, no. 2 (Summer 2007): 80–91.

[359]Daniel Dorn and Paul Sengmueller, "Trading as Entertainment?" *Management Science* 55, no. 4 (April 2009): 591–603.

---

American investors who said that they buy stocks as a hobby or because it is something they like to do.[360]

A Fidelity survey of amateur traders revealed that 54% enjoy "the thrill of the hunt," 53% enjoy learning new investment skills, and more than half enjoy sharing trading news with family and friends. "This research confirms the obvious satisfaction traders receive when generating cash from their activities, but it also highlights their desire to learn new skills and to share, teach, and mentor others," said James C. Burton, president of Fidelity's retail brokerage business.[361]

Commercials of investment companies, like commercials of vitamin companies, cater to wants of being above average, in investment returns or marathon running. The announcer in a commercial for vitamin stores denigrates "average" athletic ability. The crowning achievement of average, he says in disdain, is "everyone gets a trophy." It shows a boy in bed, whispering in his dream, "Average is good." "No," says the announcer, "average is average. You can beat it."

A commercial by an investment company denigrates index funds as average. It concludes with a man standing on a stage as a sign lights up: "Why invest in average?" And an advertisement by another investment company asks, "If passive investing was called 'Don't Try,' would you still be interested?"

## Making the Market Value Efficient and Hard to Beat by Beating It

Evidence, then, shows that investors who possess exclusively and narrowly available information are able to beat the market consistently. This finding refutes the exclusively and narrowly available information forms of the hard-to-beat efficient market hypothesis. Yet as these investors beat the market, they can make markets not only harder to beat but also more value efficient.

Prices do not move toward values by some automatic process. Instead, prices move because of the trading actions of investors. Investors estimate values—by intuition or formal models, such as discounted cash flow—compare their estimates to prices, and choose to buy or sell accordingly, selling if they conclude that prices exceed values and buying if they conclude that prices are lower than values. In the process, they can move prices closer to

---

[360]Ravi Dhar and William N. Goetzmann, "Bubble Investors: What Were They Thinking?" Yale ICF Working Paper No. 06-22 (17 August 2006). Available at SSRN: https://ssrn.com/abstract=683366.

[361]"Fidelity Research Reveals Traders' Motivations Beyond Investment Gains," Benzinga (27 January 2012). www.benzinga.com/pressreleases/12/01/b2292810/fidelity-research-reveals-traders-motivations-beyond-investment-gains#ixzz3ddLr5wIi.

values. Money managers, analysts, and other investment professionals estimate values of securities every day and act on these estimates. They would have had no employment if they accepted a premise that security prices always equal their values.

How large are typical discrepancies between prices and values? In his presidential address to the American Finance Association, Black asserted that prices regularly depart from values within a factor of 2; that is, "the price is more than half of value and less than twice value."[362] Black added that "the factor of 2 is arbitrary, of course. Intuitively, though, it seems reasonable to me, in the light of sources of uncertainty about value and the strength of the forces tending to cause price to return to value" (p. 533). Black's estimate seems reasonable even today.

Consider the lessons of **Exhibit 9.3**. On the horizontal axis is a measure of the aggregate efforts of traders to beat the market by searching for and trading on exclusively and narrowly available information. On the vertical axis is an index of value efficiency, measured as the average discrepancy

**Exhibit 9.3. Equilibrium Aggregate Effort to Beat the Market and Level of Value Efficiency**

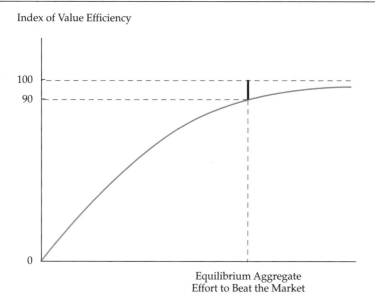

Index of Value Efficiency

Aggregate Effort to Beat the Market

---

[362]Black, "Noise."

between prices and values. A 100 index indicates a value-efficient market, with no discrepancies between prices and values.

If all investors believed that all prices already equaled values, no one would search for exclusively and narrowly available information. In such a case, markets would not be value efficient. Think of yesterday's $40 price of shares of a pharmaceutical company, equal to yesterday's value, and imagine that the FDA announced today, unexpectedly, approval of a major drug made by that company. Its value increases to $60, reflecting higher future dividends when the drug is made available to patients. If all believe that the market for shares of this company is already value efficient, then they also believe that the value of the company's shares is $40, and no investors search for information about the effect of the drug announcement on the shares' value, let alone try to beat the market by buying for $40 shares worth $60.

Some traders, however, are likely to notice that a market is not value efficient, and they can easily beat it. These traders engage in arbitrage, buying shares whose prices are lower than values and selling shares whose prices exceed values. In this case, they rush to buy shares worth $60 for $40. As traders rush in, eager to buy shares for less than their values, their buying pushes the price of shares higher, closer to their $60 value, making the market more value efficient and harder to beat.

Searching for and trading on exclusively and narrowly available information entail costs, including not only direct search and trading costs but also forgone income in alternative occupations, such as accounting, engineering, or teaching. These costs impede value efficiency. We cannot expect markets to be 100-index value efficient because traders' expected profits from efforts at beating 100-index value-efficient markets are negative. Indeed, even markets whose value efficiency is somewhat lower than 100 index, say, 95 index, might not offer discrepancies between prices and values large enough to compensate traders for their costs.

In equilibrium, the aggregate effort of traders to beat the market converges to less than 100-index value efficiency—to, say, 90-index value efficiency—leaving discrepancies between prices and values that are wide enough to allow skilled traders to beat the market by magnitudes that are at least equal to their costs. Traders who are not as skilled quit when they fail to beat the market.[363]

Value efficiency is likely to be degraded by more than just costs borne by traders. Whereas arbitrage as described in textbooks requires no capital, faces no constraints, and entails no risk, in reality, almost all arbitrage requires

---

[363]Sanford J. Grossman and Joseph E. Stiglitz, "On the Impossibility of Informationally Efficient Markets," *American Economic Review* 70, no. 3 (June 1980): 393–408.

capital, faces constraints, and is risky. These characteristics limit the willingness of traders to engage in arbitrage and, consequently, limit their ability to move prices closer to values.[364]

Disparities between prices and values are larger in some markets than in others, implying lower value efficiency. These differences can result from higher costs of searching for exclusively and narrowly available information and trading on it in some markets. For example, costs are higher in markets of small-capitalization and developing-country stocks than in markets of large-capitalization and developed-country stocks.

Some infer that lower value efficiency implies lower hard-to-beat market efficiency, making markets such as those of small-capitalization and developing-country stocks easier to beat than markets of large-capitalization and developed-country stocks. Yet this inference is unwarranted for two reasons. First, the costs of searching for exclusively and narrowly available information and trading on it are likely higher in markets of lower value efficiency, diminishing beat-the-market opportunities in such markets. Indeed, large discrepancies between prices and values in such markets are likely a *consequence* of greater costs of searching for exclusively and narrowly available information and trading on it. Second, the market-sum rule holds equally in all markets. Passive investors holding well-diversified low-fee index funds in small-capitalization and developing-country stock markets earn returns almost exactly equal to market returns. If some investors earn higher-than-market returns, other investors must earn lower-than-market returns.

In his address, Black noted that noise traders do damage to value efficiency beyond the damage they do to their own returns. Noise traders inject noise, or errors, into prices as they trade, driving markets away from value efficiency as they increase discrepancies between prices and values. Prices in markets where noise traders trade, observed Black, "reflect both the information that information traders trade on and the noise that noise traders trade on."[365] **Exhibit 9.4** illustrates increases in discrepancies between prices and values caused by noise traders.

The power of noise traders to move prices is evident in the case of United Airlines' parent company. News about the 2002 bankruptcy of United Airlines' parent company resurfaced in September 2008. Noise traders apparently perceived this old news as new and rushed to sell United Airlines' shares. The price of shares plunged by 76% within a few minutes before the NASDAQ stock exchange halted trading. The price of shares rebounded after

---

[364]Andrei Shleifer and Robert W. Vishny, "The Limits of Arbitrage," *Journal of Finance* 52, no. 1 (March 1997): 35–55.
[365]Fischer, "Noise."

**Exhibit 9.4. Aggregate Effort to Beat the Market and Levels of Value Efficiency in Markets Where Information Traders Are Joined by Noise Traders**

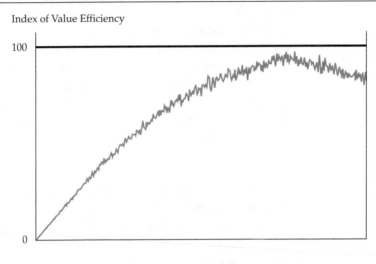

Index of Value Efficiency

Aggregate Effort to Beat the Market

the news had been identified as old but was still 11.2% lower at the end of that day.[366]

## Will the Rush to Passive Investing Reduce Value Efficiency?

Absence of attempts to beat the market, such as by widespread holdings of index funds, can increase discrepancies between prices and values if it reduces not only the number of active investors but also the overall efforts by active investors to search for discrepancies between prices and values and to trade to exploit them. Increases in the relative proportion of passive ownership during recent years heighten concern about decreases in value efficiency.

There is indeed some evidence that increases in passive ownership can decrease proportional efficiency and perhaps value efficiency, as evidenced by the decreased impact of pre-earnings announcements on trading. Economist Marco Sammon found that from 1990 to 2017, the volume of pre-earnings cumulative abnormal trading and the pre-earnings drift declined 10% and 22%, respectively. At the company level, a rise in passive ownership can explain as much as 76% of the pre-earnings volume decrease, 20% of the pre-earnings drift decrease, and 14% of the earnings-day increase in volatility.

[366]Carlos Viana de Carvalho, Nicholas Klagge, and Emanuel Moench, "The Persistent Effects of a False News Shock," *Journal of Empirical Finance* 18, no. 4 (November 2011): 597–615.

This finding may be the result of a lack of incentives for passive managers to search for and trade on company-specific information. Consistent with this possibility, a rise in passive ownership is associated with fewer analysts covering a stock, less analyst accuracy, and fewer SEC filing downloads.[367]

Yet declines in value efficiency, reflected in increased discrepancies between prices and values, attract investors eager to profit by exploiting these discrepancies. Yong Chen, Brian T. Kelly, and Wei Wu found that when the number of analysts declines because of closures and mergers of brokerage firms, hedge funds increase their search for information, trade more aggressively, and earn higher abnormal returns on the affected stocks. This way, hedge funds can mitigate value-efficiency reductions caused by decreases in the number of analysts at brokerage firms.[368]

Moreover, estimation of the proportions of active and passive investment vehicles might be erroneous. David Easley, David Michayluk, Maureen O'Hara, and Talis J. Putnins noted that many active investment vehicles are, in fact, passive "closet indexes"; likewise, many exchange-traded funds are active investments in both form and function. They found that most exchange-traded funds are active, with high active shares and tracking errors, relative to the passive market portfolio. They concluded that, overall, investors are not more passive than in the past and the market is no less efficient.[369]

An increase in the proportion of passive ownership might reduce market efficiency if it reduces incentives for activists' campaigns, tactics, and successes. Yet a study by Ian Appel, Todd A. Gormley, and Donald B. Keim found that when a greater portion of the target company's shares are held by passively managed mutual funds, activist investors are *more likely* to seek corporate control changes or influence, such as by board representation, and to forgo more incremental corporate policy changes, such as by shareholder proposals. In addition, greater passive ownership is related to greater use of hostile tactics, such as proxy fights, and a greater likelihood that activists will obtain board representation or achieve sale of the target company. Overall,

---

[367]Marco Sammon, "Passive Ownership and Market Efficiency" (22 February 2019). Available at SSRN: https://ssrn.com/abstract=3243910 or http://dx.doi.org/10.2139/ssrn.3243910.

[368]Yong Chen, Bryan T. Kelly, and Wei Wu, "Sophisticated Investors and Market Efficiency: Evidence from a Natural Experiment," Mays Business School Research Paper No. 3117188; 29th Annual Conference on Financial Economics & Accounting 2018; Yale ICF Working Paper No. 2018-05 (19 September 2018). Available at SSRN: https://ssrn.com/abstract=3117188 or http://dx.doi.org/10.2139/ssrn.3117188.

[369]David Easley, David Michayluk, Maureen O'Hara, and Talis J. Putnins, "The Active World of Passive Investing," Western Finance Association Annual Meeting 2018 (29 July 2018). Available at SSRN: https://ssrn.com/abstract=3220842 or http://dx.doi.org/10.2139/ssrn.3220842.

the findings indicate that large ownership stakes of passive investors mitigate free-rider problems and ultimately increase the likelihood of success by activists.[370]

Moreover, sometimes active investors act to widen disparities between prices and values rather than narrow them. This activity is evident in bubbles, where disparities between prices and values are large and persist for months or years. In "positive" bubbles, prices exceed values, whereas in "negative" bubbles, prices are lower than values.

The usual arbitrage argument is that traders' actions narrow disparities between prices and values as they "attack" bubbles—pressing down share prices as they sell shares when prices exceed values and pushing up share prices as they buy shares when prices are short of values. Yet economists Markus Brunnermeier and Stefan Nagel found that hedge funds chose to "ride" the technology bubble of the late 1990s, inflating it further, and "dismounted" the bubble in time as it deflated.[371]

## The Joint Hypothesis: Market Efficiency, Asset Pricing, and "Smart Beta"

The efficient market hypothesis cannot be tested on its own. As Fama noted, the hypothesis must be tested jointly with an asset pricing model, such as the CAPM, the three-factor model, or the five-factor model.[372] In other words, there must be some objective standard of value with which one can compare the price. Abnormal returns of stocks of highly profitable companies, when measured by the three-factor model, might indicate that either the market is not efficient or the three-factor model is a faulty model of expected returns.

To understand the nature of the joint hypothesis, imagine shopping for a bag of flour at your local grocery store. Each bag on the store's shelf says that it weighs 5 pounds and its price is $1.90. You place one bag on a scale next to the shelf, and the scale's needle points to 5 pounds. You place another bag on the scale, and the needle points to 6 pounds.

One possibility is that the market for flour bags is not value efficient. If the value of a 5-pound bag is equal to its $1.90 price, then the value of a 6-pound bag cannot be equal to its $1.90 price; there must be a discrepancy between the price and the value of the first bag, the second bag, or both bags.

---

[370]Ian Appel, Todd A. Gormley, and Donald B. Keim, "Standing on the Shoulders of Giants: The Effect of Passive Investors on Activism" (30 June 2018). Available at SSRN: http://ssrn.com/abstract=2693145.

[371]Markus K. Brunnermeier and Stefan Nagel, "Hedge Funds and the Technology Bubble," *Journal of Finance* 59, no. 5 (October 2004): 2013–40.

[372]Fama, "Efficient Capital Markets: II."

Moreover, this market for flour bags is easy to beat. You can easily buy the 6-pound bag for the price of a 5-pound bag, gaining a 1-pound "abnormal return." This abnormal return is an "anomaly," indicating that the market is neither value efficient nor hard-to-beat efficient.

Alternatively, both bags weigh 5 pounds, implying that the market for flour bags is both value efficient and hard to beat but the scale is faulty, sometimes pointing to 5 pounds and sometimes to 6 pounds when a 5-pound bag is placed on it. A faulty scale is analogous to a faulty asset pricing model.

The problem of the joint hypothesis is the problem of determining two variables with one equation. We can overcome the problem by assuming one variable and determining the other. We can assume that markets are value efficient and determine an asset pricing model. Or we can assume an asset pricing model and determine whether markets are value efficient.

The CAPM was accepted as the correct asset pricing model as long as it served to show that markets are hard to beat and value efficient. But the CAPM was largely replaced by the three-factor model when the former indicated that markets are not efficient, yielding abnormal returns to investors in small-capitalization and value stocks.

The three-factor model was judged as faulty when it failed to account for abnormal returns yielded by the momentum factor. And the four-factor model was declared faulty when it failed to account for abnormal returns associated with investment and profitability, idiosyncratic volatility, and net stock issues, among many others.[373]

Empirical asset pricing models, such as the three-factor model, imply a decision to overcome the joint hypothesis problem by assuming that markets are value efficient and using this assumption to determine correct asset pricing models—models that yield no abnormal returns. This is a good choice in investment asset markets, as it is in other markets, whether for cars, restaurant meals, or watches.

When we observe watches showing the same time but selling at prices that range between $10 and $1 million, we do not rush to conclude that the market for watches is inefficient. Instead, we assume that the market for watches is efficient and proceed to infer a watch pricing model. Did we remember to add a prestige factor into the model? Did we remember to add a beauty factor? Did we remember to add a factor accounting for display of moon phases and other "complications"?

The joint hypothesis underlies debates about "smart beta." Smart beta strategies involve allocations that differ from those in an index where

---

[373]Kewei Hou, Chen Xue, and Lu Zhang, "Digesting Anomalies: An Investment Approach," *Review of Financial Studies* 28, no. 3 (March 2015): 650–705.

allocations are proportional to market capitalizations. The proportion allocated to a small-capitalization stock might be 1% in a portfolio where allocations are made by market capitalization. But the proportion allocated to the same small-capitalization stock might be 3% in a smart beta portfolio. We can regard abnormal returns of smart beta strategies as evidence that markets are not efficient or, as I prefer, as guides to better asset pricing models.

## Conclusion

Discussions about market efficiency are unfocused when they conflate the *value-efficient market hypothesis* with the *hard-to-beat market hypothesis*. And such discussions are incomplete when they fail to explain why so many amateur investors with nothing but widely available information perceive markets as easy to beat even though, more often than not, it is the markets who beat the investors. Behavioral finance contributes to these discussions by distinguishing the value-efficient market hypothesis from the hard-to-beat market hypothesis and by explaining why so many investors perceive that markets are easy to beat even though, in truth, they are not.

Behavioral finance joins standard finance in providing evidence that markets are not value efficient. And behavioral finance describes the cognitive and emotional errors that mislead investors possessing nothing but widely available information into believing that markets are easy to beat and the wants, beyond errors, that induce them into efforts to beat markets.

# Conclusion

A coffee commercial shows a man walking out of his house on a winter morning, surprised to find his car covered in ice. He scrapes the ice with his briefcase and hands, slips on the ice, gets up, and continues to scrape. Finally, smiling in satisfaction, he presses the remote key button, only to see the lights blinking on the car parked in front of the one he just scraped clean.

People laugh, as I did, when they see the man, incredulous, press the remote key button again. We laugh at ourselves more than at the man in the commercial, because we can remember similar stories where we played the starring role.

The man in the commercial is normal, as normal as the rest of us. We recognize his wants as normal wants. This morning he wants nothing more than to get in his car and drive to his office. We also recognize that, like us, the man is likely generally normal-knowledgeable and normal-smart. But this time he acted as normal-ignorant and normal-foolish, as the rest of us sometimes do.

The man committed the cognitive error of representativeness, whereby we assess situations by representativeness or similarity. The car the man scraped, when covered in ice, looks similar to his car. And the location of the car is similar to the place where he parked his car the night before. The cognitive error of representativeness had misled this man into acting as normal-ignorant and normal-foolish.

This man likely engages hindsight, now that he observes the sad outcome of his actions. In hindsight, he knows that he should have pressed the remote key button before beginning to scrape rather than after. And he likely feels regret for not having done so. Hindsight and regret are generally good teachers, teaching us to think before acting and taking us some distance from normal-ignorant to normal-knowledgeable and from normal-foolish to normal-smart.

The story of the man in the commercial also illustrates the path of the field of finance from proto-behavioral finance, preceding standard finance, to standard finance and to the first and second generations of behavioral finance. Proto-behavioral finance was the "obese" era of finance. Its dual focus was the behavior of people and the behavior of markets. Proto-behavioral finance was aware of people's normal wants for the utilitarian, expressive, and emotional benefits of freedom from poverty, prospects for riches, caring for children and families, staying true to values, gaining high social status, and more. And proto-behavioral finance was aware of the common cognitive and emotional shortcuts and errors on the way to satisfying these wants. Proto-behavioral finance, however, was largely unstructured and unfit, too often proceeding directly from anecdotes to general conclusions.

The *World's Work* magazine summed up people's wants and cognitive and emotional shortcuts and errors more than a century ago, saying, "Human nature is human nature." The magazine initiated an advice column for investors in 1906, and its editor wrote in 1911, "In these five years of close and often intimate intercourse with investors of all sorts and descriptions the editor of this department has learned a great many things about the habits and state of mind of the individual investor. . . . One minor conclusion from all this data and experience is that the very small investor is the most inveterate bargain hunter in the world. . . . It is the small investor who always wants 100 percent on his money and who is willing to take the most astounding chances to get it."[374]

Standard finance ruled in the "anorexic" era of finance. It diverted our eyes from the dual focus on people and on markets to a sole focus on markets. Moreover, proponents of standard finance warned against exploration of the behavior of people, lest it distract us from the sole focus on the behavior of markets.

For example, Merton Miller, a founder of standard finance, wrote, "Stocks are usually more than just the abstract 'bundles of return' of our [economic] models. Behind each holding may be a story of family business, family quarrels, legacies received, divorce settlements, and a host of other considerations almost totally irrelevant to our theories of portfolio [selection]. That we abstract from all these stories in building our models, is not because the stories are uninteresting but because they may be too interesting and thereby distract us from the pervasive market forces that should be our principal concern" (p. S467).[375]

The behavior of the man in the commercial would have been of no interest to proponents of standard finance. This is not only because his behavior is not in the direct context of finance and not only because his cognitive errors indicate that he is not rational; it is mainly because of the concern that exploration of people's behavior would distract us from the sole focus on the behavior of markets.

Merton Miller and Franco Modigliani described rational investors as ones who "always prefer more wealth to less and are indifferent as to whether a given increment to their wealth takes the form of cash payments or an increase in the market value of their holdings of shares" (p. 412). Indifference

---

[374]C.M. Keys, "The Bargain Hunter," in *World's Work*, Vol. XXII, edited by Walter H. Page and Arthur Wilson Page, 14922–24 (Garden City, NY: Doubleday, Page & Company, 1911).
[375]Merton Miller, "Behavioral Rationality in Finance: The Case of Dividends," *Journal of Business* 59 (1986): S451–S468.

to the form of wealth indicates immunity to the cognitive errors of framing. A more comprehensive description of rational investors includes immunity to all cognitive and emotional errors.

Behavioral finance is still under construction today, as we strive for a "muscular and fit" finance. The first generation of behavioral finance largely accepted Miller and Modigliani's first premise, that the wants of investors are confined to the utilitarian benefits of wealth. But that first generation rejected the second premise, that investors are immune to cognitive and emotional errors on their way to the utilitarian benefits of the wealth. The first generation of behavioral finance described the behavior of people not only as irrational but also as predictably irrational. To this day, mention of behavioral finance brings to most minds the first generation of behavioral finance, especially the list of cognitive and emotional errors that diminish wealth, such as chasing past returns and trading too much.

The wants of the man in the commercial according to the first generation of behavioral finance are the utilitarian benefits of wealth earned by arriving to his office on time and adding to his wealth by being paid for his work. And the concern in the first generation is about cognitive and emotional errors, such as representativeness errors, committed by the man as he scraped the ice off someone else's car.

The second generation of behavioral finance rejects not only the second premise of Miller and Modigliani, that investors are immune to cognitive and emotional errors on their way to the utilitarian benefits of the wealth. It also rejects that first premise, that the wants of investors are confined to wealth and its utilitarian benefits. Indeed, the second generation elucidates everyday trade-offs people make between utilitarian, expressive, and emotional benefits, often sacrificing the utilitarian benefits of wealth for expressive and emotional benefits, whether those of sincere social responsibility or high social status. The second generation of behavioral finance is also aware of the cognitive and emotional errors people commit on their way to their wants, but it distinguishes errors from wants.

In the second generation of behavioral finance, the man in the commercial bears not only the utilitarian costs of arriving late to his office but also the expressive costs of his image as a fool, scraping the ice off someone else's car, and the emotional costs of frustration and embarrassment.

The second generation of behavioral finance underlies the five foundational blocks of behavioral finance:

1. People are normal, pursuing normal wants and their utilitarian, expressive, and emotional benefits. People trade off among utilitarian, expressive, and

**167**

emotional benefits. And people use cognitive and emotional shortcuts and commit cognitive and emotional errors on the way to satisfying their wants.

2.  People construct portfolios as described by behavioral portfolio theory, where people's portfolio wants extend beyond the utilitarian benefits of high wealth and low risk to expressive and emotional benefits, such as those of sincere social responsibility and high social status.

3.  People save and spend as described by behavioral life-cycle theory, striving to satisfy wants and overcoming cognitive and emotional errors, such as insufficient or excessive self-control, that make it difficult to save and spend in the right way.

4.  Expected returns of investments are accounted for by behavioral asset pricing theory, where differences in expected returns reflect wants, shortcuts, and errors, beyond differences in risk.

5.  Markets are not efficient in the sense that price always equals value in them, but they are efficient in the sense that they are hard to beat. Investors seek to satisfy wants for utilitarian, expressive, and emotional benefits from investments and investment activities and often commit cognitive and emotional errors on the way to their wants.

*Vest*, as in clothing, is the root of investment. Investment professionals clothe themselves in vests of knowledge that distinguish them from investment amateurs.

Investors, both professionals and amateurs, share common wants, use common cognitive and emotional shortcuts, and are susceptible to common cognitive and emotional errors. Vests of knowledge, however, enable investment professionals to be better at identifying wants, using shortcuts correctly, and avoiding errors on the way to satisfying wants.

The second generation of behavioral finance directs investment professionals to a dual focus on the behavior of people and the behavior of markets. And that second generation informs investment professionals about altering their vests by knowledge and tailoring vests of knowledge for investment amateurs.

People's reluctance to realize losses, a reluctance common to investment professionals and amateurs alike, is one example of alterations that improve the fit of vests of knowledge. Howard Snyder strove to educate investment professionals about that reluctance during the proto-behavioral finance era. The title of his 1957 article was "How to Take a Loss and Like It." He explained that realizing losses increases wealth by reducing taxes: "There is no loss without collateral compensation." However, he also noted that normal investors are reluctant to realize losses: "Human nature being what it is, we are loath to take a loss until we are forced into it. Too often we believe that by ignoring a loss we will someday glance at the asset to find it has not only recovered its original value but has shown some appreciation."[376] Hersh Shefrin and I described that reluctance to realize losses in 1985, during the early years of behavioral finance, as the "disposition effect" in our article "The Disposition to Sell Winners Too Early and Ride Losers Too Long: Theory and Evidence."[377]

Investment professionals still struggle to overcome the disposition effect, but they overcome it more effectively than amateur investors. They do so by wearing vests of knowledge that include framing, mental accounting, and self-control rules that compel them to realize losses that reach some predetermined percentage, such as 10%, and outside-control rules that compel them to realize losses as well as gains by the end of each trading day. Investment professionals tailor similar vests of knowledge for investment amateurs, such as by persuading them to "harvest" their losses by realizing them.

This book offers vests of knowledge about the behavior of investors, both professionals and amateurs, including wants, shortcuts, and errors, and about the behavior of financial markets. Investment professionals can serve investment amateurs by clothing them in vests of knowledge.

---

[376]W. Howard T. Snyder, "How to Take a Loss and Like It," *Financial Analysts Journal* 13, no. 2 (May 1957): 115–16.
[377]Hersh Shefrin and Meir Statman, "The Disposition to Sell Winners Too Early and Ride Losers Too Long: Theory and Evidence," *Journal of Finance* 40, no. 3 (July 1985): 777–90.

# Epilogue: My Way to the Second Generation of Behavioral Finance

My way from standard finance to the first and second generations of behavioral finance illustrates the ongoing general transition. I was a student at the Hebrew University in Jerusalem in the late 1960s, in a building housing the economics and finance faculty. I majored in economics and statistics in my undergraduate program and finance in my MBA program.

Daniel Kahneman and Amos Tversky were doing their pioneering work on cognitive shortcuts and errors in the building right next to mine, which housed the psychology faculty. Yet I had no idea who Kahneman and Tversky were, and none of my economics, statistics, or finance professors mentioned their names or referred to their work. It was the time of standard economics and finance.

I would walk over to the psychology building from time to time to earn pocket money by participating in psychological experiments. Speaking with Kahneman and Tversky many years later, I found out that none of the experiments I remembered were theirs. One experiment called for writing stories when presented with Rorschach inkblots. Another was a "prisoner dilemma" type of experiment I played long before I knew its name. I let the student on the other side of the partition win five games and hoped that he or she would reciprocate by letting me win five, so we would both win at the expense of the experimenter. But that student never reciprocated. I remember the smirk on his face as we left the building.

The experiments taught me further what I had known before, that human behavior has more components than just those taught in my economics and finance courses. Yet they did not teach me how to incorporate those components into economics and finance.

I got a job as a financial analyst at a high-technology company when I completed my Hebrew University studies. The job was interesting for a while, and then it was not. I would say later that projects lasted much longer than my interest in them. Yet I gained many insights about human behavior in that job and have incorporated some into my research, including those about excessive optimism regarding the likely success of new projects, the games people play as they champion their projects, and the disposition to throw good money after bad by continuing projects that should be terminated. I remember the head of the company saying that engineers regularly championed complex projects that included components yet to be developed. He was adamant in turning down pleas from such project champions.

I quit my job in late August 1973 and came to New York City to study for my PhD at Columbia Business School. The October 1973 Yom Kippur War and subsequent energy crisis caught me by as much surprise as it caught the long lines of drivers hoping that gas pumps would not run dry before they reached them. Reading the *New York Times* became a daily practice.

"Stockholders and Pickets Score Con Ed Management" was the headline of a May 1974 article by Ernest Holsendolf in the *New York Times*.[378] Above the headline was a photograph of a packed Commodore Hotel ballroom. More than 4,000 Consolidated Edison (Con Ed) shareholders overflowed the ballroom into two auxiliary suites, leaving many shareholders outside, including Sydell Pflaum, a 76-year-old widow who relied on her $90 Con Ed quarterly dividend for precious financial support.

The May 1974 Con Ed shareholder meeting was the first since the company's April 1974 announcement that it was suspending its quarterly dividend, something it had never done since it started paying dividends in 1885. Con Ed attributed its decision to an urgent need to conserve cash reserves severely depleted by soaring fuel prices in the wake of the Arab oil embargo. But Con Ed's reasoning did not sway Ms. Pflaum.

Fuming with anger, Ms. Pflaum paid $189 to fly from Miami Beach to New York City for the Con Ed meeting. "Where is Luce? Since I can't get in, maybe he'll at least pay my way back home," she said, referring to Charles F. Luce, the utility's chairman.

I remember being struck by the fury of the shareholders at the Con Ed meeting. I knew that the behavior of Con Ed's shareholders contradicted standard finance theory. In my finance courses at the Hebrew University, we studied the 1961 article by Merton Miller and Franco Modigliani that proved that rational investors do not care whether a company pays dividends or not. According to them, rational investors who expect company-paid dividends but do not receive them substitute for them "homemade" dividends they create by selling as many shares of stock as necessary to yield the same amount.[379]

Why then were Con Ed's shareholders fuming when they did not receive their dividends? This is what Fischer Black called the "dividend puzzle" in a 1976 article.[380] "Why do corporations pay dividends? Why do investors pay

---

[378]Ernest Holsendolph, "Stockholders and Pickets Score Con Ed Management," *New York Times* (21 May 1974). www.nytimes.com/1974/05/21/archives/stockholders-and-pickets-score-con-ed-management-where-is-luce-some.html.

[379]Merton Miller and Franco Modigliani, "Dividend Policy, Growth, and the Valuation of Shares," *Journal of Business* 34, no. 4 (October 1961): 411–33.

[380]Fischer Black, "The Dividend Puzzle," *Journal of Portfolio Management* 2, no. 2 (Winter 1976): 5–8.

attention to dividends? . . . The harder we look at the dividend picture, the more it seems like a puzzle, with pieces that just don't fit together" (p. 8).

I joined Santa Clara University at the end of 1979 and some months later heard Hersh Shefrin speak about joint work with Richard Thaler on framing, mental accounting, and self-control and their relation to saving behavior.[381] Richard Thaler was the 2017 Nobel Prize winner in economics, but in 1979, he must have been wondering if he would ever get tenure.

I could see the link to the dividend puzzle. Normal investors with imperfect self-control are concerned that they might give in to temptation and turn a 3% homemade dividend into a 30% homemade dividend. They bolster their self-control by framing their money into separate mental accounts, one for income and one for capital, and use a rule—"spend income but don't dip into capital"—to prevent spending too much and saving too little. Rational investors have perfect self-control, obviating any need for framing, mental accounting, and spending rules.

It turned out that Shefrin was thinking along the same lines, and we decided to collaborate. We offered a solution to the dividend puzzle in "Explaining Investor Preference for Cash Dividends," built on framing, mental accounting, self-control, regret aversion, and prospect theory.[382] I asked Con Ed for the transcript of the 1974 meeting, and we included in our paper illuminating questions and statements by shareholders and Mr. Luce's responses.

We submitted our paper to the *Journal of Financial Economics* in early 1982. We used Fischer Black's dividend puzzle as a platform for our discussion and found out later that he was our paper's reviewer. The opening words of Black's review still make me blush: "This paper is brilliant. It rings both new and true in my ears." The last sentence of the review said, "Please spell my name right." We had spelled Black's first name without the "c."

William Schwert, the journal's editor, accepted Black's recommendation after "some non-trivial soul-searching," as he described it in our personal correspondence. Much later, we learned that some of the journal's associate editors objected vociferously to the paper's publication, and a few threatened never to submit any paper to the journal if our paper was published. This surely was the era of standard finance.

I presented the dividends paper at the 1982 European Finance Association meeting at the Hebrew University in Jerusalem. Audience reactions were mostly bewilderment, but Avraham Beja, one of my former

---

[381]Richard H. Thaler and Hersh Shefrin, "An Economic Theory of Self-Control," *Journal of Political Economy* 89, no. 2 (February 1981): 392–406.
[382]Hersh M. Shefrin and Meir Statman, "Explaining Investor Preference for Cash Dividends," *Journal of Financial Economics* 13, no. 2 (June 1984): 253–82.

Hebrew University professors, liked it. "This is a pretty mischievous paper," he said with a smile.

At the 1983 European Finance Association meeting at INSEAD in Fontainebleau, France, I presented a paper that contained the basics of two other papers I subsequently wrote with Shefrin, "The Disposition to Sell Winners Too Early and Ride Losers Too Long: Theory and Evidence" and "Behavioral Aspects of the Design and Marketing of Financial Products."[383] The discussant did not like the paper much, dismissing it by pointing out that Shefrin and I argue, in effect, that investors perceive a half-full glass as holding a different amount of water than a half-empty glass. Rational people like himself, he said, know and teach their students that the two glasses contain identical amounts of water.

Black was elected president of the American Finance Association and planned its December 1984 meeting. Shefrin and I offered to organize a session at the meeting, and he accepted. The session included our paper "The Disposition to Sell Winners Too Early and Ride Losers Too Long" and Werner De Bondt and Richard Thaler's paper "Does the Stock Market Overreact?" Black chose to publish both papers in the *Journal of Finance* in 1985.[384]

Peter Bernstein accepted my invitation to serve as the discussant of De Bondt and Thaler's paper at the December 1984 meeting, and I accepted Bernstein's invitation to serve as a discussant in a session he organized. I ended my discussion of that paper with what reads like a manifesto: "Finance is full of puzzles and it seems as if one is added every day. It is clear, as stated by William Schwert, that we need new theory. However, unlike Schwert, I see no reason why this new theory must be consistent with rational maximizing behavior on the part of all actors in the model. We should develop descriptive (positive) theories. If evidence shows that models allowing actors to display cognitive biases and changing perceptions explain the world of finance better than models allowing only rational behavior, so be it."[385]

Two University of Chicago Booth School of Business professors—Melvin Reder, an economist, and Robin Hogarth, a psychologist—organized a conference at the University of Chicago in October 1985, pitting behavioral economics against standard economics. Shefrin and I were there but without

---

[383]Hersh Shefrin and Meir Statman, "The Disposition to Sell Winners Too Early and Ride Losers Too Long: Theory and Evidence," *Journal of Finance* 40, no. 3 (July 1985): 777–90; Hersh Shefrin and Meir Statman, "Behavioral Aspects of the Design and Marketing of Financial Products," *Financial Management* 22, no. 2 (Summer 1993): 123–34.

[384]Shefrin and Statman, "The Disposition to Sell Winners Too Early and Ride Losers Too Long"; Werner F. M. De Bondt and Richard Thaler, "Does the Stock Market Overreact?" *Journal of Finance* 40, no. 3 (July 1985): 793–805.

[385]Meir Statman, "Discussion," *Journal of Finance* 40, no. 3 (July 1985): 719–21.

speaking roles. At the reception on the evening before the conference's start, I heard a man behind me say to Reder, "If you see Shefrin or Statman, please point them out to me." Reder touched my shoulder and said, "Here is Meir Statman." The man said, "Hi, I'm Merton Miller." Being introduced to God would have made a greater impression on me, but being introduced to Merton Miller came close.

On the morning of the first day of the conference, the Swedish Academy announced that it had awarded the Nobel Prize in Economics to Franco Modigliani, in part for the article on dividends he wrote with Miller.[386] Newspaper reporters from around the world called Miller early that morning, asking for a one-sentence description of this joint work. Miller, known for his wit, said with a chuckle, "Moving money from your left pocket to the right won't make you rich. Franco and I proved it rigorously!"

Later that day, Miller devoted his entire presentation to an attack on the dividends paper Shefrin and I had written.[387] He mistakenly identified us as psychologists, perhaps because he could not conceive of economists writing a paper that incorporated psychology. Demonstrating his wit again, he said, "So here come two boy scouts, Shefrin and Statman, who want to help me cross the street. But I don't want to cross the street!"

In the conference volume published in 1986, following the conference, Miller wrote the following:

> As the title ["Behavioral Rationality in Finance: The Case of Dividends"] suggests, this paper attempts to get to the specifics of the behavioral rationality theme of this conference by focusing on an area in the main core of finance, namely, the demand and supply of dividends, where, by common consent, the essentially "rationalist" paradigm of the field seems to be limping most noticeably. Important and pervasive behavior patterns on both the paying and the receiving ends have despairingly been written off as "puzzles" even by theorists as redoubtable as Fischer Black (see especially his much-cited 1976 article).
>
> Behaviorists have homed in on precisely these same dividend related soft spots in the current body of theory (see especially Shefrin and Statman 1984). We seem to have, in sum, an ideal place to look for signs of an imminent "paradigm shift" in the behavioral direction of precisely the kind envisioned by some of the other contributors to this conference. (p. S451)[388]

---

[386]Merton Miller and Franco Modigliani, "Dividend Policy, Growth, and the Valuation of Shares," *Journal of Business* 34, no. 4 (October 1961): 411–33.
[387]Shefrin and Statman, "Explaining Investor Preference."
[388]Merton Miller, "Behavioral Rationality in Finance: The Case of Dividends," *Journal of Business* 59 (1986): S451–S468.

Miller downplayed the likelihood of a "paradigm shift":

How much concern should they show at this point about our dividend anomalies? Less, I will argue here, after a fresh look at the evidence, than I and others in finance may once have thought (see, e.g., the introduction to Miller and Scholes [1978]). This is not to say that we do not have our share and more of still-unsolved problems. Finance, after all, is one of the newer specialty areas in economics. But I do not see us in such disarray, even on the much-mooted dividend issues, that we must think of abandoning or even drastically modifying the basic economics/finance paradigm on which the field has been built. (p. S452)[389]

I would argue that "a fresh look at the evidence" points to a "paradigm shift in the behavioral direction," a shift that was "imminent" only in 1986, when Miller downplayed it, but is clearly evident today.

The optimism of investors as they buy stocks has an analog in the optimism of project champions as they pitch investment projects, and the disposition of investors to hold on to losing stocks has an analog in the disposition of project champions to throw good money after bad into losing projects. In the second half of the 1980s, I examined this managerial behavior and its reflection in the stock market, collaborating with colleagues in the marketing, management, and accounting departments.[390]

Investors use the term "sentiment" when speaking about optimism and pessimism. They speak of optimism, especially excessive optimism, as "bullish sentiment" and of pessimism, especially excessive pessimism, as "bearish sentiment."

In the mid-1980s, I noticed statements about the Bearish Sentiment Index, calculated as the ratio of the number of writers of investment newsletters who are bearish on the stock market to the number expressing an opinion. A contrarian use of the index calls for buying stocks when it is high and selling when it is low. The index was discussed frequently in the financial press at the time. For example, John Andrew wrote in the *Wall Street Journal* in 1984, "In recent years, the numbers [of the Bearish Sentiment Index] have become one of the most popular contrary indicators in investment circles. On the theory that the stock market generally does the opposite of what most

---

[389]Miller, "Behavioral Rationality in Finance."
[390]Meir Statman and Tyzoon T. Tyebjee, "Optimistic Capital Budgeting Forecasts: An Experiment," *Financial Management* 14, no. 3 (Autumn 1985): 27–33; Meir Statman and David Caldwell, "Applying Behavioral Finance to Capital Budgeting: Project Terminations," *Financial Management* 16, no. 4 (Winter 1987): 7–15; Meir Statman and James F. Sepe, "Project Termination Announcements and the Market Value of the Firm," *Financial Management* 18, no. 4 (Winter 1989): 74–81.

people think it will do, a high percentage of bullish advisers is considered bearish for the market. If most advisers are bears, then the stock market is supposed to be poised for a big rally."[391]

There was little interest in investor sentiment among investment academics at the time, but I thought that investor sentiment might help us understand the behavior of both investors and markets. I received the Bearish Sentiment Index data from the publisher, and fellow economist Michael Solt and I proceeded to find a significant relation between past stock returns and subsequent sentiment, teaching us about the behavior of investors, but no significant relation between sentiment and subsequent returns, teaching us about the behavior of the stock market.[392]

I also wondered at the time whether a range of return "regularities"—from market value of equity to price-to-earnings ratios, price-to-book ratios, and measures of company "neglect" and "excellence"—proxy for a preference for stocks of "good" companies over stocks of "bad" companies, in the mistaken belief that good stocks are stocks of good companies. The exploration was published as "Good Companies, Bad Stocks."[393] That paper is not explicit in attributing the preference for stocks of good companies to the "affect heuristic," but my subsequent work was explicit about it, including "Affect in a Behavioral Asset Pricing Model."[394]

My article "A Behavioral Framework for Dollar-Cost Averaging" was published in 1995, but its origins go back to the early 1980s.[395] I found the practice of dollar-cost averaging interesting because it is not consistent with rational behavior, yet it is persistent. The subtitle of that article is "Dollar-Cost Averaging May Not Be Rational Behavior, But It Is Perfectly Normal Behavior." I ended the article as follows: "It might be time to move on to a positive theory that is consistent with the evidence, and to remember that a normative theory is useless if investors cannot be persuaded to follow it. Meanwhile, I offer a hypothesis. The practice of dollar-cost averaging will persist" (p. 77).

---

[391]John Andrew, "Popularity of Contrary Indicator Judgment: Persistence in the Illusion of Validity, Spurs Questions about Usefulness," *Wall Street Journal* (28 November 1984).

[392]Michael E. Solt and Meir Statman, "How Useful Is the Sentiment Index?" *Financial Analysts Journal* 44, no. 5 (September/October 1988): 45–55.

[393]Michael E. Solt and Meir Statman, "Good Companies, Bad Stocks," *Journal of Portfolio Management* 15, no. 4 (Summer 1989): 39–44.

[394]Meir Statman, Kenneth L. Fisher, and Deniz Anginer, "Affect in a Behavioral Asset-Pricing Model," *Financial Analysts Journal* 64, no. 2 (March/April 2008): 20–29.

[395]Meir Statman, "A Behavioral Framework for Dollar-Cost Averaging: Dollar-Cost Averaging May Not Be Rational Behavior, But It Is Perfectly Normal Behavior," *Journal of Portfolio Management* 22, no. 1 (January 1995): 70–78.

Socially responsible investments caught my attention at about the same time, as I was reading newspaper reports about investors following social responsibility principles. They did so by excluding from their portfolios "sin" stocks, such as those of tobacco, alcohol, and gambling companies, and by favoring stocks of companies demonstrating concern for employees, communities, and the environment.

I found social responsibility investment criteria especially relevant to my thinking because they cannot be reasonably classified as proxies of risk or expected return. Instead, they stand for wants of socially responsible investors for the expressive and emotional benefits of staying true to their values, even when sacrificing the utilitarian benefits of higher returns and lower risk. This was an opening for discussing a wider range of investors' wants, such as wants for social status or fairness.

Few financial studies about socially responsible mutual funds were conducted at the time, despite availability of data about their returns. Standard finance academics neglected these funds likely because they do not fit within standard finance. And standard finance professionals were generally dismissive of, even hostile to, incorporating social responsibility criteria into their investments. Indeed, socially responsible mutual funds were first offered by small mutual fund companies specializing in them.

Fellow economists Hoje Jo and Sally Hamilton and I examined the performance of socially responsible mutual funds in "Doing Good While Doing Well? The Investment Performance of Socially Responsible Mutual Funds."[396] We found that the returns of socially responsible funds were no different from those of conventional funds. The most important part of the article for me, however, was introducing ideas about investor wants into a mainstream finance journal. We ended the article with a quote from the provost of a Quaker college who was asked why the college does not invest in manufacturers of armaments: "Our board isn't out to change the world. We're seeking a oneness between ourselves and our Lord."

Also, in the late 1980s, Shefrin and I wondered about the rationale for financial regulations such as those that mandate disclosure, restrict margin loans, or prohibit insider trading. We asked, What are the roles of cognitive and emotional shortcuts and errors? And what are the roles of wants for fairness?

Baruch Lev, one of my finance professors at the Hebrew University, adhered to standard accounting and finance. In 1988, he presented a

---

[396]Sally Hamilton, Hoje Jo, and Meir Statman, "Doing Well While Doing Good? The Investment Performance of Socially Responsible Mutual Funds," *Financial Analysts Journal* 49, no. 6 (November/December 1993): 62–66.

framework explaining regulations mandating disclosure by companies as influenced by considerations of fairness, but he rejected "moralistic" notions of fairness. He wrote, "The equity-orientation of disclosure regulation advanced here differs markedly from the traditional, moralistic concepts of equity in accounting, which are generally phrased in terms of maintaining fairness, eliminating fraud, and protecting the uninformed investors against exploitation by insiders. In contrast to such vague, anachronistic, and unattractive notions, the equity concept advanced here is state of the art and operational, being linked directly to recent theoretical developments in economics and finance" (p. 1).[397]

Shefrin and I noted that Lev's concept of fairness may be state of the art and operational, but it is too narrow to provide a framework for merit regulations, suitability regulations, margin regulations, trading halts, insider trading regulations, or even mandatory disclosure regulations. We argued instead that a framework consistent with the wide range of regulations in financial markets requires broader notions of fairness. We were inspired by the work of Daniel Kahneman, Jack Knetch, and Richard Thaler, who explored the role of fairness in economic choices.[398]

Shefrin and I argued, for example, that margin regulations protect investors from their own cognitive and emotional errors, because low margins facilitate speculation and resulting losses. We quoted a passage from the deliberations underlying the Securities Exchange Act of 1934: "A Federal judge furnished this committee with instances from his long experience on the bench, indicating that a large proportion of business failures, embezzlements and even suicides in recent years were directly attributable to losses incurred in speculative transactions."[399]

I explored fairness further in the context of insider trading using vignettes of the kind used by Kahneman, Knetch, and Thaler, such as one about "Paul Bond," whose story corresponds to that of James O'Hagan, who was found guilty of insider trading by the US Supreme Court. Justice Ruth Bader Ginsburg addressed fairness in the court's decision as she stressed that "an investor's informational disadvantage vis-à-vis a misappropriator with

---

[397]Baruch Lev, "Toward a Theory of Equitable and Efficient Accounting Policy," *Accounting Review* 63, no. 1 (January 1988): 1–22.

[398]Daniel Kahneman, Jack Knetch, and Richard Thaler, "Fairness as a Constraint on Profit Seeking: Entitlements in the Market," *American Economic Review* 76, no. 4 (September 1986): 728–41.

[399]Hersh Shefrin and Meir Statman, *Ethics, Fairness, Efficiency and Financial Markets* (Charlottesville, VA: Research Foundation of the Institute of Chartered Financial Analysts, 1992); Hersh Shefrin and Meir Statman, "Ethics, Fairness, Efficiency and Financial Markets," *Financial Analysts Journal* 49, no. 6 (November 1993): 21–29.

material, nonpublic information stems from contrivance, not luck; it is a disadvantage that cannot be overcome with research or skill." The first of the resulting articles was titled "Fair Trading."[400]

I broadened the exploration of investor wants by specifying their benefits. In "Behavioral Finance: Past Battles and Future Engagements," published in 1999, I divided benefits into utilitarian and value expressive. Later, in my 2011 book *What Investors Really Want: Discover What Drives Investor Behavior and Make Smarter Financial Decisions* and my 2017 book *Finance for Normal People*, I divided benefits into utilitarian, expressive, and emotional.

My current project focuses on well-being, exploring the utilitarian, expressive, and emotional benefits that enhance it and the utilitarian, expressive, and emotional costs that detract from it. My first article on the topic, "Financial Advisers as Well-Being Advisers," was published in the *Journal of Financial Planning* in September 2019.[401]

Well-being in the context of finance usually implies financial well-being. And discussions about enhancing well-being are usually about enhancing financial well-being, such as by saving during our working years to sustain us in retirement. Well-being, however, is broader than financial well-being, and enhancing well-being entails more than enhancing financial well-being. The domains of well-being also include those of family, friends, and communities, health—both physical and mental—work, and other activities.

My September 2019 article draws from interviews with investors, including Divya, a 33-year-old woman, who said, "My financial status enabled us to purchase this home that is well out of reach for many individuals in my age group and place in life. I felt proud that my family could make the decision to purchase this type of home." This home provides Divya utilitarian benefits as shelter; expressive benefits as an emblem of high social status, "well out of reach for many individuals in my age group and place in life"; and emotional benefits in pride "that my family could make the decision to purchase this type of home." Moreover, finances underlie all these benefits. Divya said, "My financial status enabled us to purchase this home."[402]

---

[400]Meir Statman, "Fair Trading," *Journal of Portfolio Management* 32, no. 1 (Fall 2005): 76–84.
[401]Meir Statman, "Financial Advisers as Well-Being Advisers: Enhance Your Clients' Well-Being by Understanding Its Four Domains," *Journal of Financial Planning* (September 2019): 48–56.
[402]Statman, "Financial Advisers as Well-Being Advisers."

# References

Adelino, Manuel, Antoinette Schoar, and Felipe Severino. 2018. "Perception of House Price Risk and Homeownership." Working paper (24 July). Available at https://ssrn.com/abstract=3197973 or doi:10.3386/w25090.

Agarwal, Sumit, Souphala Chomsisengphet, Stephan Meier, and Xin Zou. 2019. "In the Mood to Consume: Effect of Sunshine on Credit Card Spending." Columbia Business School Research Paper No. 17-104 (13 May). Available at https://ssrn.com/abstract=3014541 or http://dx.doi.org/10.2139/ssrn.3014541.

Agarwal, Sumit, Vyacheslav Mikhed, and Barry Scholnick. 2018. "Does the Relative Income of Peers Cause Financial Distress? Evidence from Lottery Winners and Neighboring Bankruptcies." FRB of Philadelphia Working Paper No. 18-16 (24 May). Available at https://ssrn.com/abstract=3192154 or doi:10.21799/frbp.wp

Agarwal, Sumit, Wenlan Qian, Tien Foo Sing, and Poh Lin Tan. 2018. "Dragon Babies." Georgetown McDonough School of Business Research Paper No. 3032575 (22 November). Available at https://ssrn.com/abstract=3032575 or http://dx.doi.org/10.2139/ssrn.3032575.

Allen, Franklin, Marlene Haas, Eric Nowak, and Angel Tengulov. 2019. "Market Efficiency and Limits to Arbitrage: Evidence from the Volkswagen Short Squeeze." Swiss Finance Institute Research Paper No. 17-64 (14 April). Available at https://ssrn.com/abstract=2977019 or http://dx.doi.org/10.2139/ssrn.2977019.

Anderson, Anders. 2013. "Trading and Under-Diversification." *Review of Finance* 17 (5): 1699–741.

Andonov, Aleksandar, and Joshua D. Rauh. 2019. "The Return Expectations of Institutional Investors." Stanford University Graduate School of Business Research Paper No. 18-5 (1 February). Available at https://ssrn.com/abstract=3091976 or http://dx.doi.org/10.2139/ssrn.3091976.

Andrew, John. 1984. "Popularity of Contrary Indicator Judgment: Persistence in the Illusion of Validity, Spurs Questions about Usefulness." *Wall Street Journal* (28 November).

Andrews, Travis M., and Lindsey Bever. 2017. "'My Pipe Dream Finally Came True': This Woman Won the Second-Largest Powerball Jackpot Ever."

*Washington Post* (24 August). www.washingtonpost.com/news/morning-mix/wp/2017/08/24/the-second-largest-jackpot-in-powerball-history-has-a-winner/?utm_term=.face2e9227ff.

Ang, James S., Gregory Leo Nagel, and Jun Yang. 2014. "The Effect of Social Pressures on CEO Compensation" (17 November). Available at https://ssrn.com/abstract=1107280 or http://dx.doi.org/10.2139/ssrn.1107280.

Anik, Lalin, Lara B. Aknin, Michael I. Norton, and Elizabeth W. Dunn. 2009. "Feeling Good About Giving: The Benefits (and Costs) of Self-Interested Charitable Behavior." Harvard Business School Marketing Unit Working Paper No. 10-012 (6 August). Available at https://ssrn.com/abstract=1444831 or doi:10.2139/ssrn.1444831.

Anthony, Andrea Therese, Kristine Beck, and Inga Chira. 2017. "Does the Source of Money Determine Retirement Investment Choices?" (23 August). Available at https://ssrn.com/abstract=3024533 or doi:10.2139/ssrn.3024533.

Antoniou, Constantinos, Alok Kumar, and Anastasios Maligkris. 2018. "Terrorist Attacks, Analyst Sentiment, and Earnings Forecasts." Working paper (5 April). Available at https://ssrn.com/abstract=2702051 or http://dx.doi.org/10.2139/ssrn.2702051.

Antoniou, Constantinos, Alok Kumar, and Lizhengbo Yang. 2018. "Seeing Is Believing: Travel, Familiarity and International Equity Investments." Working paper (22 August). Available at https://ssrn.com/abstract=3270813 or doi:10.2139/ssrn.3270813.

Appel, Ian, Todd A. Gormley, and Donald B. Keim. 2018. "Standing on the Shoulders of Giants: The Effect of Passive Investors on Activism." Working paper (30 June). Available at http://ssrn.com/abstract=2693145.

Argo, Jennifer J., and Darren W. Dahl. 2018. "Standards of Beauty: The Impact of Mannequins in the Retail Context." *Journal of Consumer Research* 44 (5): 974–90.

Ashraf, Nava. 2009. "Spousal Control and Intra-Household Decision Making: An Experimental Study in the Philippines." *American Economic Review* 99 (4): 1245–77.

Ashraf, Nava, Dean Karlan, and Wesley Yin. 2010. "Female Empowerment: Further Evidence from a Commitment Savings Product in the Philippines." *World Development* 38 (3): 333–44.

Azoulay, Pierre, Christian Fons-Rosen, and Joshua S. Graff Zivin. 2019. "Does Science Advance One Funeral at a Time?" *American Economic Review* 109 (8): 2889–920.

Baele, Lieven, Geert Bekaert, Koen Inghelbrecht, and Min Wei. 2013. "Flights to Safety." National Bureau of Economic Research Working Paper No. w19095 (May).

Bailey, Donald and J. William G. Chettle. 2017. *Your Legacy of Care: Providing for Your Special Needs Child Today, Tomorrow & Always.* San Jose, CA: Loring Ward.

Baker, Malcolm, Stefan Nagel, and Jeffrey Wurgler. 2007. "The Effect of Dividends on Consumption." *Brookings Papers on Economic Activity* (1): 231–91.

Baker, Malcolm P., Jeffrey Wurgler, and Brendan Bradley. 2010. "A Behavioral Finance Explanation for the Success of Low Volatility Portfolios." NYU Working Paper No. 2451/29537 (January). Available at http://ssrn.com/abstract=2284643.

Banz, Rolf W. 1981. "The Relationship between Return and Market Value of Common Stocks." *Journal of Financial Economics* 9 (1): 3–18.

Barber, Brad M., Yi-Tsung Lee, Yu-Jane Liu, and Terrance Odean. 2014. "The Cross-Section of Speculator Skill: Evidence from Day Trading." *Journal of Financial Markets* 18:1–24.

Barber, Brad M., and Terrance Odean. 2000. "Trading Is Hazardous to Your Wealth: The Common Stock Investment Performance of Individual Investors." *Journal of Finance* 55 (2): 773–806.

———. 2008. "All That Glitters: The Effect of Attention and News on the Buying Behavior of Individual and Institutional Investors." *Review of Financial Studies* 21 (2): 785–818.

Barrett, Clear. 2016. "Best of Money: Why Do Most Women Fear the Stock Market?" *Financial Times* (3 June). www.ft.com/content/b681b8e6-2705-11e6-8b18-91555f2f4fde.

Bartlett, Robert P., Adair Morse, Richard H. Stanton, and Nancy E. Wallace. 2017. "Consumer Lending Discrimination in the FinTech Era." UC Berkeley Public Law Research Paper (7 December). Available at https://ssrn.com/abstract=3063448 or https://dx.doi.org/10.2139/ssrn.3063448.

Basu, Sanjoy. 1977. "Investment Performance of Common Stocks in Relation to Their Price-Earnings Ratios: A Test of the Efficient Market Hypothesis." *Journal of Finance* 32 (3): 663–82.

Bazley, William J., Yosef Bonaparte, George M. Korniotis, and Alok Kumar. 2018. "Social Risk and Portfolio Choice." 7th Miami Behavioral Finance Conference 2016 (4 December). Available at https://ssrn.com/abstract=2863351 or http://dx.doi.org/10.2139/ssrn.2863351.

Bazley, William J., Henrik Cronqvist, and Milica Milosavljevic Mormann. 2019. "Visual Finance: The Pervasive Effects of Red on Investor Behavior." Swedish House of Finance Research Paper No. 17-16, SMU Cox School of Business Research Paper No. 18-4, University of Miami Business School Research Paper No. 2992812 (13 March). Available at https://ssrn.com/abstract=2992812 or http://dx.doi.org/10.2139/ssrn.2992812.

Ben-David, Itzhak, Justin Birru, and Viktor Prokopenya. 2016. "Uninformative Feedback and Risk Taking: Evidence from Retail Forex Trading." National Bureau of Economic Research Working Paper No. w22146 (April). Available at http://ssrn.com/abstract=2762097.

Ben-David, Itzhak, Justin Birru, and Andrea Rossic. 2019. "Industry Familiarity and Trading: Evidence from the Personal Portfolios of Industry Insiders." *Journal of Financial Economics* 132:49–75.

Benz, Christine. 2013. "The Error-Proof Portfolio: OK, People—What Have We Learned? The Bull Market Is Entering Its Fifth Year, but How Have Investors Done since the Market Recovered?" *Morningstar* (28 October). http://news.morningstar.com/articlenet/article.aspx?id=616424.

Berk, Jonathan B., and Jules H. Van Binsbergen. 2012. "Measuring Managerial Skill in the Mutual Fund Industry." National Bureau of Economic Research Working Paper No. 18184 (June). Available at https://ssrn.com/abstract=2089256.

Bhattacharya, Utpal, Daisy J. Huang, and Kasper Meisner Nielsen. 2017. "Spillovers in Asset Prices: The Curious Case of Haunted Houses." 8th Miami Behavioral Finance Conference 2017 (27 November). Available at https://ssrn.com/abstract=3077951 or doi:10.2139/ssrn.3077951.

Binkley, Christina. 2009. "How to Sell a $35,000 Watch in a Recession: Salespeople Study Distracting the Wife, Avoiding Talk of 'Price' and Other Tactics." *Wall Street Journal* (23 July). www.wsj.com/articles/SB10001424052 9702035173045743043227071263 80.

Black, Fischer. 1976. "The Dividend Puzzle." *Journal of Portfolio Management* 2 (2): 5–8.

———. 1986. "Noise." *Journal of Finance* 41 (3): 528–43.

———. 1993. "Beta and Return." *Journal of Portfolio Management* 20 (1): 8–18.

Blanchett, David. 2017. "Save More Today: Improving Retirement Savings Rates with Carrots, Advice, and Nudges." *Journal of Retirement* 5 (1): 69–95.

Blankespoor, Elizabeth, Ed deHaan, John Wertz, and Christina Zhu. 2018. "Why Do Individual Investors Disregard Accounting Information? The Roles of Information Awareness and Acquisition Costs." *Journal of Accounting Research* 57 (1): 53–84.

Borgers, Arian C.T., Rachel A.J. Pownall, and Louis Raes. 2015. "Exposure to Bankers: Networks and Stock Market Participation." Working paper (1 October). Available at http://ssrn.com/abstract=2783360 or http://dx.doi.org/10.2139/ssrn.2783360.

Bradley, Daniel, Sinan Gokkaya, and Xi Liu. 2017. "Before an Analyst Becomes an Analyst: Does Industry Experience Matter?" *Journal of Finance* 72 (2): 751–92.

Brenner, Suzanne A. 1995. "Why Women Rule the Roost: Rethinking Javanese Ideologies of Gender and Self-Control." In *Bewitching Women, Pious Men: Gender and Body Politics in Southeast Asia*, edited by Aihwa Ong and Michael G. Peletz, 19–50. Berkeley: University of California Press.

Brooks, John. 1999. *The Go-Go Years: The Drama and Crashing Finale of Wall Street's Bullish 60s*. New York: Wiley Investment Classics.

Brown, James R., J. Anthony Cookson, and Rawley Heimer. 2016. "Growing Up Without Finance." 7th Miami Behavioral Finance Conference 2016 (8 September). Available at https://ssrn.com/abstract=2809164 or doi:10.2139/ssrn.2809164.

Brown, Martin, Jan Schmitz, and Christian Zehnder. 2017. "Social Norms and Strategic Default." University of St. Gallen, School of Finance Research Paper No. 2016/08 (June). Available at http://ssrn.com/abstract=2743278 or http://dx.doi.org/10.2139/ssrn.2743278.

Brown, Stephen, Yan Lu, Sugata Ray, and Melvyn Teo. 2018. "Sensation Seeking and Hedge Funds." *Journal of Finance* 73 (6): 2871–914.

Brunnermeier, Markus K., and Stefan Nagel. 2004. "Hedge Funds and the Technology Bubble." *Journal of Finance* 59 (5): 2013–40.

Bursztyn, Leonardo, Thomas Fujiwara, and Amanda Pallais. 2017. "'Acting Wife': Marriage Market Incentives and Labor Market Investments." *American Economic Review* 107 (11): 3288–319.

Byun, Suk-Joon, and Jihoon Goh. 2017. "The Role of Psychological Barriers in Lottery-Related Anomalies." Working paper (21 November). Available at https://ssrn.com/abstract=3144907 or doi:10.2139/ssrn.3144907.

Card, David, Alexandre Mas, Enrico Moretti, and Emmanuel Saez. 2012. "Inequality at Work: The Effect of Peer Salaries on Job Satisfaction." *American Economic Review* 102 (6): 2981–3003.

Carvalho, Carlos Viana de, Nicholas Klagge, and Emanuel Moench. 2011. "The Persistent Effects of a False News Shock." *Journal of Empirical Finance* 18 (4): 597–615.

Chague, Fernando Chague, Rodrigo De-Losso, and Bruno Giovannetti. 2017. "The Price Tag Illusion." Department of Economics Working Paper No. 2017-31, University of Sao Paulo (16 November).

Chang, Tom Y., David H. Solomon, and Mark M. Westerfield. 2016. "Looking for Someone to Blame: Delegation, Cognitive Dissonance, and the Disposition Effect." *Journal of Finance* 71 (1): 267–302.

Chapman, Gretchen B., and Eric J. Johnson. 2002. "Incorporating the Irrelevant: Anchors in Judgments of Belief and Value." In *Heuristics and Biases: The Psychology of Intuitive Judgment*, edited by Thomas Gilovich, Dale W. Griffin, and Daniel Kahneman, 120–138. New York: Cambridge University Press.

Chapman, Jonathan, Erik Snowberg, Stephanie Wang, and Colin F. Camerer. 2018. "Loss Attitudes in the U.S. Population: Evidence from Dynamically Optimized Sequential Experimentation (Dose)." CESifo Working Paper No. 7262. Available at https://ssrn.com/abstract=3275438.

Chava, Sudheer, Soohun Kim, and Daniel Weagley. 2018. "Revealed Heuristics: Evidence from Investment Consultants' Search Behavior." Georgia Tech Scheller College of Business Research Paper No. 18-44; 14th Annual Mid-Atlantic Research Conference in Finance (2 November). Available at https://ssrn.com/abstract=3277424 or doi:10.2139/ssrn.3277424.

Chen, Yong, Bryan T. Kelly, and Wei Wu. 2018. "Sophisticated Investors and Market Efficiency: Evidence from a Natural Experiment." Mays Business School Research Paper No. 3117188; 29th Annual Conference on Financial Economics & Accounting 2018; Yale ICF Working Paper No.

**185**

2018-05 (19 September). Available at https://ssrn.com/abstract=3117188 or doi:10.3386/w24552.

Cheng, Evelyn. 2016. "Wall Street Reacts: Here's What the Markets Will Do after the Election." *Yahoo! Finance* (7 November). https://finance.yahoo.com/news/wall-street-reacts-heres-markets-144110170.html.

Choi, James J., David Laibson, Brigitte C. Madrian, and Andrew Metrick. 2002. "Defined Contribution Pensions: Plan Rules, Participant Decisions, and The Path of Least Resistance." In *Tax Policy and the Economy*, Vol. 16, edited by James M. Poterba, 67–114. Cambridge, MA: MIT Press.

Cici, Gjergji, Monika Gehde-Trapp, Marc-André Goericke, and Alexander Kempf. 2017. "The Investment Value of Fund Managers' Experience Outside the Financial Sector." Working paper (10 June). Available at https://ssrn.com/abstract=2498797 or http://dx.doi.org/10.2139/ssrn.2498797.

Clark, Robert L., Robert G. Hammond, Melinda Sandler Morrill, and Christelle Khalaf. 2017. "Nudging Retirement Savings: A Field Experiment on Supplemental Plans." National Bureau of Economic Research Working Paper No. 23679 (August).

Clarke, Roger G., Scott Krase, and Meir Statman. 1994. "Tracking Errors, Regret, and Tactical Asset Allocation." *Journal of Portfolio Management* 20 (3): 16–24.

Clarke, Roger G., and Meir Statman. 2000. "The DJIA Crossed 652,230." *Journal of Portfolio Management* 26 (2): 89–92.

Clovestar. "I'm Taiwanese American." 2007. Comment on "Raise Your Children to Rely on Them—Asian Culture and Finances," Make Love, Not Debt (8 May). www.makelovenotdebt.com/2007/05/raise_your_children_to_rely_on_them_asian_culture_and_finances.php.

Cohn, Alain, Jan Engelmann, Ernst Fehr, and Michel André Maréchal. 2015. "Evidence for Countercyclical Risk Aversion: An Experiment with Financial Professionals." *American Economic Review* 105 (2): 860–85.

Cole, Shawn Allen, Martin Kanz, and Leora F. Klapper. 2015. "Incentivizing Calculated Risk-Taking: Evidence from an Experiment with Commercial Bank Loan Officers." *Journal of Finance* 70 (2): 537–75.

Cordes, Henning, Bryan Foltice, and Thomas Langer. 2019. "Misperception of Exponential Growth: Are People Aware of Their Errors?" *Decision Analysis*, Forthcoming. Available at https://ssrn.com/abstract=3138109 or http://dx.doi.org/10.2139/ssrn.3138109.

Cortés, Kristle Romero, Duchin Ran, and Denis Sosyura. 2016. "Clouded Judgment: The Role of Sentiment in Credit Origination." *Journal of Financial Economics* 121 (2): 392–413.

Cox, Ruben, and Peter de Goeij. 2017 "What Do Investors Learn from Advertisements?" Working paper (8 September). Available at https://ssrn.com/abstract=3034144 or doi:10.2139/ssrn.3034144.

Cronqvist, Henrik, Richard H. Thaler, and Fang Yu. 2018, "When Nudges Are Forever: Inertia in the Swedish Premium Pension Plan." *AEA Papers and Proceedings*, Vol. 108 (May): 153–58.

Cross, Cassandra. 2016. "'They're Very Lonely': Understanding the Fraud Victimisation of Seniors." *International Journal for Crime, Justice and Social Democracy* 5 (4): 60–75.

Cuffe, Harold E., and Christopher G. Gibbs. 2015. "The Effect of Payday Lending Restrictions on Liquor Sales" (26 August). Available at http://ssrn.com/abstract=2652018 or doi:10.2139/ssrn.2652018.

Cvijanovic, Dragana, and Christophe Spaenjers. 2018. "'We'll Always Have Paris': Out-of-Country Buyers in the Housing Market." Kenan Institute of Private Enterprise Research Paper No. 18-25; HEC Paris Research Paper No. FIN-2018-1311 (3 October). Available at https://ssrn.com/abstract=3248902 or doi:10.2139/ssrn.3248902.

Da, Zhi, Xing Huang, and Lawrence J. Jin. 2019. "Extrapolative Beliefs in the Cross-Section: What Can We Learn from the Crowds?" (4 May). Available at https://ssrn.com/abstract=3144849 or http://dx.doi.org/10.2139/ssrn.3144849.

Dagher, Veronica. 2016. "When an Elderly Parent Has Been Scammed." *Wall Street Journal* (12 June). www.wsj.com/articles/when-an-elderly-parent-has-been-scammed-1465783683#comments_sector.

Das, Sanjiv, Harry Markowitz, Jonathan Scheid, and Meir Statman. 2010. "Portfolio Optimization with Mental Accounts." *Journal of Financial and Quantitative Analysis* 45 (2): 311–34.

Das, Sanjiv R., Harry Markowitz, Jonathan Scheid, and Meir Statman. 2011. "Portfolios for Investors Who Want to Reach Their Goals while Staying on the Mean–Variance Efficient Frontier." *Journal of Wealth Management* 14 (2): 25–31.

Das, Sreyoshi, Camelia M. Kuhnen, and Stefan Nagel. 2017. "Socioeconomic Status and Macroeconomic Expectations." National Bureau of Economic

Research Working Paper No. 24045; *Review of Financial Studies*, Forthcoming (13 November). Available at https://ssrn.com/abstract=3009941 or doi:10.3386/w24045.

Davidoff, Thomas. 2014. "Reverse Mortgage Demographics and Collateral Performance." Working paper (25 February). Available at http://ssrn.com/abstract=2399942 or doi:10.2139/ssrn.2399942.

Deason, Stephen, Shivaram Rajgopal, and Gregory B. Waymire. 2015. "Who Gets Swindled in Ponzi Schemes?" Working paper (28 March). Available at http://ssrn.com/abstract=2586490 or doi:10.2139/ssrn.2586490.

Deaton, Angus. 2005. "Franco Modigliani and the Life Cycle Theory of Consumption." Working paper (March). Available at https://ssrn.com/abstract=686475 or doi:10.2139/ssrn.686475.

De Bondt, Werner F. M., and Richard Thaler. 1985. "Does the Stock Market Overreact?" *Journal of Finance* 40 (3): 793–805. www.jstor.org/stable/2327804.

Della Vedova, Josh, Andrew R. Grant, and P. Joakim Westerholm. 2018. "Investor Behavior at the 52 Week High." 30th Australasian Finance and Banking Conference 2017; 9th Conference on Financial Markets and Corporate Governance 2018 (20 May). Available at https://ssrn.com/abstract=3021585 or http://dx.doi.org/10.2139/ssrn.3021585.

Dhar, Ravi, and William N. Goetzmann. 2006. "Bubble Investors: What Were They Thinking?" Yale ICF Working Paper No. 06-22 (17 August). Available at https://ssrn.com/abstract=683366.

Dichev, Ilia D. 2007. "What Are Stock Investors' Actual Historical Returns? Evidence from Dollar-Weighted Returns." *American Economic Review* 97 (1): 386–401.

Ditto, Peter H., and David F. Lopez. 1992. "Motivated Skepticism: Use of Differential Decision Criteria for Preferred and Nonpreferred Conclusions." *Journal of Personality and Social Psychology* 63 (4): 568–84.

Dorn, Daniel, and Paul Sengmueller. 2009. "Trading as Entertainment?" *Management Science* 55 (4): 591–603.

Du, Mengqiao, Alexandra Niessen-Ruenzi, and Terrance Odean. 2018. "Stock Repurchasing Bias of Mutual Funds" (10 September). Available at https://ssrn.com/abstract=3247066 or doi:10.2139/ssrn.3247066.

Duhigg, Charles. 2019. "Why Are We So Angry?" *Atlantic (Boston, Mass.)* (January/February): 62–75.

Easley, David, David Michayluk, Maureen O'Hara, and Talis J. Putnins. 2018. "The Active World of Passive Investing." Western Finance Association Annual Meeting 2018 (29 July). Available at https://ssrn.com/abstract=3220842 or doi:10.2139/ssrn.3220842.

Easterlin, Richard A. 1973. "Does Money Buy Happiness?" *Public Interest* 30 (Winter):3–10.

Eberhardt, Wiebke, Elisabeth Brüggen, Thomas Post, and Chantal Hoet. 2018. "Framing the Future: Using Investment and Assurance Frames to Encourage Retirement Information Search." Working paper (4 July). Available at https://ssrn.com/abstract=3060519 or http://dx.doi.org/10.2139/ssrn.3060519.

Edmans, Alex. 2011. "Does the Stock Market Fully Value Intangibles? Employee Satisfaction and Equity Prices." *Journal of Financial Economics* 101 (3): 621–40.

Egan, Mark. 2019. "Brokers versus Retail Investors: Conflicting Interests and Dominated Products." *Journal of Finance* 74 (3): 1217–60.

Egan, Mark, Gregor Matvos, and Amit Seru. 2016. "The Market for Financial Adviser Misconduct." National Bureau of Economic Research Working Paper No. w22050 (February). Available at http://ssrn.com/abstract=2739590.

———. 2018. "When Harry Fired Sally: The Double Standard in Punishing Misconduct." Harvard Business School Finance Working Paper No. 19-047 (8 August). Available at https://ssrn.com/abstract=2931940 or http://dx.doi.org/10.2139/ssrn.2931940.

———. 2019. "Arbitration with Uninformed Consumers." Harvard Business School Finance Working Paper No. 19-046 (June). Available at https://ssrn.com/abstract=3260442 or http://dx.doi.org/10.2139/ssrn.3260442.

Eisenberg, Richard. 2018. "Parents' Support to Adult Kids: A Stunning $500 Billion a Year: Are boomers and Gen Xers harming their retirement due to their generosity?" *Next Avenue* (2 October). www.nextavenue.org/parents-support-adult-kids/.

Epley, Nicholas, and Thomas Gilovich. 2016. "The Mechanics of Motivated Reasoning." *Journal of Economic Perspectives* 30 (3): 133–40.

Erev, Ido, Thomas S. Wallsten, and David V. Budescu. 1994. "Simultaneous Over- and Underconfidence: The Role of Error in Judgment Processes." *Psychological Review* 101 (3): 519–27.

Ertan, Aytekin, Stephen A. Karolyi, Peter Kelly, and Robert C. Stoumbos. 2019. "Earnings Announcement Return Extrapolation." Paper, 7th Miami Behavioral Finance Conference 2016 (25 May). Available at https://ssrn.com/abstract=2720573 or http://dx.doi.org/10.2139/ssrn.2720573.

Fadel, Leila. 2016. "Migrants Wait in Moroccan Forest for a Chance to Cross into Europe." *NPR* (21 April). www.npr.org/2016/04/21/475079102/migrants-wait-in-a-moroccan-forest-for-a-chance-to-cross-into-europe.

Fair, Ray. 2002. "Events That Shook the Market." *Journal of Business* 75 (4): 713–31.

Fama, Eugene F. 1965. "Random Walks in Stock Market Prices." *Financial Analysts Journal* 21 (5): 55–59.

———. 1965. "The Behavior of Stock-Market Prices." *Journal of Business* 38 (1): 34–105.

———. 1991. "Efficient Capital Markets: II." *Journal of Finance* 46 (5): 1575–617.

Fama, Eugene F., and Kenneth R. French. 1992. "The Cross-Section of Expected Stock Returns." *Journal of Finance* 47 (2): 427–65.

———. 2010. "Luck versus Skill in the Cross-Section of Mutual Fund Returns." *Journal of Finance* 65 (5): 1915–47.

———. 2015. "A Five-Factor Asset Pricing Model." *Journal of Financial Economics* 116 (1): 1–22.

———. 2018. "Volatility Lessons." *Financial Analysts Journal* 74 (3): 42–53.

Faraji-Rad, Ali, and Leonard Lee. 2016. "Banking Happiness." Working paper (4 February). Available at https://ssrn.com/abstract=2728061 or doi:10.2139/ssrn.2728061.

Farrell, Diana, Fiona Greig, and Amar Hamoudi. 2019. "Tax Time: How Families Manage Tax Refunds and Payments." Working paper (6 March). Available at https://ssrn.com/abstract=3348019 or doi:10.2139/ssrn.3348019.

Fender, Rebecca, Renée B. Adams, Brad M. Barber, and Terrance Odean. 2016. "Gender Diversity in Investment Management: New Research for Practitioners on How to Close the Gender Gap." CFA Institute Research Foundation 2016B-5 (1 September). Available at https://ssrn.com/abstract=2978151.

Fischhoff, Baruch. 1982. "Debiasing." In *Judgment under Uncertainty: Shortcuts and Biases*, edited by Daniel Kahneman, Paul Slovic, and Amos Tversky, 422–444. Cambridge, UK: Cambridge University Press.

Fisher, Kenneth L., and Meir Statman. 1997. "The Mean–Variance-Optimization Puzzle: Security Portfolios and Food Portfolios." *Financial Analysts Journal* 53 (4): 41–50.

Foohey, Pamela. 2017. "Calling on the CFPB for Help: Telling Stories and Consumer Protection." *Law and Contemporary Problems* 80 (3): 177–209.

Frankel, Jeffrey A., and Ayako Saiki. 2016. "Does It Matter If Statistical Agencies Frame the Month's CPI Report on a 1-Month or 12-Month Basis?" HKS Working Paper No. 16-011 (12 March). Available at http://ssrn.com/abstract=2749123 or http://dx.doi.org/10.2139/ssrn.2749123.

Freeman, Andrea. 2013. "Payback: A Structural Analysis of the Credit Card Problem." *Arizona Law Review* 55 (1): 151–199. Available at http://ssrn.com/abstract=2231738.

Friedman, Milton. 1957. *A Theory of the Consumption Function*. Princeton, NJ: Princeton University Press.

Friess, Steve. 2018. "From the Poker Table to Wall Street." *New York Times* (27 July). www.nytimes.com/2018/07/27/business/vanessa-selbst-poker-bridgewater.html?smprod=nytcore-ipad&smid=nytcore-ipad-share.

Frydman, Cary, and Colin Camerer. 2016. "Neural Evidence of Regret and Its Implications for Investor Behavior." *Review of Financial Studies* 29 (11): 3108–3139

Fungáčová, Zuzana, Iftekhar Hasan, and Laurent Weill. 2016. "Trust in Banks." BOFIT Discussion Paper No. 7/2016; Gabelli School of Business, Fordham University Research Paper No. 2782358 (13 May). Available at http://ssrn.com/abstract=2782358.

Ganzach, Yoav. 2000. "Judging Risk and Return of Financial Assets." *Organizational Behavior and Human Decision Processes* 83 (2): 353–70.

Garbinsky, Emily N., and Joe J. Gladstone. 2019. "The Consumption Consequences of Couples Pooling Finances." *Journal of Consumer Psychology* 29 (3): 353–69.

Geczy, Christopher, David Levin, and Robert Stambaugh. 2005. "Investing in Socially Responsible Mutual Funds." Working paper (October). Available at https://ssrn.com/abstract=416380 or http://dx.doi.org/10.2139/ssrn.416380.

Getmansky, Mila, Ravi Jagannathan, Loriana Pelizzon, Ernst Schaumburg, and Darya Yuferova. 2018. "Stock Price Crashes: Role of Slow-Moving Capital." SAFE Working Paper No. 227 (16 July). Available at https://ssrn.com/abstract=3239440 or http://dx.doi.org/10.2139/ssrn.3239440.

Gino, Francesca, Michael I. Norton, and Dan Ariely. 2010. "The Counterfeit Self: The Deceptive Costs of Faking It." *Psychological Science* 21 (5): 712–20.

Gjersoe, Nathalia. 2016. "The Ebbinghaus Illusion: Small, or Very Far Away?" *The Guardian* (22 August). www.theguardian.com/science/head-quarters/2016/aug/22/the-ebbinghaus-illusion-small-far-away-circles-father-ted.

Goetzmann, William, and Nadav Peles. 1997. "Cognitive Dissonance and Mutual Fund Investors." *Journal of Financial Research* 20 (2): 145–58.

Gomelsky, Victoria. 2014. "How Switzerland Came to Dominate Watchmaking." *New York Times* (20 November). www.nytimes.com/2014/11/21/style/international/what-enabled-switzerland-to-dominate-watch-making.html.

Grossman, Sanford J., and Joseph E. Stiglitz. 1980. "On the Impossibility of Informationally Efficient Markets." *American Economic Review* 70 (3): 393–408.

Gurun, Umit G., Gregor Matvos, and Amit Seru. 2016. "Advertising Expensive Mortgages." *Journal of Finance* 71 (5): 2371–416.

Gurun, Umit G., Noah Stoffman, and Scott E. Yonker. 2017. "Trust Busting: The Effect of Fraud on Investor Behavior." Kelley School of Business Research Paper No. 15-70 (24 May). Available at http://ssrn.com/abstract=2664307 or http://dx.doi.org/10.2139/ssrn.2664307.

Hackethal, Andreas, Christine Laudenbach, Steffen Meyer, and Annika Weber. 2018. "Client Involvement in Expert Advice: Antibiotics in Finance?" SAFE Working Paper No. 219 (23 July). Available at https://ssrn.com/abstract=3178664 or doi:10.2139/ssrn.3178664.

Hakim, Danny. 2001. "On Wall St., More Investors Push Social Goals." *New York Times* (11 February). www.nytimes.com/2001/02/11/business/on-wall-st-more-investors-push-social-goals.html.

Hamilton, Sally, Hoje Jo, and Meir Statman. 1993. "Doing Well While Doing Good? The Investment Performance of Socially Responsible Mutual Funds." *Financial Analysts Journal* 49 (6): 62–66.

Han, Bing, David A. Hirshleifer, and Johan Walden. 2019. "Social Transmission Bias and Investor Behavior." Rotman School of Management Working Paper No. 3053655 (31 May). Available at https://ssrn.com/abstract=3053655 or http://dx.doi.org/10.2139/ssrn.3053655.

Hartzmark, Samuel M., and Kelly Shue. 2018. "A Tough Act to Follow: Contrast Effects in Financial Markets." *Journal of Finance* 73 (4): 1567–1613.

Hartzmark, Samuel M., and Abigail B. Sussman. 2019. "Do Investors Value Sustainability? A Natural Experiment Examining Ranking and Fund Flows." *Journal of Finance* (9 August).

He, Jia, Haoming Liu, Tien Foo Sing, Changcheng Song, and Wei-Kang Wong. 2018. "Superstition, Conspicuous Spending, and Housing Market: Evidence from Singapore." Working paper (9 February). Available at https://ssrn.com/abstract=3120932 or doi:10.2139/ssrn.3120932.

Hershfield, Hal, Stephen Shu, and Shlomo Benartzi. 2019. "Temporal Reframing and Participation in a Savings Program: A Field Experiment." Working paper (2 February). Available at https://ssrn.com/abstract=3097468 or http://dx.doi.org/10.2139/ssrn.3097468.

Herzenstein, Michal, Sharon Horsky, and Steven S. Posavac. 2015. "Living with Terrorism or Withdrawing in Terror: Perceived Control and Consumer Avoidance." *Journal of Consumer Behaviour* 14 (4): 228–36.

Hilary, Gilles, and Sterling Huang. 2015. "Trust and Contracting." INSEAD Working Paper No. 2015/42/ACC (11 May). Available at https://ssrn.com/abstract=2604974 or doi:10.2139/ssrn.2604974.

Hirshleifer, David A., and Yaron Levi, Ben Lourie, and Siew Hong Teog. 2017. "Decision Fatigue and Heuristic Analyst Forecasts." Working paper (19 July). Available at https://ssrn.com/abstract=3005757 or http://dx.doi.org/10.2139/ssrn.3005757.

Hoffmann, Arvid O. I. 2007. "Individual Investors' Needs and the Investment Professional: Lessons from Marketing." *Journal of Investment Consulting* 8 (2): 80–91.

Hoffmann, Arvid O. I., Zwetelina Iliewa, and Lena Jaroszek. 2017. "Wall Street Crosses Memory Lane: How Witnessed Returns Affect Professionals' Expected Returns." Paris December 2017 Finance Meeting EUROFIDAI – AFFI (22 January). Available at https://ssrn.com/abstract=2877366 or doi:10.2139/ssrn.2877366.

Holsendolph, Ernest. 1974. "Stockholders and Pickets Score Con Ed Management." *New York Times* (21 May). www.nytimes.com/1974/05/21/archives/stockholders-and-pickets-score-con-ed-management-where-is-luce-some.html.

Hong, Harrison, and Marcin Kacperczyk. 2009. "The Price of Sin: The Effects of Social Norms on Markets." *Journal of Financial Economics* 93 (1): 15–36.

Hong, Harrison, and Leonard Kostovetsky. 2012. "Red and Blue Investing: Values and Finance." *Journal of Financial Economics* 103 (1): 1–19.

Hou, Kewei, Chen Xue, and Lu Zhang. 2015. "Digesting Anomalies: An Investment Approach." *Review of Financial Studies* 28 (3): 650–705.

Hsu, Jason C. 2012. "Selling Hope." *Rotman International Journal of Pension Management* 5 (2): 6–7.

Huberman, Gur, and Tomer Regev. 2001. "Contagious Speculation and a Cure for Cancer: A Nonevent That Made Stock Prices Soar." *Journal of Finance* 56 (1): 387–96.

Hurd, Michael D., Angela Duckworth, Susann Rohwedder, and David R. Weir. 2012. "Personality Traits and Economic Preparation for Retirement." Working paper (1 September). Available at http://ssrn.com/abstract=2239766.

Hurwitz, Abigail, and Orly Sade. 2017. "An Investigation of Time Preferences, Life Expectancy and Annuity versus Lump-Sum Choices – Can Smoking Harm Long-Term Saving Decisions?" Working paper (19 February). Available at https://ssrn.com/abstract=2742652 or http://dx.doi.org/10.2139/ssrn.2742652.

Hyytinen, Ari, and Hanna Putkuri. 2012. "Household Optimism and Borrowing." Bank of Finland Research Discussion Paper No. 21/2012 (8 May). Available at https://ssrn.com/abstract=2101025 or doi:10.2139/ssrn.2101025.

Ifcher, John, and Homa Zarghamee. 2011. "Happiness and Time Preference: The Effect of Positive Affect in a Random-Assignment Experiment." *American Economic Review* 101 (7): 3109–29.

Israeli, Doron, Ron Kasznik, and Suhas A. Sridharan. 2019. "Unexpected Distractions and Investor Attention to Corporate Announcements." Working paper (13 May). Available at https://ssrn.com/abstract=3057278 or http://dx.doi.org/10.2139/ssrn.3057278.

Jagolinzer, Alan D., David F. Larcker, Gaizka Ormazabal, and Daniel J. Taylor. 2017. "Political Connections and the Informativeness of Insider Trades." Rock

Center for Corporate Governance at Stanford University Working Paper No. 222 (29 July). Available at https://ssrn.com/abstract=2836053 or http://dx.doi.org/10.2139/ssrn.2836053.

Jefremovas, Villia. 2000. "Women Are Good with Money: The Impact of Cash Cropping on Class Relations and Gender Ideology in Northern Luzon, Philippines." In *Women Farmers and Commercial Ventures: Increasing Food Security in Developing Countries*, edited by Anita Spring, 131–150. Boulder, CO: Lynne Reinner.

Jiang, Wenxi, and Mindy Z. Xiaolan. 2017. "Growing Beyond Performance." Working paper (15 July). Available at https://ssrn.com/abstract=3002922 or doi:10.2139/ssrn.3002922.

Jorion, Philippe. 2000. "Risk Management Lessons from Long-Term Capital Management." *European Financial Management* 6 (3): 277–300.

Kahan, Dan M., and Martha C. Nussbaum. 1996. "Two Conceptions of Emotion in Criminal Law." *Columbia Law Review* 96 (2): 269–374.

Kahneman, Daniel. 2011. *Thinking, Fast and Slow*. New York: Farrar, Straus and Giroux.

Kahneman, Daniel, Jack Knetch, and Richard Thaler. 1986. "Fairness as a Constraint on Profit Seeking: Entitlements in the Market." *American Economic Review* 76 (4): 728–41.

Kahneman, Daniel, and Amos Tversky. 1979. "Prospect Theory: An Analysis of Decision under Risk." *Econometrica* 47 (2): 263–92.

Kaplanski, Guy, and Haim Levy. 2010. "Sentiment and Stock Prices: The Case of Aviation Disasters." *Journal of Financial Economics* 95 (2): 174–201.

Karadas, Serkan. 2019. "Trading on Private Information: Evidence from Members of Congress." *Financial Review* 54 (1): 85–131.

Kaufman, Gena. 2012. "Apparently THIS Is the Age Most People Feel Like Adults... (Do You Feel Like a Grownup Yet?)." *Glamour* (2 August). www.glamour.com/story/apparently-this-is-the-age-mos.

Kaustia, Markku, and Elias Rantapuska. 2012. "Rational and Behavioral Motives to Trade: Evidence from Reinvestment of Dividends and Tender Offer Proceeds." *Journal of Banking & Finance* 36 (8): 2366–78.

Ke, Da. 2018. "Who Wears the Pants? Gender Identity Norms and Intra-Household Financial Decision Making." Working paper (4 August).

Available at https://ssrn.com/abstract=2909720 or http://dx.doi.org/10.2139/ssrn.2909720.

Keim, Donald B., and Olivia Mitchell. 2018. "Simplifying Choices in Defined Contribution Retirement Plan Design: A Case Study." *Journal of Pension Economics and Finance* 17 (3): 363–84.

Kettley, Sebastian. 2017. "Nostradamus 2018 Prediction: The END OF THE WORLD Is Coming Next Year Warns Famed Prophet." *Express.co.uk* (30 December). www.express.co.uk/news/weird/898132/nostradamus-2018-prediction-end-of-the-world-prophecy.

Keys, C. M. 1911a. "The Bargain Hunter." In *The World's Work*, vol. XXII, edited by Walter H. Page and Arthur Wilson Page, 14922–14924. Garden City, NY: Doubleday, Page & Company.

———. 1911b. "The Nervous Investor and the News." In *The World's Work*, Vol. XXI, edited by Walter H. Page, 14081–14083. Garden City, NY: Doubleday, Page & Company.

Khanna, Arun. 1998. "The Titanic: The Untold Economic Story." *Financial Analysts Journal* 54 (5): 16–17.

Kilgannon, Corey. 2018. "96-Year-Old Secretary Quietly Amasses Fortune, Then Donates $8.2 Million." *New York Times* (6 May). www.nytimes.com/2018/05/06/nyregion/secretary-fortune-donates.html?hp&action=click&pgtype=Homepage&clickSource=story-heading&module=second-column-region&region=top-news&WT.nav=top-news.

Kleinfield, Sonny. 1983. *The Traders*. New York: Holt, Rinehart and Winston.

Kogan, Shimon, Tobias J. Moskowitz, and Marina Niessner. 2019. "Fake News: Evidence from Financial Markets." Working paper (15 April). Available at https://ssrn.com/abstract=3237763 or http://dx.doi.org/10.2139/ssrn.3237763.

Korn, Olaf, and Marc Oliver Rieger. 2017. "Hedging with Regret." Working paper (16 August). Available at https://ssrn.com/abstract=3020006 or doi:10.2139/ssrn.3020006.

Kruger, Justin, and Jeremy Burrus. 2004. "Egocentrism and Focalism in Unrealistic Optimism (and Pessimism)." *Journal of Experimental Social Psychology* 40 (3): 332–40.

Kruger, Justin. 1999. "Lake Wobegon Be Gone! The 'Below-Average Effect' and the Egocentric Nature of Comparative Ability Judgments." *Journal of Personality and Social Psychology* 77 (2): 221–32.

Kuchler, Theresa, and Basit Zafar. 2015. "Personal Experiences and Expectations About Aggregate Outcomes." FRB of NY Staff Report No. 748 (1 October). Available at https://ssrn.com/abstract=2677572.

Kurtzleben, Danielle. 2015. "How Americans Define 'Rich,' in One Chart." *Vox* (2 March). www.vox.com/2015/3/2/8125629/middle-class-rich-US.

Lancaster, Kelvin J. 1966. "A New Approach to Consumer Theory." *Journal of Political Economy* 74 (2): 132–57.

Langevoort, Donald. 1999. "Rereading Cady, Roberts: The Ideology and Practice of Insider Trading Regulation." *Columbia Law Review* 99:1319–41.

Lazarus, Richard S. 1991. *Emotion and Adaptation*. New York: Oxford University Press.

LeBoeuf, Robyn A., and Michael I. Norton. 2012. "Consequence-Cause Matching: Looking to the Consequences of Events to Infer Their Causes." *Journal of Consumer Research* 39 (1): 128–41.

Lee, Eunju, and Natalia Scotto Piqueira. 2019. "Behavioral Biases of Informed Traders: Evidence from Insider Trading on the 52-Week High." *Journal of Empirical Finance* 52:56–75.

Lerner, Jennifer S., and Dacher Keltner. 2001. "Fear, Anger, and Risk." *Journal of Personality and Social Psychology* 81 (1): 146–59.

Lerner, Jennifer S., Ye Li, and Elke U. Weber. 2013. "The Financial Costs of Sadness." *Psychological Science* 24 (1): 72–79.

Lettau, Martin, Sydney C. Ludvigson, and Paulo Manoel. 2018. "Characteristics of Mutual Fund Portfolios: Where Are the Value Funds?" National Bureau of Economic Research Working Paper No. w25381 (December). Available at https://ssrn.com/abstract=3306086.

Leuz, Christian, Steffen Meyer, Maximilian Muhn, Eugene F. Soltes, and Andreas Hackethal. 2018. "Who Falls Prey to the Wolf of Wall Street? Investor Participation in Market Manipulation." Center for Financial Studies Working Paper No. 609 (24 November). Available at https://ssrn.com/abstract=3289931 or doi:10.2139/ssrn.3289931.

Lev, Baruch. 1988. "Toward a Theory of Equitable and Efficient Accounting Policy." *Accounting Review* 63 (1): 1–22.

Lewis, Joshua, Celia Gaertig, and Joseph P. Simmons. 2019. "Extremeness Aversion Is a Cause of Anchoring." *Psychological Science* 30 (2): 159–73.

Lieberman, Debra, Joseph Billingsley, and Carlton Patrick. 2018. "Consumption, Contact and Copulation: How Pathogens Have Shaped Human Psychological Adaptations." *Philosophical Transactions of the Royal Society B* 373 (1751).

Lien, Jaimie W., and Jia Yuan. 2015. "Selling to Biased Believers: Strategies of Online Lottery Ticket Vendors." *Economic Inquiry* 53 (3): 1506–21.

Ling, David C., Yan Lu, and Sugata Ray. 2018. "How Do Personal Real Estate Transactions Affect Productivity and Risk Taking? Evidence from Professional Asset Managers." Working paper (January). Available at https://ssrn.com/abstract=3143081 or doi:10.2139/ssrn.3143081.

Linnainmaa, Juhani T., Brian Melzer, and Alessandro Previtero. 2018. "The Misguided Beliefs of Financial Advisors." Kelley School of Business Research Paper No. 18-9 (16 May). Available at https://ssrn.com/abstract=3101426 or http://dx.doi.org/10.2139/ssrn.3101426.

Linnainmaa, Juhani T., and Michael R. Roberts. 2018. "The History of the Cross-Section of Stock Returns." *Review of Financial Studies* 31 (7): 2606–49.

Liu, Clark, Tao Shu, Johan Sulaeman, and P. Eric Yeung. 2019. "Life Is Too Short? Bereaved Managers and Investment Decisions." 27th Annual Conference on Financial Economics and Accounting Paper (1 May). Available at https://ssrn.com/abstract=2658815 or http://dx.doi.org/10.2139/ssrn.2658815.

Lopes, Lola L. 1987. "Between Hope and Fear: The Psychology of Risk." *Advances in Experimental Social Psychology* 20:255–95.

Lowenstein, Roger. 1995. *Buffett: The Making of an American Capitalist.* New York: Random House.

Luttmer, Erzo F. P. 2005. "Neighbors as Negatives: Relative Earnings and Well-Being." *Quarterly Journal of Economics* 120 (3): 963–1002.

Madrian, Brigitte C., and Dennis F. Shea. 2001. "The Power of Suggestion: Inertia in 401(k) Participation and Savings Behavior." *Quarterly Journal of Economics* 116 (4): 1149–87.

Maillot, Matthieu, Nocole Darmon, and Adam Drewnowski. 2010. "Are the Lowest-Cost Healthful Food Plans Culturally and Socially Acceptable?" *Public Health Nutrition* 13 (8): 1178–85.

Makridis, Christos. 2018. "Can You Feel the Heat? Extreme Temperatures, Stock Returns, and Economic Sentiment." Working paper (26 December). Available at https://ssrn.com/abstract=3095422 or doi:10.2139/ssrn.3095422.

Malkiel, Burton G. 2003. "The Efficient Market Hypothesis and Its Critics." *Journal of Economic Perspectives* 17 (1): 59–82.

Markowitz, Harry. 1952. "Portfolio Selection." *Journal of Finance* 7:77–91.

———. 1959. *Portfolio Selection: Efficient Diversification of Investments*. New York: John Wiley & Sons.

———. 1991. "Individual Versus Institutional Investing." *Financial Services Review* 1 (1): 1–8.

———. 2010. "Portfolio Theory: As I Still See It." *Annual Review of Financial Economics* 2:1–23.

———. 2015. "Consumption, Investment and Insurance in the Game of Life." *Journal of Investment Management* 13 (3): 5–23.

McCarthy, Yvonne. 2011. "Behavioural Characteristics and Financial Distress." ECB Working Paper No. 1303 (14 February). Available at http://ssrn.com/abstract=1761570.

McLean, R. David, and Jeffrey Pontiff. 2016. "Does Academic Research Destroy Stock Return Predictability?" *Journal of Finance* 71 (1): 5–32.

Merkle, Christoph. 2016. "Financial Overconfidence over Time: Foresight, Hindsight, and Insight of Investors." AFA 2013 San Diego Meetings Paper (10 November). Available at http://ssrn.com/abstract=2001513 or http://dx.doi.org/10.2139/ssrn.2001513.

Merkley, Kenneth J., Roni Michaely, and Joseph Pacelli. 2019. "Cultural Diversity on Wall Street: Evidence from Sell-Side Analysts' Forecasts." Swiss Finance Institute Research Paper No. 19-07 (6 February). Available at https://ssrn.com/abstract=3068232 or http://dx.doi.org/10.2139/ssrn.3068232.

Mian, Atif, and Amir Sufi. 2014. "House Price Gains and U.S. Household Spending from 2002 to 2006." National Bureau of Economic Research Working Paper No. 20152.

Milkman, Katherine L., Julia A. Minson, and Kevin G. M. Volpp. 2014. "Holding the Hunger Games Hostage at the Gym: An Evaluation of Temptation Bundling." *Management Science* 60 (2): 283–99.

Milkman, Katherine L., John W. Payne, and Jack B. Soll. 2015. "A User's Guide to Debiasing." In *Wiley-Blackwell Handbook of Judgment and Decision Making*, edited by Gideon Keren and George Wu, 924–951. Chichester, UK: John Wiley & Sons, Ltd.

Miller, Merton. 1986. "Behavioral Rationality in Finance: The Case of Dividends." *Journal of Business* 59: S451–68.

Miller, Merton, and Franco Modigliani. 1961. "Dividend Policy, Growth, and the Valuation of Shares." *Journal of Business* 34 (4): 411–33.

Modigliani, Franco, and Richard Brumberg. 1954. "Utility Analysis and the Consumption Function: An Interpretation of Cross-Section Data." In *Post Keynesian Economics*, edited by K. Kurihara, 388–436. New Brunswick, NJ: Rutgers University Press.

Moore, Don. A., and Paul J. Healy. 2008. "The Trouble with Overconfidence." *Psychological Review* 115 (2): 502–17.

Morales, Paola Acevedo, and Steven Ongena. 2016. "Fear, Anger and Credit. On Bank Robberies and Loan Conditions." BAFFI CAREFIN Centre Research Paper No. 2015-10 (19 January). Available at http://ssrn.com/abstract=2653726 or http://dx.doi.org/10.2139/ssrn.2653726.

Mugerman, Yevgeny, Orly Sade, and Moses Shayo. 2014. "Long Term Savings Decisions: Inertia, Peer Effects and Ethnicity." *Journal of Economic Behavior & Organization* 106:235–53.

Mugerman, Yevgeny, Orly Sade, and Eyal Winter. 2019. "Out-of-Pocket vs. Out-of-Profit in Financial Advisory Fees: Evidence from the Lab." Hebrew University of Jerusalem Working Paper (21 March). Available at https://ssrn.com/abstract=3061020 or http://dx.doi.org/10.2139/ssrn.3061020.

Mugerman, Yevgeny, Orr Yidov, and Zvi Wiener. 2018. "By the Light of Day: The Effect of the Switch to Winter Time on Stock Markets." Working paper (16 September). Available at https://ssrn.com/abstract=3250442 or doi:10.2139/ssrn.3250442.

Mulcahy, Diane, Bill Weeks, and Harold S. Bradley. 2012. "We Have Met the Enemy . . . and He Is Us: Lessons from Twenty Years of the Kauffman Foundation's Investments in Venture Capital Funds and the Triumph of Hope over Experience." Working paper (May). Available at https://ssrn.com/abstract=2053258 or doi:10.2139/ssrn.2053258.

Mullainathan, Sendhil, Joshua Schwartzstein, and Andrei Shleifer. 2008. "Coarse Thinking and Persuasion." *Quarterly Journal of Economics* 123 (2): 577–619.

Mullainathan, Sendhil, and Eldar Shafir. 2013. *Scarcity: Why Having Too Little Means So Much*. New York: Times Books.

Nofsinger, John R., Fernando Patterson, and Corey A. Shank. 2017. "Decision-Making, Financial Risk Aversion and Behavioral Biases: The Role of Testosterone and Stress." Working paper (23 November). Available at https://ssrn.com/abstract=3017977 or doi:10.2139/ssrn.3017977.

Oehler, Andreas, Stefan Wendt, Florian Wedlich, and Matthias Horn. 2018. "Investors' Personality Influences Investment Decisions: Experimental Evidence on Extraversion and Neuroticism." *Journal of Behavioral Finance* 19 (1): 30–48.

Oster, Emily, E. Ray Dorsey, and Ira Shoulson. 2013. "Limited Life Expectancy, Human Capital and Health Investments." *American Economic Review* 103 (5): 1977–2002.

Oswald, Andrew J., Eugenio Proto, and Daniel Sgroi. 2009. "Happiness and Productivity." IZA Discussion Paper No. 4645 (22 December). Available at https://ssrn.com/abstract=1526075.

Pan, Carrie H., and Meir Statman. 2012. "Questionnaires of Risk Tolerance, Regret, Overconfidence, and Other Investor Propensities." *Journal of Investment Consulting* 13 (1): 54–63.

———. 2013. "Investor Personality in Investor Questionnaires." *Journal of Investment Consulting* 14 (1): 48–56.

Park, Jane, and Aner Sela. 2018. "Not My Type: Why Affective Decision-Makers Are Reluctant to Make Financial Decisions." *Journal of Consumer Research* 45 (2): 298–319.

Plutchik, Robert. 2001. "The Nature of Emotions: Human Emotions Have Deep Evolutionary Roots, a Fact That May Explain Their Complexity and Provide Tools for Clinical Practice." *American Scientist* 89 (4): 344–50.

Poterba, James M., Steven F. Venti, and David A. Wise. 2011 (revised 2013). "The Drawdown of Personal Retirement Assets." National Bureau of Economic Research Working Paper 16675.

Prast, Henriette, Jose Sanders, and Olga Leonhard. 2018. "Can Words Breed or Kill Investment? Metaphors, Imagery, Affect and Investor Behaviour." CentER Discussion Paper Series No. 2018-014 (17 April). Available at https://ssrn.com/abstract=3164260 or https://dx.doi.org/10.2139/ssrn.3164260.

Prast, Henriette, and Federica Teppa. 2017. "The Power of Percentage: Quantitative Framing of Pension Income." De Nederlandsche Bank Working Paper No. 578 (11 December). Available at https://ssrn.com/abstract=3086507 or http://dx.doi.org/10.2139/ssrn.3086507.

**201**

Raff, Konrad, and Linus Siming. 2016. "Knighthoods, Damehoods, and CEO Behaviour." *Journal of Corporate Finance* (11 October).

Rainwater, Lee, Richard Coleman, and Gerald Handel. 1959. *Workingman's Wife: Her Personality, World and Life Style.* New York: Oceana Publications.

Ramanathan, Suresh, and Ann L. McGill. 2007. "Consuming with Others: Social Influences on Moment-to-Moment and Retrospective Evaluations of an Experience." *Journal of Consumer Research* 34 (4): 506–24.

Ratner, Rebecca K., and Rebecca W. Hamilton. 2015. "Inhibited from Bowling Alone." *Journal of Consumer Research* 42 (2): 266–83.

Reed, Stanley. 2018. "Satellites Aid the Chase for Better Information on Oil Supplies." *New York Times* (8 October). www.nytimes.com/2018/10/08/business/search-for-better-information-on-oil-supplies.html.

Reinholtz, Nicholas, Philip M. Fernbach, and Bart De Langhe. 2018. "Do People Understand the Benefit of Diversification?" Working paper (12 July). Available at http://ssrn.com/abstract=2719144 or http://dx.doi.org/10.2139/ssrn.2719144.

Rick, Scott, Beatriz Pereira, and Katherine Alicia Burson. 2014. "The Benefits of Retail Therapy: Making Purchase Decisions Reduces Residual Sadness." *Journal of Consumer Psychology* 24 (3): 373–80.

Roll, Richard. 1988. "R2." *Journal of Finance* 43 (3): 541–66.

———. 1992. "A Mean/Variance Analysis of Tracking Error." *Journal of Portfolio Management* 18 (4): 13–22.

Rosenberg, Barr, Kenneth Reid, and Ronald Lanstein. 1985. "Persuasive Evidence of Market Inefficiency." *Journal of Portfolio Management* 11 (3): 9–16.

Rousseau, Denise M., Sim B. Sitkin, Ronald S. Burt, and Colin Camerer. 1998. "Not So Different after All: A Cross-Discipline View of Trust." *Academy of Management Review* 23 (3): 393–404.

Russell, Bertrand. 1930. *The Conquest of Happiness.* London: George Allen & Unwin.

Salam, Reihan. 2018. "Taxi-Driver Suicides Are a Warning." *Atlantic* (5 June). www.theatlantic.com/ideas/archive/2018/06/taxi-driver-suicides-are-a-warning/561926/.

Sammon, Marco. 2019. "Passive Ownership and Market Efficiency." Working paper (22 February). Available at https://ssrn.com/abstract=3243910 or http://dx.doi.org/10.2139/ssrn.3243910.

Schulze, William, Annemie Maertens, and Brian Wansink. 2013. "Eating Dogfood: Examining the Relative Roles of Reason and Emotion." *Journal of Economic Behavior & Organization* 92 (C): 202–13.

Schwed, Fred, Jr. 1995. *Where Are the Customers' Yachts? Or, A Good, Hard Look at Wall Street.* New York: John Wiley & Sons.

Sell, Aaron, Daniel Sznycer, Laith Al-Shawaf, Julian Lim, Andre Krauss, Aneta Feldman, Ruxandra Rascanu, Lawrence Sugiyama, Leda Cosmides, and John Tooby. 2017. "The Grammar of Anger: Mapping the Computational Architecture of a Recalibrational Emotion." *Cognition* 168:110–28.

Shafron, Emily. 2019. "Investor Tastes: Implications for Asset Pricing in the Public Debt Market." *Journal of Corporate Finance* 55:6–27.

Sharpe, William. 1964. "Capital Asset Prices: A Theory of Market Equilibrium Under Conditions of Risk." *Journal of Finance* 19 (3): 425–42.

Shefrin, Hersh. 2001. "Do Investors Expect Higher Returns from Safer Stocks Than from Riskier Stocks?" *Journal of Psychology and Financial Markets* 2 (4): 176–81.

———. 2008. *A Behavioral Approach to Asset Pricing*, 2nd ed. Burlington, MA: Elsevier Academic Press.

Shefrin, Hersh, and Meir Statman. 1984. "Explaining Investor Preference for Cash Dividends." *Journal of Financial Economics* 13 (2): 253–82.

———. 1985. "The Disposition to Sell Winners Too Early and Ride Losers Too Long: Theory and Evidence." *Journal of Finance* 40 (3): 777–90.

———. 1992. *Ethics, Fairness, Efficiency and Financial Markets.* Charlottesville, VA: Research Foundation of the Institute of Chartered Financial Analysts.

———. 1993. "Behavioral Aspects of the Design and Marketing of Financial Products." *Financial Management* 22 (2): 123–34.

———. 1993. "Ethics, Fairness, Efficiency and Financial Markets." *Financial Analysts Journal* 49 (6): 21–29.

———. 1994. "Behavioral Capital Asset Pricing Theory." *Journal of Financial and Quantitative Analysis* 29 (3): 323–49.

———. 2000. "Behavioral Portfolio Theory." *Journal of Financial and Quantitative Analysis* 35:127–51.

———. 2003. "The Style of Investor Expectations." In *The Handbook of Equity Style Management*. Third edition, edited by T. Daniel Coggin and Frank J. Fabozzi, 195–218. New York: Wiley.

Shefrin, Hersh, and Richard H. Thaler. 1988. "The Behavioral Life-Cycle Hypothesis." *Economic Inquiry* 26 (4): 609–43.

Shleifer, Andrei, and Robert W. Vishny. 1997. "The Limits of Arbitrage." *Journal of Finance* 52 (1): 35–55.

Shu, Suzanne B., Robert Zeithammer, and John W. Payne. 2018. "The Pivotal Role of Fairness: Which Consumers Like Annuities?" National Bureau of Economic Research Working Paper No. w25067 (September). Available at https://ssrn.com/abstract=3254042.

Sias, Richard W., Laura T. Starks, and Harry J. Turtle. 2018. "Molecular Genetics, Risk Aversion, Return Perceptions, and Stock Market Participation" (18 November). Available at https://ssrn.com/abstract=3292249 or doi:10.2139/ssrn.3292249.

Silverstein, Michael J., Kosuke Kato, and Pia Tischhauser. 2009. "Women Want More (in Financial Services)." Boston Consulting Group (October). http://image-src.bcg.com/Images/BCG_Women_Want_More_in_Financial_Services_Oct_2009_tcm9-125088.pdf.

Sini, Rozina. 2017. "At What Age Do You Feel You Have Reached Adulthood?" *BBC News* (27 April). www.bbc.com/news/education-39694563.

Snyder, W., and T. Howard. 1957. "How to Take a Loss and Like It." *Financial Analysts Journal* 13 (2): 115–16.

Solomon, David H., Eugene F. Soltes, and Denis Sosyura. 2014. "Winners in the Spotlight: Media Coverage of Fund Holdings as a Driver of Flows." *Journal of Financial Economics* 113 (1): 53–72.

Solt, Michael E., and Meir Statman. 1988. "How Useful Is the Sentiment Index?" *Financial Analysts Journal* 44 (5): 45–55.

———. 1989. "Good Companies, Bad Stocks." *Journal of Portfolio Management* 15 (4): 39–44.

St. John, Warren. 2004. "Making Sure Hollywood's Nouveau Riche Stay Riche." *New York Times* (22 August). www.nytimes.com/2004/08/22/fashion/22SPEN.html.

Stanovich, Keith E., and Richard F. West. 2000. "Individual Differences in Reasoning: Implications for the Rationality Debate?" *Behavioral and Brain Sciences* 23 (5): 645–65.

———. 2008. "On the Relative Independence of Thinking Biases and Cognitive Ability." *Journal of Personality and Social Psychology* 94 (4): 672–95.

Statman, Meir. 1985. "Discussion." *Journal of Finance* 40 (3): 719–21.

———. 1995. "A Behavioral Framework for Dollar-Cost Averaging: Dollar-Cost Averaging May Not Be Rational Behavior, but It Is Perfectly Normal Behavior." *Journal of Portfolio Management* 22 (1): 70–78.

———. 1999. "Behavioral Finance: Past Battles and Future Engagements." *Financial Analysts Journal* 55 (6): 18–27.

———. 2002. "Lottery Players/Stock Traders." *Financial Analysts Journal* 58 (1): 14–21.

———. 2004. "What Do Investors Want?" *Journal of Portfolio Management* 30 (5): 153–61.

———. 2005. "Fair Trading." *Journal of Portfolio Management* 32 (1): 76–84.

———. 2005. "Hedging Currencies with Hindsight and Regret." *Journal of Investing* 14 (2): 15–19.

———. 2005. "The Religions of Social Responsibility." *Journal of Investing* 14 (3): 14–21.

———. 2011. "Investor Sentiment, Stock Characteristics, and Returns." *Journal of Portfolio Management* 37 (3): 54–61.

———. 2011. "Is It Fair? Judging the Fairness of Insider Trading." *Journal of Investment Consulting* 12 (1): 47–59.

———. 2011. *What Investors Really Want: Discover What Drives Investor Behavior and Make Smarter Financial Decisions.* New York: McGraw-Hill.

———. 2014. "Behavioral Finance: Finance with Normal People." *Borsa Istanbul Review* 14 (2): 65–73.

———. 2015. "Culture in Risk, Regret, Maximization, Social Trust, and Life Satisfaction." *Journal of Investment Consulting* 16:20–30.

———. 2017. "A Different Kind of Financial Literacy Test." *Wall Street Journal* (23 October).

————. 2017. "Are Your Clients Not Spending Enough in Retirement?" *Journal of Financial Planning* (November): 34–37.

————. 2017. *Finance for Normal People: How Investors and Markets Behave.* New York: Oxford University Press.

————. 2017. "Financial Advertising in the Second Generation of Behavioral Finance." *Journal of Behavioral Finance* 18 (4): 470–77.

————. 2017. "The Mental Mistakes We Make with Retirement Spending." *Wall Street Journal* (24 April). www.wsj.com/articles/the-mental-mistakes-we-make-with-retirement-spending-1492999921.

————. 2019. "Financial Advisers as Well-Being Advisers: Enhance Your Clients' Well-Being by Understanding Its Four Domains." *Journal of Financial Planning* 32 (9): 48–56.

Statman, Meir, and David Caldwell. 1987. "Applying Behavioral Finance to Capital Budgeting: Project Terminations." *Financial Management* 16 (4): 7–15.

Statman, Meir, Kenneth L. Fisher, and Deniz Anginer. 2008. "Affect in a Behavioral Asset Pricing Model." *Financial Analysts Journal* 64 (2): 20–29.

Statman, Meir, and Denys Glushkov. 2009. "The Wages of Social Responsibility." *Financial Analysts Journal* 65 (4): 33–46.

————. 2016. "Classifying and Measuring the Performance of Socially Responsible Funds." *Journal of Portfolio Management* 42 (2): 140–51.

Statman, Meir, and James F. Sepe. 1989. "Project Termination Announcements and the Market Value of the Firm." *Financial Management* 18 (4): 74–81.

Statman, Meir, and Tyzoon T. Tyebjee. 1985. "Optimistic Capital Budgeting Forecasts: An Experiment." *Financial Management* 14 (3): 27–33.

Stigler, George. 1987. *The Theory of Price*, 4th ed. New York: Macmillan Publishing.

Summers, Barbara, and Darren Duxbury. 2007. "Unraveling the Disposition Effect: The Role of Prospect Theory and Emotions" (1 August). Available at https://ssrn.com/abstract=1026915 or doi:10.2139/ssrn.1026915.

Svenson, Ola. 1981. "Are We All Less Risky and More Skillful Than Our Fellow Drivers?" *Acta Psychologica* 47 (2): 143–48.

Teasdale, Aaron. 2018. "Explorer Crosses South Pole in Epic Race Across Antarctica." *National Geographic* (13 December). www.nationalgeographic.

com/adventure/2018/12/explorers-colin-obrady-louis-rudd-race-south-pole-antarctica/.

Thaler, Richard H., and Hersh Shefrin. 1981. "An Economic Theory of Self-Control." *Journal of Political Economy* 89 (2): 392–406.

Thaler, Richard H., and Cass R. Sunstein. 2008. *Nudge: Improving Decisions about Health, Wealth, and Happiness.* New Haven, CT: Yale University Press.

Thomas, Ashley J., P. Kyle Stanford, and Barbara W. Sarnecka. 2016. "Correction: No Child Left Alone: Moral Judgments about Parents Affect Estimates of Risk to Children." *Collabra* 2 (1): 12.

Thornton, Russ. 2009. "The Levers to Financial Freedom." *Advisor Perspectives* (1 September). www.advisorperspectives.com/newsletters09/pdfs/The_Levers_to_Financial_Freedom.pdf.

Toplak, Maggie E., Richard F. West, and Keith E. Stanovich. 2014. "Assessing Miserly Information Processing: An Expansion of the Cognitive Reflection Test." *Thinking & Reasoning* 20 (2): 147–68.

Tsur, Shlomit. 2017. "Billionaires Want Billionaire Neighbors." *Globes* (20 March). www.globes.co.il/en/article-billionaires-want-billionaire-neighbors-1001181577.

Venkataraman, Ayesha, and Nida Najar. 2017. "Here Comes the Bride. Now Count the Rest." *New York Times* (22 February). www.nytimes.com/2017/02/22/world/asia/india-weddings-law-inequality.html.

Venti, Steven F., and David A. Wise. 2004. "Aging and Housing Equity: Another Look." In *Perspectives on the Economics of Aging*, edited by David A. Wise, 127–180. Chicago: University of Chicago Press.

Verner, Amy. 2011. "L'Oréal's 'Because I'm Worth It' Slogan Marks a Milestone." *Globe and Mail* (2 December), www.theglobeandmail.com/life/fashion-and-beauty/beauty/loreals-because-im-worth-it-slogan-marks-a-milestone/article554604/.

Vogel, Carol. 2006. "Works by Johns and de Kooning Sell for $143.5 Million." *New York Times* (12 October), www.nytimes.com/2006/10/12/arts/design/12geff.html.

Wang, Hongchang, and Eric M. Overby. 2018. "How Does Online Lending Influence Bankruptcy Filings?" Georgia Tech Scheller College of Business Research Paper No. 17-20 (16 November). Available at https://ssrn.com/abstract=2958916 or http://dx.doi.org/10.2139/ssrn.2958916.

Wang, Yan Albert, and Michael Young. Forthcoming. "Terrorist Attacks and Investor Risk Preference: Evidence from Mutual Fund Flows." *Journal of Financial Economics*. Available at https://ssrn.com/abstract=3354764.

Weber, Elke U., and Joachim Klement. 2018. "Risk Tolerance and Circumstances." CFA Institute Research Foundation Brief (March).

Weinstein, Neil D. 1980. "Unrealistic Optimism about Future Life Events." *Journal of Personality and Social Psychology* 39 (5): 806–20.

Welling, Kathryn. 1977. "Women and Money '77: You've Come a Long Way, Baby—Further than Brokers Think." *Barron's* (10 October): 9–12.

White, Elizabeth. 2016. *Fifty-Five, Unemployed, and Faking Normal: Your Guide to a Better ~~Retirement~~ Life*. Createspace Independent Publishing.

Whitson, Jennifer A., and Adam D. Galinsky. 2008. "Lacking Control Increases Illusory Pattern Perception." *Science* 322 (5898): 115–17.

Wiesenberger, Arthur. 1952. *Investment Companies*. New York: Arthur Wiesenberger & Company.

Woolley, Suzanne. "How Much Money Do You Need to Be Wealthy in America?" *Bloomberg* (15 May 2018). www.bloomberg.com/news/articles/2018-05-15/how-much-money-do-you-need-to-be-wealthy-in-america.

Young, Maia J., Larissa Z. Tiedens, Heajung Jung, and Ming-Hong Tsai. 2011. "Mad Enough to See the Other Side: Anger and the Search for Disconfirming Information." *Cognition and Emotion* 25 (1): 10–21.

Zajonc, Robert B. 1980. "Feeling and Thinking: Preferences Need No Inferences." *American Psychologist* 35 (2): 151–75.

Zhang, Yan, Ye Li, and Ting Zhu. 2014. "How Multiple Anchors Affect Judgment: Evidence from the Lab and eBay." Columbia Business School Research Paper No. 14-62 (25 November). Available at http://ssrn.com/abstract=2530690 or doi:10.2139/ssrn.2530690.

Zhou, Frank, and Yuqing Zhou. 2017. "The Tale of Silent Dogs: Do Stock Prices Fully Reflect the Implication of News Withholding?" Working paper (4 August). Available at https://ssrn.com/abstract=3013757 or doi:10.2139/ssrn.3013757.

Zweig, Jason. 2007. *Your Money and Your Brain: How the New Science of Neuroeconomics Can Help Make You Rich*. New York: Simon & Schuster.

# Index

3Com, 148
52-week highs, 36
401(k) plans, 118

## A
abnormal return, 163
abortions, 12
accountability, 74
accounting, 158
activist investors, 161–62
adjustment errors, 34–36
admired companies, 64, 132
adult children, 11, 78, 108, 113
advertisements, xii–xiii, 9, 20–21,
    91–92, 156
    commercials, 11–12, 14, 16–17, 33,
        42, 108, 156, 165
    financial, xii, 47
    misleading, xiii
advisers, 75–77, 101–2, 104
    online, 105
aesthetics, 122–23
affect, 48, 62
Africa, 106
African-Americans, 20
airplanes, 14–15
    crashes, 124
Alberto-Culver, xiii
alcohol, 12, 14, 59, 137–38, 177
allocations
    extreme, 82–84
    zero, 84
allowance, 109
Ally, Arthur, 137
amateurs, 81, 150–51, 168
    investors, 35, 151
Amazon (company), 68, 124
ambulance, 36
American Association of Individual
    Investors (AAII), 154

American Finance Association (AFA),
    151, 157, 173
Americans, 11, 52, 90, 97, 101, 115
    credit card consumers, 20
    drivers, 44
    women, 17
analysts, 19, 62, 150, 157, 161
    professional, 68
    sell-side, 19
Anchoring, 33
Andrew, John, 175
anger, 48–49, 54–55, 65
annual returns, 83
annuities, 27, 119
    annuity dollars, 115
    deferred variable, 10
    option, 33
    payments, 115
    premiums, 27
anomaly, 163
Antarctica, 91–92, 95, 98, 106
antibiotics, 75
anti-lock brakes, 6
Appel, Ian, 161
Apple (company), 68, 70
Arab oil embargo, 171
arbitrage, 124–26, 135, 158–59, 162
    structural impediments to, 125
    trading strategies, 125
Asian culture, 12
aspirations, 98
al-Assad, Bashar, 76
asset pricing models, 127, 133, 162
    empirical, 127, 163
    five-factor, 128, 136, 138–39, 162
    one-factor, 136
    standard, 123, 140
    three-factor, 127–28, 136, 162–63
asset pricing theory, ix, xv, 162
    behavioral, xi, 122, 168
    standard, xi

proportionally, 146
elderly populations, 80
emotional benefits, xiii, 1, 14, 24, 45,
47, 51–52, 81, 84, 90–91,
107–8, 120–24, 126, 134, 137,
140, 142, 155, 167
of familiarity, 89
hypothesis, 133
of pride, 1, 14, 56, 86
of protection, 8
emotional costs, 8, 15–16, 97, 108, 137
of regret, xiv, 56
emotional errors, ix, xii–xiii, 1–4, 7,
47, 53, 65–66, 70, 72, 74–75,
78–79, 81, 89–90, 102–3, 105,
115–17, 120, 123–24, 126,
130, 136, 140, 164, 167
of excessive fear, 76
emotional loads, 4
emotional shortcuts, xi, 2–4, 6, 47,
65–66, 77
emotions, 47–49, 58–59, 96
anticipation, 55
anxiety, 48
cognitive, 55
envy, 22
muted, 61
negative, 49
sadness, 6, 48–49, 51, 53, 62
empirical associations, 129–30
employees, 79, 110, 117–19, 177
marketing, 9
marketing and sales, 8
relations, 13, 137
satisfaction, 137
employers, 79, 110
employment, 96
EMS Find (company), 36–37
engineering, 158
England, 134
Southampton, 146
English, 90, 134
entertainment, 110
EntreMed (company), 144

environment investments, 69, 137, 177
environmental damage, 69
enzyme deficiency, 32
Epley, Nicholas, 32
errors, 23–25, 27, 65–66, 83, 159
availability, 40–41, 115
avoiding, x
correcting, 99
framing, 1, 26, 66, 68, 115,
153–54
hindsight, 28–30, 68, 72, 76–77
optimism, 25
overestimation, 44
overplacement, 43–44
overprecision, 43
underestimation, 43–44
underplacement, 43–44
underprecision, 43
ESG investing (Environmental, Social,
and governance), 12–13
estimation, 42
errors, 83
ETFs, 133
Europe, 44–45, 98, 106
stocks, 83–84
Evensky, Harold, 104
events
liquidity, 16
negative, 44
positive, 44
evidence
confirming, 31–32, 72
empirical, 128, 134
exclusion, 18
exclusivity, 15–16
expectations, 39, 131
of the future return, 83, 132
positive, 59
expenses, 110–11
medical, 77
experience, 9, 26, 166
experiments, xiv, 132
lunch, 54
prisoner's dilemma, 59, 170

shortcuts, 25–27, 34, 77
wealth, 2
France, 84, 173
fraud, 58, 78
freedom, 9, 116
    financial, 11
    from poverty, ix
free-rider problems, 162
French, Kenneth, 128, 153
Friedman, Milton, x, 116
friends, 47
frustration, 22, 48
functional magnetic resonance
        imaging, xiv, 56
fund allocations, 79
fund managers, 37, 57
    mutual funds, 13, 37–38, 41, 53, 56
funds
    environmental, 69
    managed, 153
future returns, 135

**G**
Gallup, 50
gambler's fallacies, 38
gambling, 137–38
games, 170
    financial market, 26
    market-sum, 26, 150
    poker, 25–27
    poker players, 27
    zero-sum, 26
gas, 33, 110
GDP, 27
GE, 69
gender, 17
gender diversity, 19
General Motors, 73
German investors, 155
gifts, 123
    gift certificates, 74
    lavish, 12
Gilovich, Thomas, 32
Ginsburg, Ruth Bader, 178

goals, 92, 94, 104
    acceptable, 104
    ideal, 104
golden rule philosophy, 21
Google (company), 68
Google search, 54
Gormley, Todd A., 161
governments, 113, 116–17
GPS, 6
Graff Zivin, Joshua S., 32
grandchildren, 113
Grant's Interest Rate Observer, 143
Great Depression, 106
greed, 22
Griffin, Kenneth, 16
groceries, 11, 110
growth, 9
    exponential, 34
    stocks, 129, 133, 135
guilt, 49
guns, 13
gym, 74

**H**
Hamilton, Sally, 177
happiness, 48, 51–52, 76
    accumulated, 53
hard-to-beat efficient market
        hypothesis, 148, 156, 164
Harris, Sandra, 9
Hartzmark, Samuel, 34
Harvard University, 67
Healy, Paul, 42, 44
Hebrew University, 170–72, 177
hedge funds, 14–15, 57, 133, 153, 161–62
    managers, 16, 96
Henry Street Settlement, 52
Hershfield, Hal, 28
high social status, 14, 45–46, 76, 91,
        121, 123, 133, 165, 168
hindsight, 25, 28–30, 76–77, 94, 165
    shortcuts, 29, 77
historians, 29
Hogarth, Robin, 173

# Named Endowments

The CFA Institute Research Foundation acknowledges with sincere gratitude the generous contributions of the Named Endowment participants listed below.

Gifts of at least US$100,000 qualify donors for membership in the Named Endowment category, which recognizes in perpetuity the commitment toward unbiased, practitioner-oriented, relevant research that these firms and individuals have expressed through their generous support of the CFA Institute Research Foundation.

Ameritech
Anonymous
Robert D. Arnott
Theodore R. Aronson, CFA
Asahi Mutual Life Insurance Company
Batterymarch Financial
  Management
Boston Company
Boston Partners Asset Management,
  L.P.
Gary P. Brinson, CFA
Brinson Partners, Inc.
Capital Group International, Inc.
Concord Capital Management
Dai-Ichi Life Insurance Company
Daiwa Securities
Mr. and Mrs. Jeffrey Diermeier
Gifford Fong Associates
Investment Counsel Association
  of America, Inc.
Jacobs Levy Equity Management
John A. Gunn, CFA
John B. Neff, CFA
Jon L. Hagler Foundation
Long-Term Credit Bank of Japan, Ltd.
Lynch, Jones & Ryan, LLC
Meiji Mutual Life Insurance
  Company

Miller Anderson & Sherrerd, LLP
Nikko Securities Co., Ltd.
Nippon Life Insurance Company of
  Japan
Nomura Securities Co., Ltd.
Payden & Rygel
Provident National Bank
Frank K. Reilly, CFA
Salomon Brothers
Sassoon Holdings Pte. Ltd.
Scudder Stevens & Clark
Security Analysts Association
  of Japan
Shaw Data Securities, Inc.
Sit Investment Associates, Inc.
Standish, Ayer & Wood, Inc.
State Farm Insurance Company
Sumitomo Life America, Inc.
T. Rowe Price Associates, Inc.
Templeton Investment Counsel Inc.
Frank Trainer, CFA
Travelers Insurance Co.
USF&G Companies
Yamaichi Securities Co., Ltd.

## Senior Research Fellows

Financial Services Analyst Association

> For more on upcoming Research Foundation
> publications and webcasts, please visit
> www.cfainstitute.org/learning/foundation.